Significance of the Dead Sea Scrolls and other Essays

Copyright 2013 Jonathan Nkhoma

All rights reserved. No part of this publication may be reproduced, stored in a retrieval system, or transmitted by any means, electronic, mechanical, photocopying or otherwise, without prior permission from the publisher.

Published by:

Mzuni Press
P/Bag 201, Luwinga, Mzuzu 2, Malawi

ISBN: 978-99960-27-04-8 (Mzuni Press)

Mzuni Books no. 12

Mzuni Press is represented outside Africa by
African Books Collective, Oxford (orders@africanbookscollective.com)

Printed in Malawi by Baptist Publications, POB 249, Lilongwe

Significance of the Dead Sea Scrolls and other Essays

Biblical and Early Christianity Studies from Malawi

Jonathan S. Nkhoma

with a contribution by

Hilary B.P. Mijoga

Mzuni Books no. 12

2013

Contents

Preface	5
1. Significance of the Dead Sea Scrolls: History and Practice of the Qumran Community	8
2. Significance of the Dead Sea Scrolls: Theology of the Qumran Community	23
3. Old Testament and Jewish Hermeneutics	44
4. New Testament Exegesis of the Old Testament	57
5. Discipleship in Matthew: A Redaction-Critical Study	90
6. "Love Your Enemies": A Study of Luke 6:27-35	96
7. Table Fellowship in Luke	104
8. Acts as History in Ancient Historiography	111
9. History of the Johannine Community	121
10. Water as a Revelatory Symbol in John 1-12	126
11. Ignatius: Martyrdom or Suicide? A Study in Light of his Letter to the Romans	130
12. Martyrdom of Perpetua: Public Spaces and the Early Christian Martyrs	138
13. Ritual and Symbolism as Hermeneutical Approach	150
14. The Use of 'Hallelujah!' (הללויה) and the Malawian Context	160
15. Gender differentiation in the Bible: Created and Recognized (By Hilary B.P. Mijoga)	174

Abbreviations for Qumran Literature

1QH	:	The Thanksgiving Hymns
1QpHab	:	Commentary on Habakkuk
1Qsa	:	The Community Rule or Manual of Discipline
Iv. Qpls[a]	:	The Messianic Rule or Two-Column Document
Iv QFlor	:	A textual fragment from Cave 4.
4QMMT	:	*Miqsat ma'ase hatorah* ("Some precepts of the law")
CD	:	The Qumran Damascus Rule
1QM	:	The Qumran War Rule
1Qp HAB	:	The Qumran Commentary on Habakkuk
1QS	:	The Qumran Community Rule or Manual of Discipline
4Q flor	:	A textual fragment from Cave 4
LXX	:	The Septuagint
MSS	:	Textual Manuscripts

Preface

The present book offers an opportunity to bring together selected essays prepared over the past few years. The book has fifteen essays touching on various issues in Biblical Studies and Early Christianity, ranging from the history and life of the Qumran covenanters, a Jewish religious sect that lived along the Dead Sea in the last few centuries before Christ, and possibly in the first century after Christ, through the problem of martyrdom in the early Church to the question of gender in our own times, as seen from a biblical perspective.

The first two chapters on the Dead Sea community first appeared as "Significance of the Dead Sea Scrolls (Qumran Literature) for the Study of the New Testament: An Overview," in *Malawi Journal of Biblical Studies* 2003:49-89. They trace history, life and theology of the Qumran covenanters and conclude by observing the importance of this group for our understanding of the New Testament.

The third chapter on the Old Testament focuses on the nature of quotations and Jewish hermeneutical principles which provide background to the hermeneutical practice of the New Testament writers.

The fourth chapter is on the exegesis of the Old Testament by the New Testament writers. Although most of these exegetical methods are different from our own, they help us understand how and why they arrived at the theological conclusions they made on various issues regarding Christ.

The fifth chapter studies discipleship in the Gospel of Matthew and argues for a broader perspective.

The sixth chapter examines the command to love enemies and explores its theological implications and its role in shaping Christian identity over the centuries.

The seventh chapter discusses table fellowship in Luke, primarily from a Hellenistic perspective, and investigates its implications on the gospel.

The eighth chapter examines the historiography of Acts of Apostles placing the discussion in the context of modern debate.

The ninth chapter revisits the debate on the history of the Johannine community and observes the importance of the discussion.

The tenth chapter offers a brief literary analysis of water as a theological symbol in the first twelve chapters of John and shows how the writer develops his themes as the narrative progresses.

The eleventh chapter studies the martyrdom of Ignatius and attempts a reconstruction of the meaning that Ignatius attached to his own death in light of his *Letter to the Romans*.

The twelfth chapter seeks to understand the place of martyrdom in the early church and its relationship to public space, especially the arena, in light of the martyrdom of Perpetua.

The thirteenth chapter discusses ritual and symbolism as a potential hermeneutical method for the interpretation of the New Testament in the wake of multi-disciplinary approaches to the study of the New Testament.

The fourteenth chapter is an essay on the use of the term "Hallelujah" (הללויה). It is an attempt to trace the biblical history of this term and survey its usage from biblical times to the present, with a special focus on its usage in the cotemporary Malawian religious context.

The final chapter is an essay on the question of gender, prepared by the late Hilary B.P. Mijoga, then Associate Professor of Theology and Religious Studies in the University of Malawi. It first appeared in *Journal of Humanities* No. 13 (1999): 87-113. Professor Mijoga argues that gender differentiation in the Bible is created and recognized and suggests that it is its manipulation today that has led to the marginalization of the female gender.

All these chapters have been presented, as essays, at various academic fora at the University of Malawi, Mzuzu University and Harvard University in the United States. I am therefore very grateful to the late Professor Mijoga then of the University of Malawi; Professor Klaus Fiedler of Mzuzu University; Professor François Bovon and Professor Karen King of Harvard University; and Professor Sean Freyne of Trinity College, Dublin, who was a visiting professor at Harvard in the early years of my research on Jesus and the language of mystery. I am of course solely responsible for any weaknesses that may still remain.

I dedicate this book to the late Dr. Hilary B P Mijoga, then Associate Professor in the University of Malawi, who first introduced me to Biblical scholarship in general, the Dead Sea Scrolls, and the New Testament in particular.

May 2, 2012, Mzuzu
J.S.N.

Chapter One

Significance of the Dead Sea Scrolls: History and Practice of the Qumran Community

Introduction

The initial scholarly response to the Dead Sea Scrolls was an awareness of the contribution they would make to our understanding of the Old Testament. Soon, however, scholarly opinion shifted to their significance to the New Testament as the Christian public longed for an explanation of their relationship to early Christianity. The discussion of the relationship between the Dead Sea Scrolls and the New Testament has basically involved two positions: on one hand, there are those who see an almost direct relationship between the belief and practice expressed in these scrolls and the belief and practice of early Christianity so that the advent of the latter becomes virtually one of "the successive phases of a movement."[1] On the other hand, there are those who feel that direct dependence is almost an untenable opinion in view of the current evidence despite all the similarities that have been appealed to.

In this and the following chapter, I will argue that while the similarities are so striking as to deserve the postulation of a common religious milieu as their background, the differences between the two movements are quite distinctive so that any theory that looks at the two movements as "successive phases of a single movement" can only be sustained with great difficulties.

Here, in this chapter, I will discuss the history of the Dead Sea Scrolls community commonly known as the Qumran Community, and their practical religious life and how these relate to the New Testament.

The History of the Qumran Community

It is now generally accepted to identify the Qumran Community as part of the Essene Movement, one of the three major sects of Judaism, the other two being Pharisaism and Sadduceism. The initial development of classical Jewish sectarianism can be traced back to the Babylonian Exile. A search for priestly purity even goes further back to the division of the kingdom of Israel when it became necessary to legitimize the ancestry of Judean and especially Jerusalem priesthood in

---

[1] Edmund Wilson, "The Scrolls from the Dead Sea", in James C. VanderKam, *The Dead Sea Scrolls Today*, Grand Rapids, Michigan: William B. Eerdmans, 1994, p. 160.

conscious opposition to the priesthood established by Jeroboam in the Northern Kingdom of Israel. In order to get tenure at the Jerusalem Temple, the Zadokite descent of a particular priest had to be established first.[2] The flight of northern priests to Judah following the Assyrian attack on Israel after 733 BC only intensified the question of legitimacy for purposes of service at the Jerusalem Temple.[3]

After exile the desire for a pure priesthood, a priesthood that would not only reflect but also provide a foundation for true Israel is clearly indicated in Ezra's priestly moral reforms.[4]

A century or so later, sectarianism became a major feature in Judaism owing largely to political and religious discontent generated by the poor governance of their Ptolemid and Seleucid masters and the secularization of the priesthood which was accused of apostasy for their adoption of some Hellenistic features. Matthew Black tells us that the period 300 BC - 100 AD was a "creative and fluid period in Judaism ... characterized as that of a widespread and vigorous Jewish sectarianism, a kind of Jewish non-conformity, opposed to the official Judaism of Jerusalem ... centered on the temple and the Jerusalem Sanhedrin."[5] He suggests that this sectarianism was represented in the north by anti-Jerusalem, anti-pharisaic Samaritan groups and in the south by the monastic and semi-monastic sect of the Essenes located by the Dead Sea.[6]

More specifically the rise of the Qumran Community is associated with the appearance of a reform movement during the reign of Antiochus Epiphanes (175-163 BC): the Hasidim or the "pious ones." They aligned with Mattathias, the father of Judas Maccabeus in a liberation struggle against the Syrian tyrant in 167 BC (1 Macc 2:42). The revolt was fueled by mainly religious motives: what the pious called the 'blasphemies' by the Hellenized Jews who were favored by the Syrian administration and the removal from office of Jason, a Zadokite high priest in favour of the non-Zadokite Menelaus in 172 BC (2 Macc 4:23-26).[7]

---

[2] Zadok was himself a priest at David's court who anointed Solomon as king of Israel. He was descendant of Ithamar, the younger one of Aaron's surviving two sons and traced his descent through the Shilonite Priest-hood (2 Sam.:8:17; 15:24; 20:25; 1 Kings 18, 2:35).

[3] W.F. Albright and C.S. Mann "Qumran and the Essenes: Geography, Chronology and Identification of the Sect," in Matthew Black (ed), *Theological Collection II: The Scrolls and Christianity, History and Theological Significance*, London: SPCK, 1969, pp. 16,17.

[4] Ibid., p. 18.

[5] Matthew Black, "The Dead Sea Scrolls and Christian Origins," in *Theological Collections II*, p.97.

[6] Ibid.

[7] W.F. Albright and C.S. Mann, "Qumran and the Essenes," p. 18. Also, Raymond E. Brown, "The Teacher of Righteousness and the Messiah(s)," *Theological Collections II* pp. 37f.

Following the appointment of Menelaus as high priest, a bitter strife ensued between his house and that of Jason which soon became an open civil war. Antiochus then used this state of confusion to carry out his massacres, desecrate the temple in 167 BC and completely Hellenize the city of Jerusalem. With these events the time was ripe for the rise of the Maccabees whose aim was to get independence for the Jews and then establish a new high priestly house.[8]

But the hope of the Hasidim was later lost when they realized that the Maccabees were only interested in civil independence and political power. This drift is clearly illustrated by the reactions of the two sides to the appointment of Alcimus as successor of Menelaus. Alcimus was pro-Syrian and an appointee of that throne. While the Maccabees vigorously opposed his appointment, the Hasidim accepted him because he was 'from the seed of Aaron.'[9] But his cruel slaughter of their number made them change their mind. However, this showed that the Maccabees could no longer count on their help.

Possibly many of them lost interest in the struggle once religious freedom had been granted. However, Judas and his friends felt that as long as the high priesthood was influenced by Syrian rulers who promoted Hellenistic culture, the Jewish religious heritage was in danger of syncretism or even extinction. Thus they continued to press for political freedom and a high priest who was prepared to break with the Seleucid masters.

This was achieved by 152 BC under the leadership of Jonathan (161-143 BC), Judas Maccabeus' brother.[10] Jonathan was then appointed high priest by Alexander Balas, son and successor of Antiochus Epiphanes who later made him 'general and governor of the province' (1 Macc 10:15-66).[11]

The Hasidim were seriously offended by Jonathan's acceptance of the appointment to high priesthood since he was not of the line of Zadok, and the Hasidim had fought for the purity of this office throughout. At this point part of the Hasidim separated themselves from the Maccabean Movement and united themselves under an unnamed Zadokite priest, probably an heir in the high priestly line whom they called the 'Teacher of Righteousness' or the 'Right Guide'. The group endured persecution in Jerusalem by the 'wicked priest,' a designation which suits Jonathan very well.[12]

The gap between the Hasidim and the Maccabean administration was further widened by Simon (143-135 BC), brother and successor of Jonathan. In 140 BC,

---

[8] Frank Moore Cross, *The Ancient Library of Qumran and Modern Biblical Studies*, Westport: Greenwood, 1976, p.98.
[9] *Ibid.*, p. 99
[10] Floyd V. Filson, *A New Testament History*, London: SCM, 1964, p. 14.
[11] *Ibid.*, p. 15.
[12] Raymond E. Brown, "The Teacher of Righteousness and the Messiah(s)," p. 38.

Simon accepted the high priesthood for himself 'forever' (i.e. and his children, 1 Macc 14:41-48), thus irrevocably abrogating otherwise legitimate claims to that office from those of the line of Zadok.

Meanwhile another group of Babylonian priests was fleeing from Babylonia at the time of the Parthian invasion (141-140 BC) and were seeking refuge at Damascus. It was at this time, 'after twenty years of groping for the way' (CD i, 9 f) before God 'raised up for them a Right Guide' (CD i, II.)—a reference to the preceding two decades (160-140 BC) mostly covered by Jonathan's reign, a time when the sectarians became increasingly dissatisfied but did not have an effective leader—that the Hasidim fled to Damascus where they would be out of reach for the Jerusalem high priesthood and among their supporters.

The Hasidim, properly known as the Essenes, meaning 'the poor' appear to have first settled at Qumran during the reign of John Hyrcanus (135-104 BC), son and successor of Simon, according to the findings at the site.[13] The community continued to grow and experienced its heyday during the reign of Alexander Janneus (103-76 BC). In BC 31 their building complex was destroyed by an earthquake and seems to have been abandoned until the reign of Herod Archelaus (4 BC – 6 AD) when it was restored and reoccupied by the sect until its final destruction by the Romans in June 68 AD.[14]

It appears that Qumran was their main settlement, especially for the more strict and celibate wing of the Essene sect. Josephus informs us that the Essenes lived in various places throughout the country. The group that stayed in Damascus seems to have practiced marriage though in accordance with their own discipline as the evidence from the Damascus Document shows (CD vii, 6a-9). The Qumran community is therefore a peak in an Essene Iceberg, a fairly well known group of a larger relatively unknown sectarian movement.

The Practical Religious Life of the Qumran Community

Most of the practices of the Qumran community do have some theological significance since the community understood itself in eschatological terms and believed they had a soteriological role in the history of redemption. They were a

---

[13] Kurt Schubert, *The Dead Sea Community: Its Origin and Teachings*, Westport: Greenwood, 1973, p. 25. Schubert puts the settlement in the second part of the reign. W.F. Albright and C.S. Mann, in "Qumran and the Essenes" put it in the first part dating it around 128 BC following the death of Antiochus Sidetes and John Hyrcanus' conquest of Samaria and invasion of the Transjordan (p. 20). For a full description of the building complex that was excavated by Roland de Vaux in 1951-1956, see Gaalyah Cornfield, *Archaeology of the Bible: Book by Book*, London: Adams and Charles Black, 1977, p. 258.

[14] *Ibid*.

community of the new covenant foretold by the prophet Jeremiah (31:31). These theological implications will be considered below when we discuss their exegetical methods and theological understanding over against those that appear in the New Testament. Our immediate task in this section is to present an overview of their practical way of life as can be reconstructed from the scrolls, archaeological findings and ancient historical sources.

When the Teacher of Righteousness[15] and his followers came to Qumran, they established a religious order with a very strict discipline. The members were dedicated to the will of God which they hoped to fulfil by studying the Law (Torah), trusting the Teacher's inspired exposition of the law and living a life of holiness and obedience as judged by the community in the light of its special understanding of the Torah.

The Teacher appears to be the highest in the community hierarchy. Next to him is an executive council of twelve men and three priests:

> In the formal congregation of the community, there shall be twelve laymen and three priests schooled to perfection in all that has been revealed of the entire law (1QS viii, 1).

Then there are the priests who assured leadership in any group activity. There were other officers, for instance, the *mebeqqer*, charged with special duties for the smooth running of the community (1QS vi, 13). Above all was the general assembly of all the confirmed members. Important decisions in the community like confirmation of probationers, granting approval for the provision of honours to or their withdrawal from members depending on the evaluation of their character and performance were made by the general assembly (1QS vi. 13-23; ii, 19-25). There was a wide range of status-levels. Each member was allocated a specific status and would move up or down the status ladder, depending on how the assembly rated his religious standing in the community from year to year.

The Qumran order seems to have practiced celibacy. Women who were attracted to celibate life in order to devote themselves to the will of God were accepted at Qumran. This is supported by the fact that some skeletons found in a graveyard believed to have been used by the sect turned out upon examination to be of women.[16] It is not clear whether married members were accommodated at Qumran. Although Essenes were generally celibate,[17] we know that others were allowed to

---

[15] The Teacher of Righteousness appears to be the founding leader of the community who led the first band of followers to Qumran. It however seems that this "name" developed into a title which was applied to his successors throughout the history of the community.

[16] R.K. Harrison, "The Rites and Customs of the Qumran Sect", *Theological Collections II*, p. 29.

[17] *Ibid.*

marry and raise their families in accordance with strict Essene rules as was certainly the case with the Damascus Essene community:

> If members of the community happen to be living in encampments in accordance with a usage which obtains in this country, and if they marry and beget children, they are (in such matters) to follow the precepts of the Law (Torah) and the disciplinary regulations therein prescribed for the relationship of husband to wife and of father to child (CD vii, 6a-9).

A mutilated text for the regulations of camp communities appears to suggest that divorce was not forbidden, rather the man proposing divorce had to obtain permission from the *mebeqqer* (overseer) of his camp (CD xiii, 17).[18] This could as well obtain at Qumran if married people were accepted. It is however difficult to see how married life would work out at Qumran in view of the strict if not ascetic type of discipline imposed on its members. There is an elaborate procedure of entry into the covenant community:

> If any man in Israel wish to be affiliated to the formal congregation of the community, the superintendent (*mebeqqer*) of the general membership is to examine him as to his intelligence and his actions and, if he then embark on a course of training, he has to have him enter into a covenant to return to the truth and turn away from all perversity (1QS vi,13).

The *mebeqqer* then explains to the initiate all the rules of the community. It appears that once the *mebeqqer* is satisfied with the candidate's preliminary qualifications, he joins the community as a probationer. It is not clear whether the formal congregation is consulted for the 'general vote' to give finality to the candidate's admission or rejection immediately following the initial interview with the *mebeqqer*. Whatever the case, after a one year probationary period 'his spiritual attitude and his performance' with regard to the community's doctrine and practice are thoroughly reviewed by the entire membership.

If his understanding and performance are found satisfactory by the general membership he is asked to bring 'all his property and the tools of his profession.' These are handed over to the community's 'minister of works' who records them but they are not made use of until the completion of the second year of probation. After the completion of the second year of probation, the candidate is reviewed further by the general membership and if voted into the community he is registered into the appropriate rank he is to occupy among the members in the community. At this point all the rights of full membership are conferred upon him. Henceforth, his property becomes the community's property and is now open for common use. His judgment and counsel is now to be consulted on all matters pertinent to the life of the community including doctrinal matters, 'judicial procedure, degree of purity and

---

[18] F.F. Bruce, "Jesus and the Gospel in the Light of the Scrolls," *Theological Collections* II, p. 73.

share in the common funds,' all this in accordance to the rank assigned him. He would participate in all deliberations and voting (1QS vi, 13-23).

The candidates are formally accepted at a solemn function at which the priests and Levites bless God for his salvation and the revelation of his truth, and recount the great acts and mercies of God to Israel as well as the iniquities of the children of Israel that are committed 'through the dominion of Belial.' The candidates say 'Amen' to all this and proceed to confess their sins:

> We have acted perversely, we have transgressed, we have sinned, we have done wickedly, ourselves and our fathers before us, in that we have gone counter to the truth. God has been right to bring His judgment upon us and upon our fathers. Howbeit always from ancient times He also bestowed His mercies upon us, and so will He do for all time to come (1QS I, 16-ii, 18).

The priest then invokes the Aaronic blessing upon them: 'May he bless thee ... keep thee ... illuminate ... grace thee ... lift up his ... countenance towards thee ...' adding interpretive comments in between these words, while the Levites invoke a curse upon all that have cast their lot with Belial:

> Cursed art thou for all thy wicked guilty works ... cursed art thou beyond hope of mercy ... May God show thee no favor when thou callest, neither pardon to forgive thine iniquities ... may no man wish thee peace of all that truly claim their patrimony (QS i, 16-ii, 18).

The invocation concludes by cursing everyone who enters the covenant 'with the taint of idolatry in his heart ... saying: may it go well with me, for I shall go on walking in the stubbornness of my heart' to which all the initiates say 'Amen.'

Central to the activities at Qumran was the study of the law. Wherever, there were ten men enrolled in the community there was always to be one, a priest, to interpret the Law to them 'at any time of day or night, for the harmonious adjustment of their human relations.' The members were to be awake 'for a third of all the nights of the year reading books (or the Book of the Law) studying the Law and worshipping together' (1QS vi. 1-8). It was their primary duty to discuss matters pertaining to the apprehension of God's truth and his righteous judgments, so as to

> Guide the minds of the members of the community, to give them insight into God's inscrutable wonders and truth, and to bring them to walk blamelessly each with his neighbor in harmony with all that has been revealed to them. For this is the time when 'the way is being prepared in the wilderness' and it behoves them to understand all that is happening (1QS ix, 16-21).

Thus, for the Qumran covenanters, studying and observing the law, as interpreted by the Teacher of Righteousness and his priests was the fulfillment of Isaiah's prophecy which refers to the preparations for the Lord (Messiah) in the wilderness (Isa 40:3). However, they are sternly warned not to discuss any matters, pertaining to the Law with non-members:

> And in the company of forward men everyone is to abstain from talk about (i.e. keep

hidden) the meaning of the Law (Torah) (1QS ix, 16-21).

The community was esoteric. Its teachings concerning the meaning of the Law and the prophets were kept secret and could only be passed on to the initiates. Not only were the members obliged to guard their teaching from the public but also they were enjoined to hate all the 'sons of darkness' that is non-members. The member:

> Is to bear unremitting hatred towards all men of ill repute, and be minded to keep in seclusion from them (1QS ix, 21-26).

They also had an elaborate penitential code prescribing punitive measures to a wide range of offences that could be committed by the covenanters. Certain crimes warranted expulsion with no room for return. These included mentioning the Name (YHWH), slandering the entire community, complaining against the very basis of the community, defecting after twelve years and any association with such a defector. Another group of offences included being out of state of purity as punishment in addition to decreasing the food ration of the offender for a specific period, usually one to two years. These included lying about wealth, nursing anger against the priests, slandering one's neighbour and apostasy. There were many other minor offences like rudeness against one's superior, indecent talk, interrupting a speaker at a public session, leaving the session for three times without proper reasons, sleeping or spitting at a public session, indecent dress, indecent laughter and many others. Punishment for these offences consisted mainly of reducing the food ration for a specific period of time ranging from 10 days to six months (1QS vi, 23-vii, 5-25).

Every year at the time when the feast of weeks or Pentecost was celebrated in mainline Judaism, the covenanters held their annual convention where affairs of the community were fully deliberated:

> Their spiritual attitudes and there performance are to be reviewed, however, year by year, some being promoted by virtue of their (improved) understanding and the integrity of their conduct, and others demoted for their waywardness (1QS v. 20-24).

Those who appear to be more advanced in their understanding and practice of the law as interpreted by the community were appointed leaders, preachers and 'apostles' of the sect at this occasion.[19]

The members took their meals together. Each of them took their seats in order of rank or class with the priests occupying the first place. None would start eating before the blessing from a priest. They also indulged in regular lustrations which also appear to have a sacral significance.

Their feasts and ceremonies were based on a calendar different from the one used in official Judaism at Jerusalem. Theirs was a luni-solar calendar which is

---

[19] Theodor H. Gaster, *The Dead Sea Scriptures, in English Translation with Introduction and Notes*, Garden City, New York: Doubleday, 1956.

depicted in the Book of Jubilees adopted by many other sectarian Jews. They appear to have discontinued the practice of offering sacrifices. The daily lustrations seem to have replaced these offerings.

The sectarians produced their food and tanned skin for leather ware and parchment at Ein Feshka, one and half miles south of the settlement.[20] It also appears that there were a lot of dates in the area at the time of their occupation. Archaeology has shown that there are trunks of date trees now fossilized under the sea and this suggests that the strip of water in which these are fond formed part of the seashore in their day.

It is sufficient at this point to briefly look at some similarities and differences between the Qumran community and the early Church in terms of their practice. Common to both communities was the 'church idea,' a sense of being a community called by God as a new people of God in fulfillment of prophecy. Both referred to themselves as 'the poor,' or 'the way'. The role of the *mebeqqer* is almost identical with that of the overseer or bishop in the early church. Both operated independently from the temple although a wing of the early Christian community continued with their temple services including James, Peter and John. Confession and repentance were necessary conditions for entry into each of the communities. The twelve apostles in the primitive Church recall the council of twelve laymen and three priests at Qumran. The members of the primitive church participated in the decision making processes through participation in deliberating and voting just as the Qumran members did. The study of scriptures and devotions were a central activity in both communities. Both practiced some kind of baptism whether as an initiation rite or as a regular practice for maintaining ritual purity.

The common meals at Qumran correspond to the earliest form of the Lord's Supper in the Palestine tradition when it was still a full meal. Both communities were founded by leaders who were believed by their followers to possess a new revelation of the mysteries of God and his kingdom. Hence, the manner in which these leaders understood and interpreted scripture was crucial to the foundation and development of the communities. Both communities also shared their property through the central administration of each community.

There were some crucial differences, however, in their practice. While the Qumran community still looked forward to the coming of the Messiah, for the Christians the Messiah had already come. The Teacher of Righteousness was neither a Messiah nor any of the eschatological figures. The priestly emphasis of Qumran is lacking in the early church. While the Qumran covenanters withdrew from the general public and kept their teaching secret, the early church was established among the public and proclaimed its good news to all. Entry into the Qumran

---

[20] Gaalyah Cornfeld, *Archaeology of the Bible*, p. 258.

community involved a vigorous process of a lengthy period. Entry into the primitive church is almost immediate at the declaration of faith in Jesus.

The penitential code of Qumran has been compared to the ethical code in the 'Sermon on the Mount' in the gospel of Matthew 5-7. But a casual reading of the two 'codes' is enough to show that the Christian 'code' is far from being a 'practical' one.[21]

The Biblical Exegesis of the Qumran Community

The importance of the Dead Sea Scrolls found at Qumran is not limited to the New Testament. The scrolls have also contributed much to the critical studies of the Old Testament.[22] However, our interest is in their exegesis as it relates to the New Testament. It has been observed that 'there is no hermeneutical principle of interpretation in the New Testament which cannot be exactly matched in the Qumran literature.'[23] Our task, therefore, in this section is to look at the presupposition which governed their exegesis then proceed to see how it works out in practice, and then relate this to what we find in the New Testament exegetical tradition.

Their Presupposition

The basic presupposition to their biblical exegesis is their understanding that the word of God as presented in the Law and the prophets (i.e. the Hebrew Bible) remains a divine mystery (Heb, 'raz', Gk: 'mysterion'). In order to understand its meaning, therefore, there is need for a divinely inspired interpretation ('pesher') and that such an interpretation can not be attained by ordinary human wisdom.[24] Since the real meaning of scripture is veiled in divine mystery, God's divine purpose cannot be properly understood unless its 'pesher' has been revealed as well. So far in redemptive history God only gave his word to the prophets in its mystery dress. It is only in their day that its pesher was made known to His chosen interpreter, the Teacher of Righteousness, the founder of the community.

---

[21] These apparent similarities and differences are almost certainly found in any text on the Dead Sea Scrolls. Here we can mention Millar Burrows, *More Light on the Dead Sea Scrolls and New Interpretations with Translations of Important Recent Discoveries*, London: Secker and Warburg, 1958, Chapter X, F.F. Bruce, *Second Thoughts on the Dead Sea Scrolls*, Carlisle: Paternoster, 1961, Chapter XII; J.M. Allegro, *The Dead Sea Scrolls*, Harmondsworth: Penguin 1959, Chapter 11.

[22] For a thorough treatment of their contribution to Old Testament Studies, see Millar Burrows, *The Dead Sea Scrolls with Translation by the Author*, New York: Viking Press, 1961, pp. 301-324; F.F. Bruce, *Second Thoughts on the Dead Sea Scrolls*, pp. 56-69.

[23] Allegro, *The Dead Sea Scrolls*, p. 137.

[24] F.F. Bruce, *Biblical Exegesis in the Qumran Texts*, London: Tyndale, 1960, p. 8.

From this basic understanding of the nature and history of revelation we can outline three principles:

1. That God revealed his divine will to His servants the prophets. However, this revelation could not be understood in terms of its manner and time of fulfillment until its meaning was revealed to the Teacher of Righteousness.
2. Since all prophecy could only be meaningful through its interpretation by the Teacher of Righteousness, who himself appeared in the last days, all prophecy referred to the End-time.[25] It is to that age of fulfilment that its real meaning belonged.
3. The time of the end is at hand.[26] But the community sees itself as already living in this age of fulfilment. The real meaning of all prophecy veiled throughout prophetic history is now, therefore, to be known and applied to the history of the sect and its contemporaries.

It is in the light of these exegetical presuppositions that biblical prophecies of varying dates and references are interpreted as directly applying to the commentators' own day. Texts are 'atomized' in order to make them meaningful to current situations, and textual variants are put to the service of the commentators' purpose. Where the text does not seem to suggest an immediate relationship to the commentators' situation, allegory is resorted to.[27]

Thus, the Old Testament Scriptures at Qumran are freely adapted and modified in various ways, as the examples below will show, in order to get from them a meaning that they considered real and relevant to their own historical situation without any regard to what a modern critic would call the original context of the biblical text. For according to them the text did not have any 'real' meaning in that context, or at least it could in that context be unknown.

---

[25] Other scholars have seen three different types of interpretation. They have seen the explanation of the texts as referring to (1) the history of the sect, (2) a different ethnic group in the framework of contemporary history, (3) eschatological events, as three distinctive types of interpretation. However, it seems to me better to consider all these as falling under one type of interpretation—historical interpretation—since all the three aspects mentioned can fit that type of interpretation as M. Burrows suggests: the history of the sect, the contemporary framework as well as the eschatological aspects are "historical" because they are all in the "now" of the Qumran community or at least begin there since the community conceived of itself as an eschatological entity. See Burrows, *More Light on the Dead Sea Scrolls*, p. 166.
[26] Bruce, *Biblical Exegesis in the Qumran Texts*, pp 9-10. Cf. Bruce, *Second Thought on the Dead Sea Scrolls*, p. 77.
[27] Bruce, *Second Thoughts on the Dead Sea Scrolls*, p.77.

The Exegetical Practice

The free adaptation and modification of scripture for a liturgical purpose is seen in the manner the Aaronic blessing (Numbers 6:24-26) is employed. The text of the Bible reads:

> May He bless you and preserve you, May He lighten your heart, May he raise His Merciful face towards you for everlasting bliss.

However, the covenanters add certain interpretive phrases to these words so that their version reads:

> May He bless you with all good and preserve you from all evil! May he lighten your heart with life-giving wisdom and grant you eternal knowledge! May He raise His merciful face towards you for everlasting bliss![28]

The text of Habakkuk as quoted by the commentator in some cases appears in one form while its explanation seems to presuppose a different form of the text. In the standard text Hab 1:11 reads:

> Then shall he sweep by as a wind, and shall pass over, and be guilty; even he whose might is his god.

And the text in the commentary reads:

> Then the wind sweeps by and passes: and another whose might is his god, proceeds to wreak devastation.

Then the interpretation reads:

> This refers to the rules of the Kittaeans. In their guilt-ridden Council House they keep replacing those rulers one after another.

Now, notice that in the standard text there is a reference to the concept of guilt. This idea is not found in the text as quoted by our commentator. Yet the concept of guilt is reflected in his interpretation.

In Hab 2:15 the standard text has 'their nakedness.' But our commentator introduces a slight orthographic change to it to become 'their festivals or feats or seasons.' Then, he introduces a root verb meaning 'exile'. And then, in his interpretation, says it applies to the Teacher of Righteousness who was pursued and persecuted in 'exile' on the 'season' of rest, that is, on Atonement Day. Also in Hab 2:16, the standard text has 'be uncircumcised' while the quote in the commentary reads 'stagger' and yet in his interpretation the idea of circumcision is brought up: 'because he did circumcise the foreskin of his heart.' These are cases of changing a text of quotation and then use both the old and the new reading in the interpretation.

Hab 1:12-23 and 2:5 provide us with instances where a text is 'atomized' or changed in order to make it fit to a new historical situation. In both verses of the first

---

[28] This textual translation is taken from G. Vermes, *The Dead Sea Scrolls in English*, London: Penguin.

text, according to the original context of Habakkuk, it is the prophet who is addressing God. The commentator interprets it accordingly in verse 12. However, the commentator wants verse 13 not to address God but those who did not support the Teacher of Righteousness during his persecution by the wicked priest (or the man of lies). To suit this new application, therefore, the commentator changes the 'thou' (singular) of the original text which refers to God to 'you' (plural) which is now made to refer to the members of the 'House of Absalom.' Similarly in Hab 2:5, the commentator replaces the word of wine *(hyyn)* by another for wealth *(hwn)* so that the text should speak about the greed of the wicked priest in contrast to the holy poverty of the sect.

An allegorical interpretation is involved on the Habakkuk pesher (1Qp Hab xi, 17xii, 5) for Hab 2:17.

> The violence of Lebanon shall overwhelm thee and the assault of wild beasts shall crush you.....'

The statement refers to the wicked priest and means that God will mete out to him the treatment that he meted out to the needy. 'Lebanon' stands here for the Communal Council, and 'wild beasts' for the single-minded Jews who carry out the Law.

In the historical setting, however, Habakkuk refers to the cutting down of the cedars of Lebanon by Chaldeans for military and other use, and to the hunting of animals living there.

Another way in which they used scripture is re-interpretation of the Old Testament writings. Habakkuk 1:6 begins: 'For, lo, I raise up the Chaldeans, that bitter and hasty nation...' In the *pesher* this is interpreted as referring to the Kittaens (Kittim) who are generally believed to be either the Seleucids or the Romans. But Habakkuk appears to be himself interpreting for his own day Isaiah's warning concerning the Assyrian invasion of Judah (Isa 29:13f).

In a Qumran *Testimonia*, there is a compound quotation of Deut 5:28-29 and Deut 18:18, and the latter text is also quoted in Acts 3:22, 7:37 where again Acts 3:22 combines the 'threat' motif from Deut 18 and the 'promise' motif form Genesis 12:3.[29]

Other methods of interpretation include splitting words and then proceed to use their two parts in the interpretation, and using more than one meaning of a term and proceed to comment on both.

Let us now turn to New Testament exegesis to see how New Testament writers also freely adapt and modify the Old Testament text to favour their interpretations. It

---

[29] For a thorough discussion of these compound quotations, see Allegro, *The Dead Sea Scrolls*, pp. 138f; Barnabas Lindars, *New Testament Apologetic. The Doctrinal Significance of the Old Testament Quotations*: London: SCM, 1961, pp. 207-210.

is probably important to note at the outset that the *pesher* form of interpretation appears to be found in the New Testament especially in the Gospel of Matthew and the Gospel of John particularly on the Psalms and the prophetic books.[30]

Matt 2:6 appears to be a pesher on Micah 5:2. Matthew's quote reads:

> And you, O Bethlehem, in the land of Judah, are by no means least among the rulers of Judah, for from you shall come a ruler, who will govern my people Israel.

And the Old Testament text reads:

> But you, O Bethlehem Ephrathah who are little to be among the clans of Judah from you shall come forth for me one who is to be ruler in Israel.

Apparently Matthew's aim is to show that the birth of Jesus in Bethlehem was already foretold by the prophets. In order to fit this text to the birth of the Messiah, Matthew identifies the geographical term 'Ephrathah' with 'Land of Judah,' changes the whole sentence structure to imply that Bethlehem is not the least while the original text says she is, changes 'clans of Judah' to 'rulers of Judah'; omits 'for me' and elaborates 'Israel' by the phrase 'my people Israel.'

Matthew also finds an explanation for Jesus' use of parables in Psalms 78:2 in relation to the "mystery" nature of God's revelation, a significant motif in the New Testament. Matthew quotes it as:

> I will open my mouth in parables, I will utter what has been hidden since the foundation of the world (13:35).

But the Old Testament text has:

> I will open my mouth in a parable, I will utter dark sayings from of old, things that we have heard and known, that our fathers have told us.

Thus, in order to emphasize the newness of the revelation that has come through Jesus' life and teaching, Matthew takes 'dark sayings from of old' to mean 'hidden since the foundation of the world' and neglects verse 3 which explains that these dark or hidden things have already been explained by the fathers and are quite well known.

Matthew also finds the events of Palm Sunday fulfilling two separate prophecies which he brings together into a composite quotation and at the same time changes the original structure of one of the quotations to imply there were two animals involved. Matthew's quote reads:

> Tell the daughter of Zion, Behold, your king is coming to you, humble and mounted on an ass, and on a colt, the foal of an ass (21:5)

The Zechariah 9:9 passage says:

> Rejoice greatly, O daughter of Zion! Shout aloud, O daughter of Jerusalem! Lo, your king comes to you, triumphant and victorious is he, humble and riding on an ass, on a colt, the foal of an ass.

---

[30] Lindars, *New Testament Apologetic*, pp. 259-272.

While the Isaiah 62:11 passage reads:

> Say to the daughters of Zion, 'Behold, your salvation comes…

This is a case of a compound quotation. Matthew's free structural changes of his quotation from Zachariah, however, leads him to a strange suggestion in verse 7 where he presents Jesus as sitting on both animals.

An allegorical use of the Old Testament in the New Testament is found in Paul's letter to the Galatians (4:22-27) where he interprets the two wives of Abraham, Sarah and Hagar as the two covenants, one spiritual and heavenly and the other earthly and of the flesh.

Conclusion

In this chapter I have discussed the historical background of the Qumran community which was primarily rooted in political and religious discontent generated by the poor governance of the Ptolemid and Seleucid regimes and the secularization of the priesthood, a situation that was not sufficiently addressed by the Hasmonean dynasty who later replaced these foreign regimes. I have also discussed their religious life at Qumran and how they interpreted their scriptures. From the examples of their exegetical practice provided in this chapter, it can be concluded that the Qumran covenanters and the New Testament writers share a similar exegetical tradition. However, there are significant differences between the two groups even in this area. When the latter prophets of the Old Testament and the New Testament writers echoed the words of their predecessors they meant that the words which were applicable in the context of their original proclamation appear to be applicable and relevant to the contemporary situation. This sense is lacking in Qumran literature.[31] It is also significant to note that while the sect considered its interpretation of the law to be very important and deserving to be "preserved without change and strictly enforced," Jesus criticized the traditional interpretation of the Pharisees, in many ways less strict than those of the covenanters, charging scribes of making God's law ineffective by these traditions. Jesus himself interpreted scriptures freely but 'according to its inner intent.'[32]

---

[31] Bruce, *Biblical Exegesis in Qumran Texts*, p. 17.
[32] Burrows, *Dead Sea Scrolls*, p. 251. For an illustration of how Jesus interpreted Scripture, see Bruce, "Jesus and the Gospels in the Light of the Scrolls," *Theological Collections II*, pp. 72-3.

Chapter Two
Significance of the Ddead Sea Scrolls: Theology of the Qumran Community

Introduction

In the previous chapter, I discussed the history of the Qumran community and some of their practices. The community also achieved significant developments in theological reflection. In this chapter I shall look at their theological perspectives in relation to the New Testament. I will focus on dualism, eschatology, sacraments, the after-life and on religious language.

1. Dualism

The basic philosophical and religious concept that shaped the religious and theological outlook of the Qumran covenanters is the belief in the powers of the two spirits: The Prince of Light and the Angel of Darkness whom God created before the foundation of the world. At the root of their understanding of the powers of these two spirits is the concept of predestination. There is a clear statement of pre-determinism in Enoch 81:1,2: "And he said unto me: 'Observe, Enock, these heavenly tablets and read what is written thereon and mark every individual fact.' And I observed the heavenly tablets ... of all deeds of mankind, and of all children of the flesh that shall be upon the earth to the remotest generation.."[1] This sense is echoed in 1QS 3:15f:

> All that is and ever was comes from a God of Knowledge. Before things came into existence, He determined the plan of them; and when they fill their appointed roles, it is in accordance with His glorious design that they discharge their function. Nothing can be changed.

The pesher on Habakkuk 2:3b reads "for all the ages of God reach their appointed end as he determines for them in the mysteries of his wisdom." The War Scroll (1QS 1: 4) speaks of the day appointed for the destruction of the sons of darkness. The Hymn Scroll tells us that all that happens is engraved in the tablets of remembrance (1QH 1:24).

Human destiny is also included in this predestination. Josephus tells us:

> But the sect of the Essenes affirm that fate governs all things, and that nothing befalls

---

[1] Schubert, *The Dead Sea Community*, p. 59.

men but what is according to its determination.[2]

Man is born in iniquity right from the mother's womb (1QH 4:29f) and that he can only take the right way by divine illumination (4:5). The members of the Qumran community are the *bene rashon* (sons of divine good pleasure) or the *bechire rashon* (the elect of divine good pleasure) (4:3; 1QS 8:6).

Thus the whole world is divided into two opposing camps, one under the Prince of Light and the other under the Angel of Darkness. Man therefore behaves in accordance with the spirit apportioned to him:

> Thus far, the spirits of truth and perversity have been struggling in the heart of man. Men have walked both in wisdom and in folly. If a man casts his portion with truth, he does righteously and hates perversity; if he casts it with perversity, he does wickedly and abominates truth (1Qsiii, 13-iv. 26).

Allegro informs us of a document which suggests that these spirits are apportioned at birth depending on the position of the stars and that the propositions within man can be numerically calculated.[3] However, this predestination does not appear to be absolute. Man is still able to make almost independent choices which then lead to either punishment or reward. The wicked are reserved for 'the day of slaughter,' because:

> They walk in the way of the bad and spurn thy covenant and their soul abhors thy statutes and they take no pleasure in all thou has commanded, but choose that which thou hatest (1QH xv, 19-26).

While the wicked are destroyed for choosing that which God hates, the elect, the members of the Qumran community, voluntarily 'declare their readiness to run away from evil and adhere to all that God in His good pleasure has commanded' (1QS, v. 1). It therefore appears that to become a member of the 'elect' according to Qumran understanding is not the case of either predestination or free will (free choice) but rather one of both predestination and free will. Allegro has a similar understanding of the community. 'But the Qumran covenanter has his answer. For all men there was one way of salvation depending on his will and the mercy of God.'[4] Also the statements which emphasize the importance of good works, those that blame men for yielding to temptation and indulgence in sinful behaviour - like CD 3:7, 4:9-10 on the evil who are punished for rejecting God's will and do their own; 1QS iii, 1 on those who deliberately reject the sectarian interpretation of the Torah; 1QS v, 11

---

[2] Flavius Josephus, 'Antiquities of the Jews, '12, 15, 19 in William Whiston (transl.), *The Complete Works of Josephus*, Grand Rapids: Kregel, 1981.
[3] Allegro, *The Dead Sea Scrolls*, pp. 125-125.
[4] Ibid., p. 126. See also Schubert, *The Dead Sea Community*, p. 59.

where the wicked commit both 'unknown sins' and 'deliberate sins' - do suggest free will, also the emphasis on repentance does not favour absolute predestination.[5]

E.P. Sanders also suggests that predestination and free will in Qumran religious thought should not be seen as alternative theological positions but as different explanations of the community's self-understanding:

> Just as from one point of view the members of the community are said to be the elect of God, they are from another point of view, said to elect God or to volunteer.[6]

Therefore, to say that wickedness is caused by the Angel of Darkness is not to deny that it is a result of man's sin. A similar dualism is basic to the New Testament thought particularly expressed in the Johannine writings and to some extent in Pauline literature. The forces of Light and Darkness; Truth and Falsehood are usually pictured in a state of opposition:

> God is light and in him is no darkness at all. If we say we have fellowship with him while we walk in darkness, we lie and do not live according to the truth; but if we walk, in the light, as he is in the light, we have fellowship with one another (1 Jn 1:5-7).

The spirits need to be tested to discern the one from God:

> Do not believe every spirit, but test the spirits to see whether they are of God ... By this you know the spirit of God, every spirit which confesses that Jesus Christ has come in the flesh is of God and every spirit which does not confess Jesus is not of God ... By this we know the spirit of truth and the spirit of error (1 Jn 4:1-3, 6).

Also in the prologue to the fourth gospel:

> In him was life, and the life was the light of men. The light shines in the darkness and the darkness has not overcome it ... The true light that enlightens every man was coming into the world (John 1:4-5, 9).

The problem of temptation and sin in the New Testament is to be understood as rooted in this state of opposition and conflict between God and Satan. Because of this state of affairs the believer is in constant danger of being tempted. Paul sends Timothy to the Thessalonians to be ensured of their faith. He fears 'that somehow the tempter had tempted you and that our labour would be in vain' (1 Thes 3:5); Paul advises couples in the Corinthian Church not to separate too long 'lest Satan tempt you...' and warns the Galatian believers to restore an apostate brother with gentleness 'lest you be tempted' (Gal 6:1).

---

[5] For a thorough discussion of the same view, see Raymond E. Brown, 'The Qumran Scrolls and the Johannine Gospels and Epistles,' in Krister Stendahl (ed.), *The Dead Sea Scrolls and the New Testament*, Westport: Greenwood Press, 1975, p. 191.

[6] E.P. Sanders, *Paul and Palestinian Judaism A Comparison of Patterns of Religion*, London: SCM, 1977, p. 282.

On account of the same basic dualistic outlook, Jesus sees his ministry, teaching, and even death in the framework of a struggle between God and Satan in the world:

> And the scribes who came down from Jerusalem said, 'He is possessed by Beelzebul, and by the prince of demons he casts out demons.' And he said to them ... How can Satan cast out Satan? If a kingdom is divided against itself, that kingdom cannot stand ... but is coming to an end. But no one can enter a strong man's house and plunder his goods, unless he first binds the strong man.' (Mark 3:22-27; also Lk 11:15-22).

At this point it is significant to note that the concept of dualism as found in both Qumran and the New Testament is lacking in the Old Testament where the struggle is rather between an individual and his attempts at fulfilling the Law.[7] It has been argued by many scholars that this dualism has its origin in Zoroastrianism where there is one God, 'Ahura Mazda,' two opposing spirits which are co-existent from all eternity, and the apocalyptic end of the world that envisages an end to all evil. It has been suggested, especially by K.G. Kuhn, that this dualism has been modified through its contact with the doctrine of creation in Judaism[8] so that the Qumran concept of two created spirits is a result of a synthesis of both Persian and Jewish lines of religious thought.

Whatever source it has, Qumran dualism presents us with a background framework for understanding the dualism of the New Testament. It provides the missing link between the Old Testament and the New Testament religious thought.

> Hellenistic Gnosticism as a source does not suit the nature of Qumran dualism. The former dualism is physical (between spirit and matter) while the latter is both ethical (moral and spiritual) and eschatological[9] looking forward to the defeat of the spirit of perversity at the end-time through God's intervention in support of the spirit of truth.

However, there are significant differences between Qumran and New Testament dualism which almost completely rule out any suggestion for a relationship or dependence between the two movements. While the spirit of truth in Qumran is a created spirit, in the New Testament the Spirit is a third member of the Trinity who

---

[7] Brown, *The Scrolls and the New Testament*, p. 185; see also Max Wilcox, 'Dualism, Gnosticism and other Elements in the Pre-Pauline Tradition,' *Theological Collections II*, p. 85.

[8] Kuhn's view of seeing the difference basically lying in Jewish doctrine of creation has been criticized on the following grounds: (1) Lack of precise information regarding age, actual content and development of ancient Persian religion. (2) The men of Qumran regarded themselves as Jews who sincerely believed were being faithful to the faith of their fathers, (3) Mere similarity in language and thought forms is not sufficient to prove that the literature under consideration is a product of a particular age. See Wilcom 'Dualism, Gnosticism and other Elements in Pre-Pauline Tradition,' *Theological Collections II* pp. 86-87.

[9] *Ibid.*, p. 88.

is himself uncreated. While in Qumran it is the Angel of Light who leads men to salvation, in the New Testament it is God himself who is the light and who comes into the world to lighten it through the person of Jesus Christ.

Secondly, becoming a 'son of light' in Qumran is achieved through good works of the Law and acceptance of the Teacher's interpretation of it. In the New Testament, however, it is only through faith in the person of Jesus Christ.

It is above all the Christological factor, which makes the New Testament distinctive. With the coming of Jesus darkness already passes away. The struggle is already won and hence the combatants no longer engage at equal footing as do the forces in the scrolls. Victory is already at hand. In Qumran the opposing camps engage each other with equal strength to the very end although they will partake in the bringing down of judgment upon the wicked (a feature now anticipated in their present cursing of Belial and hating all his followers). Victory is still future. Christ makes the difference.

II Eschatology

From its beginning, the Qumran community was conscious of its eschatological character. It was an end-time community called by God out of apostate Israel into the wilderness to prepare the way for their coming messiah. Their mission is to be understood in the context of their understanding of the prophecy of Isaiah which differs significantly from that of John the Baptist although both are eschatological. In 1QS iii, 13-16, Isaiah is quoted:

> They are to be kept apart from any consort with forward men, to the end that they indeed go into the wilderness to prepare the way, 'i.e., do what scripture enjoins when it says, 'prepare in the wilderness the way...make straight in the desert a highway for our God' (Isaiah 40:3).

The reference is to the study of the Law which God commanded through Moses to the end that, as occasion arises, all things may be done in accordance with what is revealed through God's Holy Spirit.

John the Baptist's quote of Isaiah 40:3 reads:

> The voice of one crying in the wilderness: prepare the way of the Lord, make his paths straight.

The Old Testament Isaiah 40:3 text says:

> A voice cries: 'In the wilderness prepare the way of the Lord, make straight in the desert a high way for our God.'

Notice that the Qumran commentator drops the first three words: 'A voice cries' which John elaborates as 'the voice of one crying' and applies it to himself. Thus from the same prophecy, Qumran covenanters see a call upon themselves to prepare for the coming Messiah through strict obedience of the Law in a monastic setting keeping their teaching secret. Their emphasis is on 'prepare in the wilderness the way.' John, however, sees himself as the 'voice' that cries in the wilderness. Hence, he primarily sees himself as a herald or preacher whose role is to spread the news that the Lord is coming hence people should repent of their sins. There are no legalistic and esoteric elements in John, elements that are basic to the covenanters. Nor does John establish a monastic community of followers.

III Sacramental Aspects

1. Ritual washing: To enter the community is to become a member of an eschatological community, a people called out to prepare for the Messiah. The initial acceptance of a ritual washing or a baptism was a mark of entry into such a community.

The ritual character of these washings which were regular and self-administered is attested by the strict requirements prescribed for the purification water:

> Now, concerning purification by water. No one is to bathe in dirty water or in water which is too scant to produce a ripple. No man is to purify himself with water drawn in a vessel or in a rock-pool where there is insufficient (water). If an unclean person comes in contact with such water, he merely renders it unclean (CD x, 10-13).

The covenanters were to wash themselves before the common meals, after visiting a toilet and even when touched by a younger member.[10] The excavations of the cisterns at Qumran also testify to the significance of these washings to the covenanters.[11]

However, these washings could only be effective and meaningful when accompanied by genuine repentance and complete turn to God:

> Anyone who refuses to enter the ideal society of God and persists in walking in the stubbornness of his heart shall not be admitted to this community of God's truth... He cannot be cleared by mere ceremonies of atonement, nor cleansed by any waters of ablution, not sanctified by immersion in lakes or rivers nor purified by any bath. Unclean, unclean he remains as long as he rejects the government of God and refuses the discipline of communion with Him. For it is only through the spiritual apprehension of God's truth that man's ways can be properly directed... Only by a spirit of uprightness and humility can his sin be atoned (1QS ii, 25-iii 6).

Thus the moral qualities that obtain at Qumran to make the washings effective are the same as those that John the Baptist called for in his preaching. The washing at Qumran takes a sacral character. Josephus says about John the Baptist:

> (He) was a good man, and commanded the Jews to exercise virtue, both as to righteousness towards one another, and piety towards God, and so to come to baptism

---

[10] Shubert, *The Dead Sea Community*, p. 54.
[11] Kathleen M. Kenyon, *The Bible and Recent Archaeology*, London: British Museum Publications, 1978, p. 94.

for that the washing (with water) would be acceptable to him if they made use of it, not in order to put away (or the remission) of some sins (only), but for the purification of the body: supposing still that the soul was thoroughly purified before hand by righteousness.[12]

Apparently Josephus appears to be inconsistent with Mark 1:4 which says John preached 'a baptism of repentance for the forgiveness of sins.' But it is probable that Josephus is only implying that the forgiveness of sins can only be realized by fulfilling moral conditions of cleansing not through the ritual act by itself.

The opening to the quote above (1QS ii, 25-iii, 6) however appears to imply that salvation for Qumran is strongly and practically associated with the community itself.

Both at Qumran and for John the Baptist, baptism has an eschatological significance, pointing to the outpouring of the Holy Spirit in the Messianic era which was just at hand:

> I baptize you with water for repentance, but he who is coming after me is mightier than I ... He will baptize you with the Holy Spirit and with fire. (Mt 3:11-12).[13]

In the scrolls the idea of cleansing with the spirit is found in 1QS iv, 20, 21:

> God will purge all the acts of man in the crucible of His truth, and refine for himself all the fabric of man, destroying every spirit of perversity from within his flesh and cleansing him by the Holy Spirit from all the effects of wickedness. Like waters of purification, he will sprinkle upon him the spirit of truth.

However, there are differences even in the area of baptism and lustration. For John, the rite of water baptism was administered once for all, prefiguring more directly the baptism of 'The Coming One' while for Qumran, they were daily washings, self-administered and even more than once each day. While John's call for repentance and the proclamation of the coming one was addressed to all, only the initiate would have access to the esoteric teaching of Qumran. While for Qumran fulfilling the moral requirement of repentance was to strictly follow the Torah as interpreted by the Teacher of Righteousness, for John it was more ethical than legal duty which would prepare the people by rendering them well disposed to faith in Jesus.

It has been questioned whether the reference to holy spirit in 1QS iv, 20, 21, should be understood in the New Testament sense. Davies has argued that in this text the spirit is impersonal and that it lacks the dynamic eschatological power associated with the Holy Spirit in both the Old and the New Testament where he is

---

[12] Josephus, 'Antiquities,' 18, 5, 2.

[13] For the argument that John is referring to two baptisms, one of the endowment of the Holy Spirit upon God's people and another of fire (judgment) upon the wicked although an element of purifying is also present in the baptism of the Spirit, see Charles H.H. Scobie, 'John the Baptist'. *Theological Collections* II, pp. 59-61.

personal and a third member of the Godhead.[14] Coupled with the fact that it is only here in the scrolls that the Holy Spirit is mentioned in an eschatological setting, it can be concluded that the sect does not have a developed teaching on the role of the Spirit at the end of the time as does the New Testament. The phrase "holy spirit" could as well only amount to a literary expression referring to a good disposition to God's truth.

2. Sacral meals

The second sacramental aspect is their meals. It appears that the Qumran covenanters discontinued sacrificial offerings but continued with the daily baths and sacral meals both of which acquired a deeper religious significance. While originally washings were a means to secure cultic purity they now mediate divine forgiveness of sins as has been shown above.

The common meal at Qumran was strictly regulated. Our ancient source, Josephus, again appears to provide us with authentic witness at this point.

> After the purification they assemble in a special room which none of the uninitiated is permitted to enter; pure now themselves, they repair to the refectory as to some sacred shrine. When they have seated themselves in silence, the baker serves the loaves in order, and the cook sets before each one plate with a single course. Before the meal, the priest gives the blessing, and it is unlawful to partake before the prayer. The meal ended, he offers a further prayer; thus at the beginning and at the close they do homage to God as the bountiful giver of life (Bell 2,8,5).[15]

At this occasion, as at all public sessions, members only speak in order of their rank (1Qs vi, 10). They also take up their seats according to their respective ranks (1QS vi 8). Food is also served according to the same principle (1QS vi 4). Before they start eating the priest invokes a blessing, and it is unlawful to start eating before this is done (1QS vi 5). Further no one who is not initiated into the community could partake in these meals. None is allowed to touch it before the priest (1QSa ii, 18f). These prescriptions, together with the requirement of at least 10 men and a bath before every meal appear to give the common meal a sacral character.

This view is further supported by the manner in which the messianic banquet is described in 1Qsa ii, 18f where the two messiahs are present. The messianic expectations will soon be discussed. At this point it is sufficient to note that some scholars have questioned the sacral character of the meals of Qumran on account of the last statement in the Messianic Rule (1Qsa): "This rule is to obtain at all meals

---

[14] W.D. Davies, "Paul and the Dead Sea Scrolls: Flesh and Spirit, "*The Scrolls and the New Testament*, p. 173.

[15] Karl G.Kuhn, "The Lord's Supper and the Communal Meal at Qumran," *The Scrolls and the New Testament*, p. 173.

where there are ten or more men present." Apart from the suggestion that the meals were simply ordinary as this closing statement implies, it is also argued that the word for "meal" more generally meant "arrangement."[16] Schiffman argues:

> These meals conducted regularly as part of the present-age way of life of the sect, were pre-enactments of the final messianic banquet which the sectarians expected in the soon-to-come end of days. Again the life of the sect in this world mirrored its dreams for the age to come.[17]

However, it is difficult to see how this position can be sustained. The manner in which these meals are described gives the impression that they are messianic, eschatological, generally unusual and rarely celebrated. This is especially the case with the meal described in 1Qsa, the very place where the problematic statement is found. The ceremonial aspect of these meals is further attested by the excavation findings of small pockets of animal bones buried when flesh was removed. It would appear that bones of animals eaten at those occasions could not be thrown away anyhow.[18]

Rather than to deny the general nature of the meals described in the scrolls we would here suggest that ordinary meals in a sense of a meal that does not meet all the formal prescriptions (eg. the requirement of 10 men) are simply not described in the scrolls. In support of this view, we would argue that the very prescription that at least ten men or more be present at the meal occasions described in the scrolls presupposes other situations where for some reason these could not be met in which case meals taken at such occasions could be ordinary and not formal and sacral in character. If our suggestion is correct, then the Qumran meals which are sacral in character according to the manner in which they are described can be considered "common" in the sense that they are daily meals and that they are taken at the monastic centre where the prescribed conditions could almost always be met without requiring ourselves to think that the meals described in the scrolls are the "only type" of meals partaken by the members of the sect.

The Messianic Rule (1Qsa) visualized a messianic banquet with the two messiahs at the head. However, at the actual meal the messiah of Israel was not represented for he was to come at consummation (1QS vi).

Although the texts in the scrolls do not reflect a clear interpretation of the cult meal as was the case with the washings above, that the meals had a religious significance of a sacral character is almost certain in the light of the central position of the cult meal at Qumran. From careful study of *Joseph and Asenath*, an ancient work, Kuhn has deduced the meaning of a religious Jewish meal and concludes that

---

[16] VanderKam, *The Dead Sea Scrolls Today* pp. 174, 175.
[17] Ibid., p. 175
[18] Kenyon. *The Bible and Recent Archaeology*, p. 94.

eating the bread and drinking the cup "mediates immortality and eternal life"[19] and suggests that this may as well apply to the Qumran meals.

In the New Testament the Qumran meals particularly correspond to the earliest Palestinian Christian meal fellowship which was a continuation of Jesus' meal fellowship by his disciples after his death and resurrection. While there is no consensus among scholars as to whether the Lord's Supper was a Passover celebration,[20] Jesus' last meal with the disciples where he declares he will not partake in these meals any more "until it is fulfilled in the kingdom of God," (Lk 22:15f; Mk 14:25; 1 Cor, 11:29) has a parallel in the Rule of Congregation (1Qsa, ii, 11f) where an eschatological messianic meal is described.

In the New Testament the Lord's Supper has always maintained a sacral significance although as the Church expanded from Palestine it lost its character as a full common meal to constitute only of bread and wine. There appears to be a progressive development in the Christian understanding of its meaning in relation to the Person of Christ. The earliest was one of eschatological joy, a looking forward to a Messianic banquet at the Parousia. As the awareness of the significance of Jesus' death grew the Lord's Supper became a memorial, backward looking to the atoning death on the Cross. Thus the meal mediated to the believer the salvation brought forth by Jesus' atoning death. Later, especially in Pauline churches it became a symbol of the mystical body of Christ (1 Cor 12:12-13).[21]

Despite these and other similarities, however, the most distinctive feature is that the Lord's Supper is Christological from beginning to end. It is founded on the Person of Christ and his redemptive work. To this there is no parallel in the scrolls. The scrolls appear to acknowledge faith as a medium of salvation. This is what the Habakkuk commentator has on the famous faith passage, Hab 2:46.

> But the righteous through his faithfulness shall live. This refers to all Jewry who carry out the Law (Torah). On account of their labor and of their faith in him who expounded the Law aright, God will deliver them from the house of judgment (1Qp Hab viii).

A closer look at this *pesher* shows that the concept of faith implied is different from that found in the New Testament and that the Law remains the agent of salvation and not 'him who expounded the Law aright.' Salvation is said to be offered 'on account of their labour and of their faith.' Thus the works of the Law, its strict observance, remain a basis for salvation. Their faith is not placed on the person of the expositor but on the nature of his exposition for he expounds the Law 'aright'.

---

[19] Kuhn, "The Lord's Supper and the Communal Meal at Qumran. *The Scrolls and the New Testament*, p. 76.
[20] For a thorough discussion of this problem, see Ibid., pp. 78-93.
[21] Ibid., pp. 77-78.

What is called faith here is simply trust that the meaning of the Law as expounded by the Teacher of Righteousness is indeed the correct one. This is apparently necessary if the covenanters are to keep the Law as interpreted by the Teacher.

In the New Testament, salvation comes by faith and without works of the Law, for the New Covenant, centered in the person of Jesus, has superseded the Old Covenant centered on the Law. The new Law is Jesus himself and therefore faith alone in his redemptive work is sufficient to mediate salvation. It is in this spirit that Paul can say:

> But now the righteousness of God has been manifested apart from the Law, although the Law and the prophets bear witness to it, the righteousness of God through faith in Jesus Christ for all who believe (Rom 3:21-22).

Christ is not an interpreter of the Law, but he is the Law itself, hence, he becomes the object of both faith and practice in the New Testament. The Teacher at Qumran is not the Law but simply guides his followers to the Law which alone he understands to be the basis of salvation.

Thus in both sacraments and faith, as mediums of salvation at Qumran and in the New Testament, it is the person of Jesus and his role in redemptive work that make the difference.

IV. Messianic Expectations

The problem with Qumran messianic expectations has been that the texts are not in agreement in their references to the messiah or messiahs. Some texts clearly refer to at least two messiahs:

> And they shall be ruled by the first laws with which the men of the community began to be disciplined until the coming of a prophet and the anointed ones of Aaron and Israel (1Qsa ix, 11).

1Qsa ii reads:

> The high priest as head of the entire community of Israel is to come first... After that, the anointed (king), being a layman, is to come ... If they happen to be foregathering for a common meal or to drink wine together, when the common board has been spread or the wine mixed for drinking, no one is to stretch out his hand for the first portion of the bread or wine prior to the priest ... who is to pronounce the blessing ... and is first to stretch out his hand to the bread ... After that, the anointed (king), a layman, after that the members in order of rank.

Thus the Messianic Rule (1Qsa ii) clearly refers to a messiah of Aaron who is the priestly head of the eschatological community and a messiah of Israel, a layman (Davidic, kingly), both at the head of the messianic banquet. The Damascus Document in a *pesher* on Numbers 24:17 (CD viii, 18-20) refers to the 'Star' from Jacob, the 'Interpreter of the Law', and the 'Scepter' who is 'the Prince of the whole congregation.'

Then here is another group of texts which is not as clear. These could either be understood as referring to two messiahs or as referring to one messiah who fulfills both priestly and kingly messianic functions. For instance CD xii, 23 speaks of 'the priestly and lay messiah'; CD xiv, 19 speaks of 'the priestly and lay messiah'; CD xx, 1 speaks of 'messiah from Aaron and from Israel.' CD xiv, 19 speaks of 'the priestly and lay messiah; The last group appears to refer to a single messiah: CD ii, 12 and vi which speak of 'His anointed one' (singular).

It has been suggested that the earliest Essene writings (140-110 BC) did not refer to any messiah. The first and most significant messianic reference is probably 1 Qs ix, 11 (BC 100) quoted above. The problematic references appear to have come from the middle period (110-70 BC), while the late writings clearly refer to two messiahs.[22] For instance the War Scroll mentions a prince of the whole congregation, probably a combat leader since priests do not fight (1QM v. 1). A *pesher* on Psalms mentions two figures: "The Branch of David who will arise with the interpreter of the Law ... at the end of days." The first mentioned is a Davidic messiah while the second is a priestly one. A *pesher* on Isaiah also refers to 'the Branch of David who shall arise at the end of days' and 'that priests will teach him how to render judgment'. Hence, these latter works, without specifically mentioning the messiahs of Aaron and of Israel, attest to the twofold messianic expectations.

A closer study of the texts, however, shows that the Qumran covenanters expected two messiahs and not one. One of the references to a single messiah makes better sense in its context if it were plural:

> Moreover, by the hands of Thine anointed, the men who had vision of things foreordained thou hast related unto us the warlike triumphs of thy hand (1QM xi, 7).

This text appears to refer to many anointed men in which case 'Thine anointed' could be more correctly understood as 'Thine anointed ones.'[23] Notice that the phrase 'Thine anointed' is interpreted in the next clause as 'the men who had vision of things foreordained.' The same could apply to 'His anointed' of CD ii, 12. The text: "and build for them in Israel a firmly established House" (CD iv 1") is yet another specific reference to a Davidic messiah.

We can therefore conclude that the Qumran Community expected two messiahs.[24] The priestly one was the head while the lay messiah was occupying a secondary place in rank.

---

[22] Brown, "The Teacher of Righteousness and the Messiah(s)", *Theological Collection II*, pp. 41-43.

[23] Kuhn, *The Scrolls and the New Testament*, p. 59.

[24] The association of the Prophet with the two messiahs is difficult to sustain at least for three reasons: (1) The role of this eschatological prophet is said to be interpreting the Law. But this is the role of the priestly Messiah. (2) 1QS ix, II is the only text that associates the

The expectation of the two messiahs is well founded in the Old Testament. Israelite leadership, from the post-exilic times on was characterized by both priestly and political wings. Hence, we hear about priests and 'princes' (Ezk 34:24), and the Aaronic Joshua and the Davidic Jerubbabel as the 'two anointed' of Zech 4:14; 3:8 (520 BC). Although the offices are temporarily combined after Zerubbabel due to external political circumstances, in the messianic era the ideal division of Israel leadership will again take place. Along side the messianic high priest (Ezk 45:19) there will be a Davidic prince:[25]

> It is he who shall build the temple of the Lord, and shall bear royal honor, and shall sit and rule upon his throne. And there shall be a priest by his throne, and peaceful understanding shall be between them. (Zech 6:13).

During the Maccabean period it has already been noted above that Jonathan (161 – 143 BC) accepted the high priesthood while the office was turned into a hereditary one by Simon (143-135) to the disappointment of the Hasidim. However, even with the Hasmoneans the offices of high priesthood and political government were still viewed as distinct and separate. The bearer of political power is 'the people of the Jews', 'the council of the Nation', 'the congregation of the Jews' (1 Matt 8:20; 12:3-6).[26]

In the New Testament there is no hint to two messiahs. The post-exilic expectation of two messiahs preserved at Qumran had long become classical (i.e. known only among the scholars) if not even completely forgotten or neglected. The contemporary messianic expectation referred to one messiah of the Davidic house. Practically the expectation of two messiahs was almost abandoned in Judaism. The New Testament shared the view of the common man in its messianic expectations.

Even here it is the Person of Christ that makes the Christian messianic hope quite distinctive. While at Qumran the two messiahs are no more than 'a shadowy idealization,' in the New Testament the messianic expectation is a fulfilled reality in the person of Jesus Christ.

V. The End-Time and the After-Life

Both the Qumran community and the New Testament portray a literal destruction of the universe by fire:

---

prophet with the Messiahs. He is not envisaged in other messianic and eschatological contexts. (3) The prophet is sometimes associated with the resurrected Teacher of Righteousness at the end of days. But the question of whether the community believed in resurrection is itself highly debatable. In this I differ with Kuhn who takes the Prophet to be a member of the messianic entourage. See Ibid., p. 63.

[25] Ezek. 34:24; 37:25; Zech 6:15; Jer. 23:5; 33:15.
[26] Kuhn, "the Two Messiahs, "*The Scrolls and the New Testament*, pp. 60,61.

> The torrents of Belial shall spread to all ends of the mountains. In all their channels a devouring fire shall destroy every fresh and withering tree on their banks; it shall burn fiery flames unto the end of all their destructiveness. It shall devour the foundation of the earth and dry land. The foundation of the mountain shall be blasted; roots of the rocks shall (turn) to torrents of pitch, it shall consume to the depths of the earth. (1QH iii, 29-31).

John says:

> He will baptize you with the Holy Spirit and with fire. His winnowing fork is in his hand, and he will clear his threshing floor and gather his wheat into the granary, but the chaff he will burn with unquenchable fire (Matt 3:11-12).

In Rev 21:1 we read of a 'new heaven' and a 'new earth'. This presupposes the destruction of the older. Both also refer to a cosmic war:

> For God shall thunder forth his loud rumblings, and his sacred dwellings shall thunder with the truth of his glory. The heavenly host shall give thunder and the world's foundation shall stagger and tremble. The war of the heavenly warriors shall devour the earth and it shall not return before destruction, which shall be endless and indescribable (1QH. iii, 34-36).

Similarly we hear of a cosmic struggle among the heavenly beings, earthquakes, falling stars, the darkening of sun and moon, the shaking of the heavenly bodies (Matt 24:29; Rev 6:12-14; 8:12). This cosmic struggle which affects the whole created order is deeply rooted in the Old Testament perspective of the Day of the Lord.[27]

However, Qumran and the New Testament differ significantly in their view of the after-life following the final messianic victory in the cosmic struggle with all forces of evil. What can be clearly ascertained in the scrolls is that the elect shall enjoy a millennial paradisiacal bliss as reflected in 4Q 171, iii. 1-2, a *pesher* on Psalm 37:18-19a.

> To the penitents of the desert who, saved, shall live for a thousand generations and to whom all the glory of Adam shall belong...

There is no clear reference to resurrection in the scrolls and the internal evidence usually appealed to in its support is problematic while the external evidence is contradictory. Josephus appears to suggest that the Essenes held a belief of the immortality of the soul and the dissolution of the body.[28] Josephus seems to be supported by 1QH iii, 5:

> I thank Thee, O Lord, for Thou has redeemed my soul from the pit and from the hell of Abaddon ... thou has cleansed a perverse spirit of great sin that it may stand with the host of the Holy Ones, and that it may enter into community with the congregation

---

[27] Isa. 13:10; 34:4; Ezek. 32:7; Joel 2:10; 31 Zeph. 1:15.
[28] Josephus, "Jewish War," 2.154-155.

of the sons of Heaven. Thou has allotted to man an everlasting destiny amidst the spirits of knowledge.

This may refer to the after-life. However, it can also be a mere poetic reference to the "present experience of the members of his group" in this life.[29] Hippolytus of Rome (170-236 AD) in his *Refutation of all Heresies*, 9:27 says they believed in the resurrection of the flesh and its immortality thereafter along with the soul.[30] *The Book of Jubilees* simply adds to the confusion:

> Then the Lord will heal his servants. They will rise and see great peace. He will expel their enemies. The righteous will see (this), offer praise and be very happy forever and ever. They will see all the punishments and curses on their enemies. Their bones will rest in the earth and their spirits will be very happy (23:30-31).[31]

Thus *Jubilees* while referring to the resurrection of the elect says their bones will remain in the earth while their spirits will be full of joy.

What appears to come closest to the resurrection idea are: 1QH vi, 29-30 which refers to the rising of the sons of truth at the time of judgment to overthrow the sons of darkness; 1QH v. 34 which commands those "who lie in the dust" to raise a flag, and 1QH xi, 12-14 which refers to the rising of the worm-like bodies from the dust to the eternal community.

It appears that the first two texts (1QH, vi, 29-30 and 1QH, v. 34) are no more than poetic expressions urging the living to fight for the elect or the pious dead of the past to come to their aid.[32] 1QH xi, 12-14 is closer to the Daniel text:

> that worm-like bodies may be raised from the dust to the (eternal) community, and from the perverse spirit to (thy) understanding, that he may stand before thee with the everlasting host, and with the spirits (of wisdom).

On closer observation, however, what appears as an ultimate destiny of those raised in 1QH. xi, 12-14 is to be transmuted from matter into spirit and in that state join the angelic beings.[33]

---

[29] VanderKam, *The Dead Sea Scrolls Today*, p. 80.

[30] Ibid., p. 79.

[31] Ibid., p. 80. Schubert, who holds that the covenanters believe in a bodily resurrection, thinks this view of a bodiless state in the next world presented here must not be taken literary, see p. 111. VanderKam sees proof for the belief in at least a physical resurrection in 4Q 521. See ibid p. 81.

[32] John Pryke, "Exchatology in the Dead Sea Scrolls, "*Theological Collections* II, p. 56.

[33] Ibid., pp. 55, 56. The text in which other scholars have seen a reference to resurrection in connection with the Teacher of Righteousness is the pesher on Numbers 21:18 "Until he comes who shall teach righteousness" (CD vi, 3-10). However, the last six Hebrew words in this text are so problematic that it is unsafe to construct a doctrine of resurrection on its basis. Neither is the Teacher of Righteousness a messianic figure. On this Teacher-resurrection

In the New Testament, however, the resurrection, the judgment and the after-life are explicitly portrayed as prophesied:

> And many of those who sleep in the dust of the earth shall awake, some to everlasting life, and some to shame and everlasting contempt (Dan 12:2)

In Matt 25:46, Jesus refers both to eternal life for those who are saved and to eternal punishment for those who are condemned. This judgment is said to be effected by the Son of Man seated at the right-hand of God the Father and coming with the clouds unexpectedly to gather his people for himself (Matt 42:30, 44, Mark. 14:62) as prophesied in Daniel 7:13.

There is no reference to the Son of Man and the judgment he brings in the scrolls. Here, as we have observed again and again, the Person of Jesus is the central distinctive feature. The Son of Man comes to judge in glory.[34]

VI. Language and Thought: Some Common Theological Concepts

There are certain terms which appear frequently enough in the scrolls and the New Testament to attract scholarly attention. Among these are such terms as spirit, flesh, perfection, mystery, knowledge, righteousness, light, darkness, truth and error.

Light, darkness, truth and error have been already discussed in connection with dualism. The term "flesh" appears in Rabbinical literature in the compound phrase: 'flesh and blood', and refers to the limitations of man in contrast to God. In the Old Testament it is used over against the Spirit of Yahweh denoting, probably, the frailty and mortality of man. In the scrolls, 'flesh' appears over against both the Spirit of Yahweh and the spirit of truth, where it also reflects the unworthiness of man before God (1QH iv, 29). It implies the "idea of weakness through natural inclination of man."[35]

Thus, to belong to the 'flesh' is to belong to the sphere of perversion and darkness. The "Ish" of 1QS xi, 7-10; 1QH iii, 19-36 has this moral connotation. Here, the "Ish" of the scroll has the same theological meaning as the "I" of Romans 7.[36] But this is no Hellenistic concept while the believer belongs to the realm of

---

problem and some suggestions, see also Ibid pp. 53, 54. Also Joseph A. Fitzmyer, *Responses to 101 Questions on the Dead Sea Scrolls*, London: Geffrey Chapman, 1992, pp. 62-63; Bruce, "Jesus and the Gospels in the Light of the Scrolls," *Theological Collections II*, p. 80.

[34] For a full treatment of the comparison between Jesus and the Teacher of Righteousness, see Burrows, *More Light on the Dead Sea Scrolls*, pp. 64, 74-77; Fitzmyer, *Responses to 101 Questions on the Dead Sea Scrolls*, pp. 57f, Brown, "The Teacher of Righteousness and the Messiah(s), *Theological Collections* II, p. 40.

[35] Kuhn, "New Light on Temptation, Sin and Flesh in the New Testament," *The Scrolls and the New Testament*, p. 101.

[36] Ibid., p. 102.

'flesh' because he is sinful, he is the elect of God . The believer belongs to both at the same time. This dualistic belongingness is found in both the scrolls and the New Testament.[37]

Both the scrolls and the New Testament do not appear to develop a full doctrine of 'flesh' for in both writings the term is used in relation to a discussion of personal experience of sin and not in relation to an elaborate discussion on the nature of universal corporate sin.[38]

Although the term 'spirit' appears in both literatures and may in other cases be used in the same manner,[39] there are significant differences. Paul's understanding of 'spirit' is greatly influenced by his understanding of the historical Jesus, the saviour of the world. To Paul, the Spirit is usually the Holy Spirit, the Spirit of Christ or the Spirit of God who was poured out at Pentecost to indwell those who believe in Jesus and accept him as their Saviour. He is the divine gift who gives spiritual gifts among men for the building of the body of Christ, the Church. At Qumran, however, the spirit is not given on the basis of faith to whoever believes but rather is apportioned to each person by divine predestination. Thus in Paul and the rest of the New Testament the Spirit is both Christological and existential. These two aspects are missing in the scrolls.[40]

The emphasis on the role of the 'spirit' is also different in the two literatures. In the scrolls there is an 'enduring presence and persistence until the end'. The two spiritual forces release a constant flow of spiritual power in their conflict. In the New Testament, however, there is an "in-rush of special (empowering spiritual) energy" that has an "invasive transcendent character." Thus, while in the Old Testament and New Testament, the spirit manifests his power through the eschatological gifts given to believers, in the scrolls this power is lacking although the man who is 'sprinkled' upon (1QS iv, 18ff) receives knowledge of the Most High.[41]

Hence, unlike in the New Testament, where the Spirit is personal, Christological, existential and uncreated, in Qumran the spirit is either the created member of the

---

[37] Davies, "Paul and the Dead Sea Scrolls: Flesh and Spirit, "*The Scrolls and the New Testament*, p. 162.

[38] Ibid., p. 164.

[39] For instance in the sense of being spiritual or having a spiritual disposition (Gal. 6:1, Rom 12:1,11) or in the sense of spirits (1 Cor 12:10; 14:32; 1Jm 4:1).

[40] Kuhn, "New Ligh on Temptations, Sin and Flesh in the New Testament", *The Scrolls and the New Testament*, p. 106.

[41] Davies, "Paul and the Dead Sea Scrolls: Flesh and Spirit," "*The Scrolls and the New Testament*, p. 173.

spiritual dual or it is an impersonal force, no more than a spiritual disposition as in the phrase: "Spirit of the Counsel of God."[42]

We can therefore conclude that the concept of 'spirit' in the scrolls is not fully developed as we find it in the New Testament. There is no doctrine of the Holy Spirit in the scroll as we already suggested in connection with John's baptism above.

The terms perfection, mystery, knowledge and wisdom are used by the two groups in a similar manner but referring to different aspects. For the New Testament, mystery, knowledge, perfection and wisdom are always Christological. They refer to the revelation that is embodied in the Person of Christ: that Jesus is the Son of God and Saviour of the world. Similarly in the scrolls these refer to the 'new revelation' given to the Teacher of Righteousness on the basis of which he is able to unseal the real meaning of prophecy. Hence, these terms refer to his special interpretation of the Torah and the Prophets all of whom prophesied about the things that were to take place in the End-time in which the Teacher and his contemporaries already lived.[43]

Thus we again see that Christological considerations influence the meanings of otherwise common concepts in the wider Jewish background.

Conclusion

The Qumran scrolls have shed much light on New Testament studies. Their contribution to the study of New Testament exegesis has already been considered. The scrolls lead us to reconsider some of the presuppositions of classical form criticism as argued by Bultmann and Martin Dibelius. It was assumed that the Christians of the first two centuries could not prepare a reliable tradition about Jesus either because they were not educated enough or were not willing. It was also assumed that they almost wrote nothing because they had an intense expectation of the Parousia.[44] But the scrolls provide us a different picture: The Qumran covenanters had an ardent expectation for an imminent end of the world yet they were no 'mere messengers' as they waited for the End. But rather for the very reason of their intense expectation they devoted themselves to the study of Scripture,

---

[42] A.R.C. Leaney (ed), *A Guide to the Scrolls, Notthingham Studies on the Qomran Discoveries*, London: SCM Press, 1958, pp. 87.

[43] For a thorough discussion on these terms see Max Wilcox "Dualism, Gnosticism and other Elements in the Pre-Pauline Tradition," *Theological Collections II*. Also Davies, "Paul and the Dead Sea Scrolls: Flesh and Spirit, "*The Scrolls and the New Testament*. pp. 170-180, 182.

[44] Otto Betz and Rainer Riesner, *Jesus, Qumran and the Vatican*, London: SCM Press, 1994, p. 153.

keeping "awake for a third of all the nights of the year reading books, studying the Law and worshipping together" (1QS vi, 6-8).

Secondly there is evidence that the Qumran community was literary productive throughout its history and not only in its later period.[45] Thus despite their expectation they were not discouraged from writing.

There is also evidence that the Essenes and the earliest Christians often refer to some specific groups of Old Testament texts which suggest a common exegetical tradition.[46] It therefore appears to us that there is no compelling reason for putting off the writing of the earliest documents for decades—with "Q" source as the earliest put at 50 AD[47]—in the light of the scrolls.

Also, a text, *miqsat ma'ase ha-torah* (4QMMT) believed to be a letter by the Teacher of Righteousness, shows how significant it was for the community to preserve the teaching of its founder.[48] This makes it difficult to see why no one should dare to write anything about Jesus until 20 years after the crucifixion and resurrection. This becomes even more difficult to imagine if some of the Essenes were converted to primitive Christianity just as we know from the Gospels and Acts that some Pharisees, like Nicodemus, were.

The scrolls have also significantly shed much light on Johannine critical studies. In the past, Johannine antithetical language was thought to be rooted in a Hellenistic environment because it reflected some Gnostic affinities. Since mature Gnosticism existed in the second century AD, not only was the date of authorship for the Johannine literature suggested to be sometime in second century AD but also the place of authorship was to be at one of the early Hellenistic Christian centers, away from Palestine. Now that the language of John is seen to be Jewish and local Palestinian, just as the Qumran covenanters were, the date of authorship has moved into the first century AD, and the place has moved closer to Palestine.

---

[45] Raymond E. Brown attempts a classification of the scrolls according to the period in which they were probably written. He mentions no work for the earliest period (140-110 BC) but says the literature of this period did not refer to a messiah. He suggests the manual of Discipline (1QS), the Damascus Document (CD) and the Rule for All the Congregation of Israel (1Qsa) belong to the period 110-70 BC, and that the War Scroll (QM) from 59 BC to 25 AD while a pesher on Psalms (IV Q Flor.) and another on Isaiah (IV Qp Is^a) appear to belong to the later period of 1-50 AD. See Davis, "The Teacher of Righteousness and the Messiah(s)=", *Theological Collections* II, pp. 41-43.

[46] See the section "The Biblical Exegesis of the Qumran Community" above. Also Betz and Reisner, *Jesus, Qumran and the Vatican* ,p. 153.

[47] I. Howard Marshall, *New Testament Interpretation, Essays on Principles and Methods*, Carlisle: Paternoster, 1992, p. 153.

[48] Betz and Reisner, Jesus, *Qumran and the Vatican*, p. 153.

The scrolls have also shed light on the fluidity of the Hebrew text of the Bible at the dawn of the Christian era, as well as the widespread usage of other textual recensions like the Samaritan recension of the Pentateuch which has remarkable affinities with Acts 7. This explains partly the textual problems we meet in New Testament quotations from the Old Testament that are quite different in their text form from any variants that may be preserved for us elsewhere. This problem is especially acute with the text of the Gospel of Matthew.

The use of specific texts of the Old Testament by both groups appears to support the theory of the existence of a pre-Christian collection of an eschatological *testimonia*.

The scrolls have also shed much light on the nature and extent of Jewish sectarianism at the beginning of the Christian era. They have also shed light on the history of the early Church. While in the period before the discovery of the scrolls the 'Palestine elements' and the 'Hellenistic strata' of the Gospel tradition were considered to be in opposition,[49] especially in the latter part of the primitive apostolic church, the scrolls show that these elements are both Jewish, Palestinian and early. The 'Hellenistic element' cannot be considered as a late element in the primitive church any longer.

The scrolls have also afforded us linguistic parallels that help us understand some of the Semitic expressions in the New Testament.[50]

Without doubt, therefore, some of the parallels we have met in this study between the scrolls and the New Testament are very close, almost suggesting a direct relationship. These appear to be rooted in the general character of the Jewish sectarian milieu which was united in its opposition to official Judaism. But it must be remembered that both sectarian and official Judaism had a common basis in the Old Testament tradition. Similarities, therefore, seem to be inevitable.

However when we turn to the differences, the impression one gets again and again is that the two groups of literature cannot belong to "successive phases" of a simple movement. While there may be practical, ideological and linguistic differences, the most distinctive feature that defies any direct relationship[51] is the Person of Jesus upon whom the whole Christian outlook is oriented.[52]

---

[49] The supposed opposition between "Paul's Party" and "James's Party" which, according to the History of Religious School of Tübingen, is reflected in the New Testament.

[50] A good example is the problem of the phrase translated "peace among men with whom he is pleased" in the RSV Bible in Lk. 2:14. See Ernest Vogt, "Peace among Men of God" ="Good Pleasure," *The Scrolls and the New Testament*, pp. 114-117.

[51] The complete silence of the New Testament on the Qumran Question appears to be suggestive of this lack of any formal relationship between the two religious communities

although the scrolls are likely to provide a general religious background to some aspects of the New Testament as we suggest in the footnote below.

[52] Findings from the Dead Sea Scrolls continue to shape New Testament scholarship at many points. For example, the relationship between wisdom and apocalyptic traditions is being reassessed and the results are bringing stratification theories in recent Q scholarship under severe strain. The recently published text, *4QInstruction (Musar le Mevin)*, where the phrase *raz nihyeh* occurs repeatedly, is likely to provide scholars with a fundamental conceptual background that will shape our understanding of the notion of μυστήριον in the Gospels, especially Mark. See, for example, John J. Collins, "Wisdom, Apocalypticism and Generic Compatibility", in *In Search of Wisdom: Essays in Memory of John G. Gammie*, eds., L. Perdue, B.B. Scott and W.J. Wiseman, Louisville: Westminster/John Knox, 1993, pp. 165-185; George W.E. Nickelsburg, "Wisdom and Apocalypticism in Early Judaism: Some Points for Discussion", in *Conflicted Boundaries in Wisdom and Apocalypticism*, eds., Benjamin G. Wright III and Lawrence M. Wills, SBL Symposium Series 35, Atlanta: SBL, 2005, pp. 17-37; Daniel Harrington, "The Raz Nihyeh in a Qumran Text (1Q26, 4Q415-418, 423)", *RevQ* 6 (1996) pp. 549-552; Matthew J. Goff, "Discerning Trajectories: 4QInstruction and the Sapiential Background of the Sayings Gospel Q", *Journal of Biblical Literature* 124 (2005) pp. 657-73; *idem*, "Wisdom, Apocalypticism, and the Pedagogical Ethos of 4QInstruction", in *Conflicted Boundaries in Wisdom and Apocalypticism*, pp. 57-67; Grant Macaskill, *Revealed Wisdom and Inaugurated Eschatology in Ancient Judaism and Early Christianity*, Leiden and Boston: Brill, 2007, especially pp. 1-16; John Strugnell and Daniel Harrington eds., *Qumran Cave 4 xxxiv: Sapiential Texts, Part Two, 4QInstruction (Musar le Mevin) 4Q415ff. With a Re-edition of 1Q26*, Oxford: Clarendon, 1999.

Chapter Three
The Old Testament and Jewish Hermeneutics

Introduction

There is no handy rule by which to explain the manner in which the New Testament writers use their Scriptures which to us are represented more or less by the Old Testament of the Christian Bible or the Hebrew Bible. This situation has led to misunderstanding among scholars as to how the two testaments relate to each other in terms of scriptural interpretation. Paul Joyce claims that a "careful study of the biblical texts by these methods (that is literary and historical criticism) has made very clear the important differences which exist between the original meaning of certain Old Testament material and the re-use of that same material in the New Testament."[1] Lindars is of the opinion that "Matthew inherits the formula-quotations without being aware of the issues which underlie the selection of them and are responsible for their text-form."[2] Even Rudolf Bultmann is perplexed by the fact that many Old Testament texts appealed to by the New Testament writers as having been fulfilled in the coming of Jesus Christ are not "prophetic" in the sense of being explicitly forward-looking, and seeks a solution to his dilemma by siding with J.C.K. Hofmann who concluded before him "that it is not the 'words' of the Old Testament that are really prophecy, but the 'history' of Israel to which the Old Testament testifies."[3]

However, despite the absence of a simple and explicit hermeneutical principle to explain all that is involved in the New Testament exegesis of the Old, there are some observable tendencies that offer us some clues to discern exegetical practices of the New Testament writers as well as presuppositions at work behind these hermeneutical practices. The present chapter attempts to explore these background Jewish hermeneutical practices. Seen from this perspective the New Testament use of the Old becomes a meaningful enterprise and the "important differences" between

---

[1] Paul Joyce, "The Old Testament and its Relation to the New Testament," in John Rogerson (ed), *Beginning Old Testament Study,* London: SPCK, 1983, p. 140.

[2] Barnabas Lindars, *New Testament Apologetic, the Doctrinal Significance of the Old Testament Quotations,* London: SCM, 1961, p 16.

[3] Quoted in John Goldingay, *Approaches to Old Testament Interpretation,* Leicester: Apollos, 1990, p 116

the original settings and the new meaning it acquires in its New Testament context, as Joyce observes, become strikingly sensible.[4]

In this chapter, I shall first look at the text-form of the Old Testament quotations in the New Testament. Then I will turn to Jewish literary methods and exegetical practices of the first century AD, which provide a literary background to New Testament exegesis of the Old Testament.

The Text-Form of Old Testament Quotations

One of the notoriously difficult problems in the textual study of the Old Testament is the reconstruction of an authoritative version of the first Century Bible which New Testament writers used. This section examines the nature of this difficulty and concludes that New Testament writers are early witnesses to a variety of textual traditions that existed at the time.

1. Textual Variations in Old Testament Quotations

The text-forms of the quotations used by New Testament writers take various forms of phraseology which include verbatim quotations with introductory formula, verbatim quotations without introductory formula, clear verbal allusions, clear references without verbal allusion, possible verbal allusion, allusions and possible references without verbal allusions. It is, however, not always easy to distinguish a quotation from an allusion or even a mere coincidence in phraseology. The phrase

---

[4] A discussion of the results that come out after applying the methods of literary and historical criticism to the biblical texts relevant to this study is nevertheless beyond the scope of the present inquiry. It is, however, sufficient to note that these critical methods have their own presuppositions which do not necessarily correspond to those hermeneutical presuppositions held by New Testament writers. It is, therefore, probably rash to judge first century A.D. hermeneutical practices using twenty-first century hermeneutical presuppositions which we know are alien to the biblical times. For a discussion on the need for compatibility (not identity) of our world view with the biblical view necessary for our proper understanding of New Testament hermeneutical practices, see Dan G. McCartney, "The New Testament Use of the Old Testament," in Harvie M. Conn (ed), *Inerrancy and Hermeneutic: A Tradition, a Challenge, a Debate*, Grand Rapids: Baker, 1988, p. 111. For a recent critical appraisal of Historical Criticism as a means of establishing authenticity or historicity of biblical data, especially in the Gospels, see Scot McKnight, *Interpreting the Synoptic Gospels*, Grand Rapids: Baker, 1988, pp. 62-64. Cf. R.T. France, *Jesus and the Old Testament, His Application of Old Testament Passages to Himself and His Mission*, London: Tyndale, 1971, pp. 15-22.

"And he gave him to his mother" (1 Kings 17:23; Luke 7:15b, RSV) is a good illustration of this difficulty.[5]

In the quotations found in Pauline epistles, E. Ellis observes that 19 are in agreement with LXX and the Hebrew text (e.g. Rom 3:13a, 13b; 14:17,18). 14 are in agreement with the LXX against the Hebrew text (e.g. Rom 4:3, 7-8; 1 Cor 6:2; Gal 4:27). 4 are in agreement with the Hebrew text against the LXX (Rom 11:35; 1 Cor 3:19; 2 Cor 8:15; 2 Tim 2:19). 23 are at variance with the LXX and the Hebrew text where they agree (e.g. Rom 3:10-12; 1 Cor 1:31; 2 Cor 6:17; Gal 3:8). 33 are at variance with the LXX and the Hebrew text where they vary (e.g. Rom 3:4; 9:26; 1 Cor 2:16; 15:54; Gal 3:10). Of those at variance with the LXX, 20 cases involve a slight variation (e.g. Rom 1:17; 3:18; 1 Cor 3:20; 9:9; 2 Cor 13:1; Gal 3:11, 12; Eph. 4:8). There are also cases where the variation involves word order (Rom 9:13; 10:21;15:21).[6] Of the 23 variations with LXX mentioned above the differences in Rom 11:8 and 2 Cor 6:17 involve clauses while the rest vary in the addition, omission or rendering of words.[7] Similarly, of the 33 variants mentioned above Rom 3:15-17; 9:33; 10:6-8; 14:11; 1 Cor 2:9 involve clauses while the remaining texts vary in terms of words.[8]

France also finds similar categories in his study of Old Testament quotations attributed to Jesus in the synoptic gospels.[9] He finds that the following quotations differ from both the LXX and the Hebrew text. Mark 4:12 (Isaiah 6:9-10); 9:48 (Isaiah 66:24); 10:19 (Exodus 20:12-16 = Deut. 5:16-20). 12:30 (Deut. 6:5); 12:36 (Ps 110:1); 14:27 (Zech 13:7); Matt 4:10 (Deut. 6:13); 7:23 (Ps. 6:9); Luke 4:18-19 (Isa 61:1-2; 58:6); 17:29 (Gen 19:24); 17:31 (Gen 19:17); 23:30 (Hos 10:8). The following agree with the Hebrew text against the LXX: Mark 4:29 (Joel 4:13); 10:19 (Exodus 20:12-16= Deut 5:16-20); 12:30 (Deut 6:5) 13:24-25 (Isa 13:10; 34:4); Matt 11:10 (Mal 3:1; Exodus 23:20); 11:23 (Isa 14:13,15); 11:29 (Jer 6:16; 18:16 (Deut 9:15); Luke 4:19 (Isa 61:2); 13:27 (Ps 6:9); 20:18 (Isa 8:14-15); 22:37 (Isa 53:12). In this category are also the following less certain allusions: Mark 8:38 (Dan 7:13-14); 11:15 (Zech 14:21) 13:8 (Isa 19:2); 14:24 (Isa 53:12) Matt 6:11 (Prov

---

[5] See Gerhard von Rad, "Typological Interpretation of the Old Testament," in Claus Westermann (ed), *Essays on Old Testament Hermeneutics*, Richmond: John Knox, 1963, pp. 20-21.

[6] E. Earle Ellis, *Paul's Use of the Old Testament*, Grand Rapids: Baker, 1957, Appendix 1 (A), pp. 150-152.

[7] *Ibid.*, p. 150, footnote number 2.

[8] *Ibid.*, footnote number 3.

[9] For a thorough discussion of the text-form of the quotations attributed to Jesus in the synoptic Gospels as outlined in these categories, see France, *Jesus*, pp. 25-37, especially Appendix B, pp 240-258 to whom I am deeply indebted for the section that follows.

30:8); 6:23 (Prov 28:22); 13:41 (Zech 1:3); Luke 16:15 (Prov 16:5; 6:16-17); 22:31 (Amos 9:9). Matt 4:4 (Deut 8:3) is a textual variant.

There are also those quotations which agree with one text of the LXX against another: Mark 7:6 (Isa 29:13); 7:10 (Exodus 21:17); 9:48 (Isa 66:24); 10:7 (Gen 2:24);10:19 (Deut 16:20); 12:26 (Exodus 3:6); 12:30 (Deut 6:5); 13:25 (Isa 34:4); 14:27 (Zech 13:7); Matt 4:10 (Deut 6:13); 9:13; 12:7 (Hos. 6:6) (Deut 19:15)12:30 and Luke 23:30 (Hos 10:8). Then there are those quotations which agree with the LXX against the Hebrew text. Among these are those quotations where the LXX form does not affect the sense or application of the text: Mark 4:29 (Joel 4:13); 10:8 (Gen 2:24); 10:19 (Exodus 20:12-16 = Deut 5:16-20); 12:1 (Isa 5:1-2); Matt 4:7 (Deut 6:16); 18:16 (Deut 19:15); 18:22 (Gen 4:24); 25:31 (Zech 14:5); Luke 4:18 (Isa 61:1-2); 23:46 (Ps 31:6). In the same category are those quotations whose sense may be said to depend on their LXX form: Mark 7:6-7 (Isa 29:13); 9:13 (Mal 3:23-24); Matt 21:16 (Ps 8:3); Luke 4:18 (Isa 61:1); Matt 11:5 (Isa 61:1-2). In all these cases, however, France argues convincingly for their Hebrew origin. The apocalyptic discourse also falls into this category of quotations: Mark 13:7 (Dan 2:28-29); 13:13 (Dan 12:12); 13:14 (Dan 11:31; 12:11); 13:19 (Dan 12:1); 13:24-25 (Isa 13:10; 34:4); 13:27 (Zech 2:10); Matt 24:30 (Zech 12:10-14) and Luke 21:24 (Zech 12:3).

These two studies at least show us that New Testament writers did not always quote verbatim and that despite other influencing factors they drew their quotations from more than one textual tradition

There are several factors which have contributed to these variations in the text-form of the quotations. These include the literary freedom to change a text which was not uncommon during the first century among the rabbis as well as the writers of the New Testament (e.g. Rom 1:17 = Hab 2:4; 11:2 = Ps 94:14 = 1 Sam 12:22). Conflation of texts so that they serve as "proof-texts" for apologetic reasons was another factor (e.g. Rom 9:9 = Gen 18:10-14; 9:27-28 = Isaiah 10:22ff = Hos 2:1). Sometimes these variants were created to suit a new context (e.g. Rom 2:6 = Ps 61:3; 10:7 = Ps 107:26;11:8 = Deut 29:3-4 = Isaiah 29:10); to indicate emphasis (e.g.; Rom 9:13 = Mal 1:2; 10:8 = 45:23); citations from memory as indicated by scriptural reflection (Rom 1:3 = Micah 5:2 = 2 Sam 7:16 =Ps 89:3f, 19 = Deut 33:14,18; also in 1:7; 1:8; 1:20 etc), and confusion in the quotations likely to arise from memory work (e.g. Rom 9:27-28 which Paul attributes to Isaiah while a part of it is clearly from Hos 2:1. Similar cases appear in Rom 9:20= Isaiah 29:16; 9:25 = Hos 2:25; 11:3 = 1 Kings 19:10; 11:4 = 1 Kings 19:18 etc).

Textual variations could also arise as a result of using sources like testimonia (oral or written), other versions of the LXX, Aramaic targums and *ad hoc* renderings of the Hebrew text.[10] Sometimes the variations are made to seek support of an authority (e.g. Matt 4:14) or simply for a heightened literary effect (e.g. Titus 1:12).[11]

The theory of "memory lapse" as cause of textual variations has been criticized. The importance of scriptural memorization for the Jew and, in the case of Paul, his rabbinic training and the verbal exactness of many of his quotations and their general agreement with the LXX combine to militate against this theory. Rather these would point to a conscious desire to reproduce a particular text. Hence, Krister Stendahl, while having the impression that Paul would be quoting from memory goes on to qualify it: "yet a memory which was the storehouse of more than one language, and one trained in Jewish methods of bringing together passages from books of the Old testament."[12] In addition we might note that quotations used by a particular writer are likely to have been employed by him on several occasions and thus become well-known to him, making memory lapse as a factor in textual variations highly improbable.

It has been also suggested that another cause of textual variations was that the New Testament writers were wresting texts to serve their own purpose.[13] This impression arose from the results of the early studies on Qumran literature.[14] However, later evidence from Qumran studies appears to suggest that even the sectarians did not deliberately change their received Hebrew text to suit their convictions, but rather employed received textual variants since the Hebrew text was still in a fluid state.[15] This latter view appears to be supported by the nature of the text-type of the LXX which is mainly used by New Testament writers.

---

[10] For a thorough discussion of these causes of textual variations especially as they apply to the Pauline Epistle to the Romans, see H.B.P. Mijoga, "Causes of Text Variations in Old Testament Quotations in Paul's Epistle to the Romans", *Journal of Humanities*, No. 4, October 1990, especially pp. 23-31. Cf. Ellis, *Paul's Use,* pp. 11-15.

[11] See E Earle Ellis "How the New Uses the Old", in I. Howard Marshall (ed), *New Testament Interpretation, Essays on Principles and Methods*, Carlisle: Paternoster, 1985, p. 199.

[12] Quoted in Ellis, *Paul's Use,* pp. 14f. Cf. John W. Wenham, *Christ and the Bible*, Leicester: InterVarsity, 1984, p. 92-94; Ellis, "How the New Uses the Old", p. 199.

[13] Mijoga, "Causes", *Journal of Humanities,* p. 30.

[14] The idea of wresting a text is implied in the method that F.F. Bruce calls "atomization" where a biblical text is made to fit a new historical situation regardless of its contextual meaning, see F.F. Bruce, *Biblical Exegesis in the Qumran Text,* London: Tyndale, 1960, p. 12.

[15] See W.F. Albright and C.S. Mann, *Matthew, Introduction, Translation and Notes*, Anchor Bible, New York: Doubleday, 1971, p. LIXf.

2 The Problem of the First Century Biblical Text

Two theories have been suggested to explain the origin of the LXX. The first postulates that there was an archetypal text which originated around 300 BC as a Greek translation of the Torah in a Jewish community in Alexandria and that it had three major recensions; Hesychius, Lucian and Origen. The difficulty with this theory was that it could not explain the textual variations of the Old Testament citations in Jewish writings (e.g. Philo) in the New Testament and in the writings of the early church fathers. This led to its abandonment.

The other theory postulates that there was no archetypal text. Rather the LXX started life as oral renderings of the Hebrew text in the Aramaic targums in various synagogues. These oral targumic versions were later reduced to writing which then developed into an official targum, that is the LXX.[16] Thus Kahle sees variant forms behind Origen's Hexapla, in the Old Latin version and to some extent in Philo and Josephus, while Manson sees similar Greek texts developing along regional lines. For instance, behind the Theodotion is seen a Greek Targum of Asia while Targums of Syria and Egypt are thought to lie behind Lucian and the LXX.[17] It is in the light of this theory that Manson suggests that the LXX we now possess "is the debris of primitive diversity only very imperfectly overcome rather than the record of sporadic lapses from a primitive uniformity.."[18] And Kahle concludes, "The task which the LXX presents to the scholar is not the reconstruction of an imaginative Ur-text, nor the discovery of it, but a careful collection and investigation of all the remains and traces of earlier versions of the Greek Bible which differ from the Christian standard text."[19]

In recent LXX studies, however, the theory of multiple and simultaneous development of Greek targumic texts leading to subsequent compilation of the LXX has suffered on two counts; first Kahle's treatment of the Aristeas tradition and the quotations from Philo is highly questionable. Extant Greek Targums are lacking and the manner he relates the New Testament quotations to the Greek Old Testament betrays a radical treatment. Secondly, the Qumran evidence favours an archetypal view of LXX origin.[20] J.M. Cross regards this evidence from the Dead Sea Scrolls as "decisive evidence for the older view.."[21] This view is further strengthened by the observation by most New Testament scholars that not only did New Testament

---

[16] See Ellis, *Paul's Use*, p. 16-17.
[17] Cf. *Ibid.*, p. 18.
[18] Quoted in *Ibid*.
[19] *Ibid*.
[20] See Ibid.. p. 19. For the Letter of Aristeas, see R.H. Charles, *The Aplocrypha and Pseudepigrapha of the Old Testament*, Vol. II, Oxford: Clarendon, 1969, pp. 83-122.
[21] Quoted in Ellis, *Paul's Use* p. 19, footnote number 3.

writers often approximate their quotations to LXX, but also did that in relation to a Palestinian form of LXX, that is MSS A, Q and Lucian, as over against the MSS B and X (Aleph). They also agree that New Testament writers did not make their own translation into Greek under normal circumstances. Similarly, Josephus, Philo and early Christian writers approximated their Greek texts to these MSS.[22]

The letter to the Hebrews appears to be an exception to this general tendency to approximate to a particular extant witness to LXX.[23]

Thus, while there is a tendency for quotations to approximate a certain text-type, it is still uncertain whether these were independent texts or merely revisions within a LXX family of a textual tradition, although evidence does not point to any great number of independent textual traditions or to a great majority of Greek Targums. We might as well conclude with Sanday's observation that "(there is) no sufficient evidence to say whether this (narrative) arises from a reminiscence of Hebrew text .... or from an Aramaic Targum or from the use of an earlier form of LXX text."[24] It would appear to us that the greatest difficulty is not only the question of the text behind Paul's quotations as Allis observes,[25] but indeed, the text behind the New Testament writers in general.

The question of the Hebrew text of the first century AD is even more uncertain. While the Qumran discoveries vindicated the trustworthiness of the Massoretic text,[26] pushing our knowledge of the Hebrew text a thousand years back and

---

[22] See Wenham, *Christ and the Bible*, p. 95 C.f. David F. Hinson, *Theology of the Old Testament, Old Testament Introduction 3*, London: SPCK, 1976, p. 135. France, *Jesus*, p. 31.

[23] See Harold W. Attridge, *The Epistle to the Hebrews, Hermeneia – A Critical and Historical Commentary on the Bible*, Philadelphia: Fortress, 1989, p. 23. Efforts to identify the LXX behind the Epistle to the Hebrews have become even more complicated by recent development in LXX textual studies. For instance, the recognition of the need to judge every book of LXX or groups of books or even part of a book on its own merit, implying that what is true with one book or part of a book or a group of books in the LXX is not necessarily true of all the others; the recognition that uniformity of text-type in any book cannot be assumed; disagreements among scholars as whether to speak of different forms of LXX text, or different translations of LXX. For a discussion of these and other difficulties related to Textual Criticism of the LXX in contemporary scholarship see Paul Ellingworth, *The Epistles to the Hebrews, A Commentary on the Greek Text, New International Greek Testament Commentary*, Grand Rapids: Eerdmans & Carlisle: Paternoster, 1993, p. 37.

[24] Quoted in Ellis, *Paul's Use*, p. 20.

[25] *Ibid.*' p. 19.

[26] Albright and Mann hold the view that the Hebrew originals on which the Greek text of the Old Testament (LXX) was based were more reliable than the present Hebrew text (MT). See Albright and Mann, *Matthew*, p. LX.

revealing a wonderful fidelity in scribal transmission of the text in the subsequent centuries, the case is not one of complete uniformity of the Hebrew text in the first century AD

Readings appear in the Qumran texts which have so far only been known through the LXX, especially in the historical books. Other readings appear which are only preserved in the Samaritan Pentateuch and not found in the Hebrew.[27]

This inquiry into the text-form of the first century biblical text leads us to the conclusion that the New Testament writers are themselves an early witness to important text-types found at the time. If this is true, then while these writers could modify the quoted text to fit their purpose or contention, such modifications are likely to be usually of a grammatical nature. Important variants are, however, likely to come from textual sources rather than be created by the writers. It is doubtful that a biblical writer could base a serious argument on a text of his own creation and make everyone else believe it was scriptural.

3 Jewish Literary Methods and Exegetical Practices in First Century AD

This section briefly outlines some Jewish literary and exegetical practices. These practices served as background to the way New Testament writers used the Old Testament.

(a) Jewish Literary Methods

The New Testament writers had much in common with the Jewish schools of thought in their literary heritage. When the Christian faith began its earliest witnesses proclaimed it using Jewish methods of literary expression. Several literary methods have been recognized as typically Jewish although they were shared with the Christian community. Here I shall look at some of these literary methods.

Free and Exegetical Paraphrase

This is basically an interpretive rendering of a biblical text. The Aramaic Targums are a good example of this literary style. The LXX in so far as it includes some interpretive expressions of the Hebrew text within itself can also be considered as an example of a free and exegetical paraphrase. In Rom 10:11, Paul adds the word "everyone" (The word is strangely rendered "No-one" in the RSV Bible. However, it is properly rendered in verse 13) to the Old Testament quotation as an interpretive expression that suits his argument.

---

[27] See Wenham, *Christ and the Bible,* p. 97.

Composite Quotations[28]

This is also a rabbinical literary practice. Sometimes the text of these quotations is altered to fit contemporary application, for instance, Paul's composite quotations in 1 Cor 2:9 and 2 Cor 6:16-18. However, there is significant difference in the manner composite quotations are used by both rabbinic commentators and New Testament writers. For the latter, the quotations are cited freely without necessarily adhering to the letter. The rabbis, however, strictly adhere to the letter and indicate by the formula *al tigre* whenever they depart from it.[29]

Changing Contextual Sense

Employing a quotation in a sense that differs from the original context is another rabbinical literary method. In the New Testament obvious examples of what is seemingly unnatural interpretation of texts include Matthean quotations referring to the divine call of God's son from Egypt (Matt 2:15; Hos 11:1; Ex 4:22) and the lamentation of Jerusalem over her massacred babies (Matt 2:18; Jer 31:15). Also, Paul's interpretation of "seed" (Gal 3:16; Gen 12:7), and his application of Deut 25:4 concerning a farm animal, to preachers of the Gospel (1 Tim 5:18).[30]

Daily Life Illustration

Employing illustrations from daily life was another rabbinic style. However, while New Testament writers used these for explanatory purposes, the rabbis gave them the authoritative note of proof.

Fragmentary Citations

The use of fragmentary citations with the continuance of a given portion sometimes implied. For instance, 1 Cor 2:9; Acts 2:17-21,39.[31]

---

[28] For combined or merged quotations as well as chain quotations in Pauline letters see Ellis, *Paul's Use*, Appendix III, p. 186.

[29] Cf. *Ibid*, p. 45, footnote number 5.

[30] However, it appears that behind these seemingly unnatural interpretations of the biblical text lie sound exegetical principles and assumptions so that the difficulty is more apparent than real. See Wenham, *Christ and the Bible*, pp. 99-100. Cf. R.T. France, *The Gospel According to Matthew*, Tyndale New Testament Commentary, Leicester: InterVarsity and Grand Rapids: Eerdmans, 1985, p. 68.

[31] This literary style indicates that the portion of Scripture that the writer has in mind is not necessarily limited to the amount he quotes. C.H. Dodd appeals to this fact to support his argument that a quotation in the New Testament serves as a pointer to a wider context from which it is drawn. This argument militates against Lindars' assumption that Matthew was

Insertion of Hortatory and Ethical Sections

The rabbinic scriptural interpretation known as *haggadah* allowed imaginations a free range over scriptures in order to develop religious and moral lessons that would promote piety and devotion.[32] The New Testament also has hortatory and ethical sections, for instance, the Sermon on the Mount in Matt 5-7 and in the final sections of almost all the Pauline epistles.

Introductory Formula

These usually use the verbs of "saying" and "writing," for instance "scripture has said" (John 7:38; Gal 4:30); "It is written" (Rom 9:33); "have you not read" (Luke 6:3); "the Law says" (1 Cor 14:34); "Moses says" (Rom 10:19); "Isaiah ...... say" (Rom 10:20) and many others. These introductory formulas, especially those that employ verbs of saying are also found in the Old Testament, in Qumran literature, in Philo's writings as well as in rabbinic works. These introductory formulas do usually serve a variety of purposes. They are sometimes used to locate a citation in terms of a book, writer or story from which the citation is taken (e.g. Rom 11:2; Mark 12:26; Acts 28:25). The citation may also be interpretive.

This appears to be the case when one book is named and another is quoted (Matt 27:9). The citation may be an elaboration of the text in the book named (Mark 1:2), or possibly even an incidental error. Also, the formulas emphasize the divine authority of the Old Testament. Ellis observes that such a formula as "scripture says" implies the "revelational 'word of God' character" of Scripture that is present within the current interpretation as over against its absence in the rabbinic traditional interpretations (Matt 22:29).[33]

The introductory formulas also show the New Testament writers' attitude to the Old Testament. The formula "it is written" in secular Greek culture referred to the terms of an unalterable agreement. For the Jew it referred to the unalterable nature of the Word of God. Although the human author could be cited, for instance, "Moses says" (Rom 10:19), "Isaiah says" (Rom 10:20), it is the Word of God that is quoted. For them such formulas as "God says," "Scripture says," "Moses says," are just alternative ways of expressing the same thing. To them the Old Testament is

---

ignorant of the original text from which he drew his formula-quotations, unless one assumes with Lindars that the Evangelist was detached from the apostolic tradition and that he did not know his Bible. See C.H. Dodd, *According to the Scriptures,* Cambridge: Nisbet, 1952, p. 47. Cf. Lindars, *New Testament Apologetic,* p. 16.

[32] See James D.G. Dunn, *Unity and Diversity in the New Testament, An Inquiry into the Character of Earliest Christianity,* Second Edition, London: SCM and Philadelphia: Trinity 1990, p. 62.

[33] See Ellis, "How the New Uses the Old," p. 200.

inspired and as such it was the very word of God despite their acknowledgement of the human means through which it was spoken.[34]

(b) Jewish Exegetical Practices

Just as early Christian writers shared in the conceptual framework of Jewish literary methods, they also shared in Jewish exegetical practices. Since these Jewish exegetical practices are, with a few exceptions, also employed by New Testament writers, they will be treated in detail under the chapter on New Testament exegesis below. Meanwhile, it is sufficient simply to mention these and then move to the principles of Hillel and certain features of Akiba's rival exegetical practice, which in certain cases were also employed by the New Testament writers.

The major categories of Jewish exegesis are midrash, pesher, allegory, typology and prediction-fulfillment, especially for those groups with a strong sense of being an eschatological community.[35] By the first century AD, exegetical principles, generally known as the Seven Rules of Hillel, had been standardized so that they were often used in biblical interpretation. These Seven Rules are:-

Qal Wahomer: What applies in a less important case will also apply in a more important one. It is known as *a fortiori*. This is employed by Jesus, for instance in reference to God's care for his people on the basis of his care for lower creatures (Matt 7:30), the "something greater than Jonah (Solomon) is here" passage (Matt 12:38; also Ex 22:9, 14; 1 Cor 9:9).

Gezerah Shawah: verbal analogy e.g. Rom 4:3-8 where Paul uses verbal analogy to link Gen 15:6 and Ps 32:1. Reference to Melchizedeck (Heb 7:1 and 5:6) is the basis for bringing in the Ps 110:4 reference in a discussion based on Gen 14:17-20. Also the reference to sacrificial blood (Heb 9:20; 8:8-12) is the basis for bringing together Exodus 4:8 and Jer 31:31-34 in the discussion.

Binyan ab mikathub ehad: building up a family from a single text. This rule suggests that if the same expression or phrase is found in a number of passages then a consideration found in one of them is applicable to them all.

---

[34] See Ellis, *Paul's Use*, p. 23. For a thorough discussion of the New Testament writers' view on verbal inspiration of scriptures, Cf. Wenham, *Christ and the Bible*, p. 86-91, 101-103.

[35] See Dunn, *Unity and Diversity*, p. 82-87. He lists targum as a special type in addition to those we have mentioned. However, it appears to me that a targum is not a method but a product of the use of a particular method e.g. midrash or pesher. Hayes and Holladay mention only four: *Peshat* (literal), *remez* (allegorical), *derash* (homiletical) and *sod* (mystical). See John H. Hayes and Carl R. Holladay, *Biblical Exegesis, A Beginner's Handbook*, Second Edition, London: SCM, 1988, p. 21.

Binyan ab mishene kethubim: building up a family from two texts. Here, a principle is established by relating two texts together. The principle so established can then be applied to other passages. Where two texts contradict each other, a third one must be found to reconcile them.

Kelal upherat: the general and the particular, e.g. Lev. 5:4. A general principle may be restricted by its particularization in another verse, or, conversely, a particular rule may be extended into a general principle.

Kayoze bo bemaqom aher: a difficulty in one text may be solved by comparing it with another which has points of general similarity. This is analogy of similar texts.

Debar halamed me inyano: a meaning established by its context.[36]

These rabbinical-exegetical rules are similar to Hellenistic rules of legal interpretation.[37]

In addition to emphasis on these rules, there was also an emphasis on grammatical exegesis in which grammatical details contributed to the meaning finally arrived at. There was also the practice of quoting the Law, the Prophets and the Hagiographa in succession to support a rabbinic opinion. These methods are also employed in the New Testament. For instance, Paul's argument in Gal 3:16 hinges on the singular word "seed.." Appeals to the Law, the Prophets and the Hagiographa are also found in Rom 11:8-10; 15:9-12; Luke 24:44; Matt 12:3-8; Luke 16:16,29. But these methods are much more used by Jewish commentators and only occasionally by the New Testament writers.[38]

While these methods are in themselves sound and objective, in the hands of rabbis they often led to fantastic exegetical conclusions. For instance, the rabbinic teaching that God prays to Himself so that His mercy subdues His wrath is deduced from Isa 56:7; "As it is said 'Even them will I bring to my holy mountain, and make them joyful in my house of prayer (the Hebrew is literally 'the house of my prayer') (Isa 56:7). It is not said, 'their prayer' hence we infer that the Holy One, blessed be He, prays."[39]

---

[36] See John Bowker, *The Targums and Rabbinic Literature, An Introduction to Jewish Interpretation of Scripture*, Cambridge: University Press, 1969,p. 315. Cf. Dunn, *Unity and Diversity*, p. 84; Ellis, *Paul's Use*, p. 41, Albright and Mann, *Matthew*, p. LX-LXI.

[37] See Goldingay. *Approaches*, p. 149.

[38] See Ellis, *Paul's Use*, p. 45f. For Paul's quotations from the three sections of the Hebrew Bible in succession see *Ibid*, Appendix III, p. 186. Examples of rabbinic use of the three sections of the Hebrew Bible in successive citation include: *Makkoth* 10b: Num 22:12, 20; Isa 58:17; Prov 3:34. *Baba Kamma* 92b: Gen 28:9; Judg 9:3; Sirach 13:15; Sanhedrin 90b: Deut 31:16; Isa. 26:19. See *ibid*, p. 46, footnote 6.

[39] See A. Cohen, *Everyman's Talmud*, London: J.M. Dent & Sons and New York: E.P. Dutton, 1949, pp. 18-19.

After 70 AD, a rival system of exegesis was popularized by Rabbi Akiba, and though resisted at first, it soon dominated rabbinic exegetical practice. It emphasized exegesis by letter-number equivalence (Gematria), by construction of words from the letters of a word (Notarikon) and by combination of letters to fit a secret meaning (Themoura). This method of exegesis contributed greatly to the extravagancies of later rabbinic exegesis. When outside Palestine attempts were being made to interpret Scriptures in the light of Greek philosophy, allegory emerged as an appropriate method for this task. In Alexandria, Philo, through allegorical interpretation, endeavored to show that the Pentateuch was supportive of Greek philosophical ideas.[40]

Conclusion

In this chapter I have discussed the fluidity of the first century biblical text which led to variations in the text-form of quotations used in the New Testament. I have also suggested some causes that may lie behind these variations. This situation complicates any theories of an archetypal text. I have also outlined some interpretive methods used to determine meaning.

---

[40] Referred to in Ellis, *Paul's Use,* pp. 42-45.

Chapter Four
New Testament Exegesis of the Old Testament

In this chapter I shall look at major approaches to the exegesis of the Old Testament which the New Testament writers took. It has already been hinted that these approaches were not exclusively Christian but rather that they were shared with Jewish scholarship at large.

Midrash

The Term Midrash

The term midrash is used in different senses by those who apply it to New Testament studies. When taken in its broader sense it only becomes vague. It is often not clear whether the term is formally intended to refer to a literary genre or informally to a literary technique or style. The term midrash is related to the Hebrew word "darash" which means "to seek, inquire, investigate, study." Midrash is the product of such a study. Reference to midrash is found in II Chr 13:22; 24:27 where it refers to a commentary on the Book of Kings and a commentary on the Prophet Iddo. Since these are lost to us, it is almost impossible to determine their specific character. The term also appears in Sirach 51:23 in a phrase "house of midrash." It appears again in IQS 6:23; 8:15,26; CD 20:6 where it refers to investigation, study or interpretation.[1]

A more illuminating use of the term is found in 4Q Flor 1:14. Here the term is used as a title to a passage which interprets Ps 1:1 through a number of biblical quotations that are woven together in an interpretive way.[2] However, contemporary connotations of the term "midrash" are not derived solely from this pre-Christian usage, but rather are determined by later rabbinic usage. From this a number of characteristics of midrash have been suggested. First, the essence of midrash is the pre-occupation with contemporarization of Scripture so that a particular text of Scripture becomes applicable to current situations.[3]

---

[1] See Raymond E. Brown, *The Birth of the Messiah, A Commentary on the Infancy Narratives in the Gospels of Matthew and Luke*, New York: Doubleday, 1993, pp 557, 558. Cf. Ellis, "How the New Uses the Old", p. 201.

[2] See Brown, *The Birth of the Messiah*, p. 558.

[3] Cf. Ellis, "How the New Uses the Old", p. 202.

Secondly, midrash is said to be concerned not so much with "literal" meaning as with "inner" or "hidden" meaning of a biblical text. It is typically concerned with drawing out these hidden meanings from a given text as B. Gerhadson in his *Testing on God's Son* puts it: "Midrash starts from a (sacred) text or often a single word; but the text is not simply explained—its meaning is extended and its implications drawn out with the help of every possible association of ideas."[4]

Thirdly, midrash is considered as essentially creative stories (e.g. about Jesus and the teaching attributed to him) which derive not from a "historically based tradition" but rather from a "scripturally-inspired imagination."[5] A logical implication of this third character of midrash is obviously that it is basically unhistorical. This is the common understanding of those who see midrash in Matthean and Lucan infancy narratives, although some hold a modified version of this view.[6] The wide differences in scholarly opinion as to the meaning and content of the genre midrash can probably be accounted for by how much weight each of them puts to any of these main characteristics of midrash in relation to the others. Here, we do not pretend to be exhaustive. To be sure, there are other significant characteristics of midrash besides these three. However, these provide a reasonable minimum that is sufficient for our purpose.

Goldingay has given a useful guidance to what consists the genre midrash of. He lists the following: the biblical text as modified in the course of transmission or translation e.g. the Targums and the LXX; close textual commentary e.g. Qumran pesharim;[7] discursive commentary e.g. Philo's commentary on Genesis; legal commentary; anthologizing of Scripture; homily; retelling of biblical narrative e.g. Genesis Apocryphon; expansion of biblical books; the "testaments" and visions attributed to biblical figures; literary genres which are themselves biblical and portray biblical language e.g. 1 Maccabees, or the Qumran Hodayot; community rules e.g. the Talmud or the Manual of Discipline.[8] He also observes that all these

---

[4] Quoted in Dunn, *Unity and Diversity*, p. 84.

[5] See France, *Matthew*, p. 24.

[6] For instance, Brown holds that the midrash found in the Matthean and Lucan infancy narratives contains both historical and non-historical elements. For a thorough discussion of his position and the significant role played by these narratives in the development of the concept of midrash in subsequent Christianity, see Brown, *The Birth of the Messiah*, p. 557-562.

[7] *Pesher* is a sub-genre of *midrash*. While *midrash* is a wider term for interpretive comments on a text of Scripture, *pesher* is a special type of *midrash* which employs contemporarized line-by-line re-interpretations of biblical works. See Brown, *The Birth of the Messiah*, p. 558, footnote number 3.

[8] Goldingay, *Approaches*, p. 147.

contain explicit and implicit biblical interpretation and that those works cited near the beginning show priority to the biblical text while those close to the bottom employ the text only as a vehicle for new material that may have little connection with the text.[9]

However, midrash as a genre needs to be distinguished from midrash as a technique for biblical interpretation,[10] especially in relation to the New Testament. While it is relatively easier to identify a Midrashic technique of interpretation at work in some text of the New Testament, it is relatively difficult to pronounce any given text or passage a midrash in terms of its genre because New Testament passages rarely fit neatly all the characteristics prescribed for the genre midrash.

It is, therefore, in my view proper to speak of midrashic methods of interpretation in the New Testament, rather than speak of the genre midrash in it. And by midrashic methods I refer primary to the interpretive comments on Scripture. These may be woven into the scriptural text quoted, hence, affecting its textual form (implicit midrash) or may be added as a formal text-exposition where comments are not necessarily woven into the text (explicit midrash) without assuming any inference to hidden meanings and creation of "*facts*" and stories by an inspired imagination. It is to the presence of these in the New Testament that I now turn.

Midrash in the New Testament

As a literary method employed in the use of the Old Testament by the New Testament writers, midrash was their principal tool.[11] It can be divided into two categories in the New Testament, implicit and explicit. Implicit midrash appear as "double entendre," as interpretive alterations of the Old Testament citations and in more elaborate forms. In the case of "double entendre" a play on words is involved. For instance, in the fulfillment prophecy that identifies Jesus' stay in Nazareth as a messianic fulfillment (Matt 2:23)[12] there is involved a play on the words "Nazarite" (Judg 13:5, 7 LXX) or "Netzer" (i.e. branch, Isa 11:1; cf. 49:6; 60:21). It also

---

[9] *Ibid.*

[10] Brown also acknowledges the need to draw this distinction between *midrash* as a genre and *midrash* as a process of interpretation, see Brown, *The Birth of the Messiah*, p. 558.

[11] Indeed, Goldingay sees the whole system of Jewish and Christian exegetical practice in a m*idrashic f*ramework and approaches his whole discussion on New Testament times interpretation of the Old Testament as Scripture from that perspective. See Goldingay, *Approaches,* pp. 146-153.

[12] Dunn discusses this verse under the *pesher* category. This indicates that the techniques overlap and one cannot be very dogmatic in their classification. See Dunn, *Unity and Diversity,* p. 93.

involves double meaning. The word "lift up" in John 3:14; 12:32 implies to hang or to exalt. The term alludes to the Aramaic "Zekaph" in Isa 52:13 where it has both meanings. In the synoptics the term is clarified as to "be killed and rise" (Mark 8:31; Luke 8:31). Similarly in Acts 3:22-26, the term "raise up" is employed to refer both to the Messiah's pre-resurrection ministry and to his resurrection.[13]

As interpretive alterations of the Old Testament citations, midrash is evident in Rom 10:11 where Paul adds the word "everyone" to his Old Testament citation (Isa 28:16) which has "He," in order to fit his argument (Rom 10:12). A similar case is found in Gal 4:30. The phrase "son of the free woman" is substituted for "my son Isaac" (Gen 21:10) in order to apply to his argument.

More elaborate and complex forms of implicit midrash appear in composite quotations from various Old Testament texts. These are usually altered in order to make them applicable to contemporary situations (e.g. 1 Cor 2:9; 2 Cor 6:16-18). Another complex form of implicit midrash is the description of a current event in biblical phraseology that seek to connect the contemporary event with its Old Testament counterpart. In this case, the contemporary event is of primary interest and that the Old Testament allusions are meant to explain it. This is a more subtle form of implicit midrash. This type of midrash is found in the Lucan infancy narratives (Luke 1:26-38) which allude to Isa 6:1-9:7.[14]

Other instances of implicit midrash are found in the Magnificat (Luke 1:46-55),[15] the Benedictus (Luke 1:68-79);[16] the Lord's response at his trial (Mark 14:62) and the Apocalyptic discourse (Mark 13).

There are also instances of explicit midrash in the New Testament. Probably, these originated not only as "sermons" or "homily" (i.e. in a synagogue preaching) but also as a commentary (i.e. a scholarly work). These acquired a more or less distinctive pattern employed for preaching, apologetic or didactic purposes. This type of midrash could roughly fall into two categories: the "proem" midrash and the

---

[13] See Ellis, "How the New Uses the Old", p. 202.

[14] Dodd has shown that this text of Isaiah was part of the *Testimonia* and hence a primary source for early Christian exegesis. Such an allusion to its phraseology in the infancy narratives is, therefore, perfectly natural. See Dodd, *Scriptures,* pp 78-82.

[15] For a thorough treatment of the Old Testament background to the language of the *Magnificata,* see Brown, *The Birth of the Messiah,* pp. 355-365, especially his Table XII on p. 358. In addition to canonical Old Testament sources he finds linguistic parallels in IV Ezra 9:45; Psalms of Solomon 13:11; Sirach 10:14; 1QM XIV 10-11 and Psalms of Solomon 10:4.

[16] For a thorough discussion of the Benedictus, see *Ibid.,* pp 377-392.

yelamme-denu rabbenu ("let our master teach us"). The general pattern for the "proem" midrash was as follows:[17]

    i.   The (Pentateuchal – in the case of rabbis) text for the day.

    ii.   A second text, the proem or "opening" of the discourse.

    iii.   Exposition with additional quotations from the Old Testament, parables or other explanations or illustrations and connected to the initial texts by catch words such as "stone," "tradition," etc.

    iv.   A final text, usually repeating or alluding to the text for the day. The pattern is clearly expressed in Rom 9:6-29:

           vs. 6   :   Theme and initial text, Gen 21:12

           vs. 9   :   A second, supplementary text, Gen 18:10

           vs. 10-28 :   Exposition with additional citations (13, 15, 17, 25-28) which is connected to the initial texts by the catchwords, "call," "son" (1, 2, 24, 27)

           vs. 29   :   A final text alluding to the initial text with the catch-word "children."

A similar pattern with slight variations is found in Heb 10:5 – 39; 1 Cor 1:18 – 31; 2:6 – 16. Sometimes a midrashic summary may constitute "texts" on which the whole "proem" midrash is based. For instance, in 1 Cor 10:1-13, vs. 1-5 are an implicit midrash (Exod 13f; Num 14:20). Vs 6 is an application and an additional text (Exod 32:6). Then comes an exposition and application which allude to the preceding midrash and other texts (Num 25:1–18; 21:5-6; 16:41, 49).

The examples above show how a composite, interpreted citation and an interpreted summary of a wider section of Scripture may function as a "text" in a midrash (the letter of Jude is another example of the latter—a midrash on midrash). Sometimes a short explicit midrashim functions as a text. This is the case in 1 Cor 1:18-20 which has the following sections that are linked by catchwords like "wisdom," "foolishness":

           1:18-31:   Initial text

           2:1-5 :   Exposition and application

---

[17] For the following discussion on "*proem*" midrash and the *Yelemmedenu rabbenu*' I am gratefully indebted to Ellis, "How the New Uses the Old", p. 203-206.

> 2:6-16: Additional "text"
>
> 3:1-17: Exposition and application
>
> 3:18-20: Concluding texts: Job 5:13; Ps 94:11

Similar exegetical patterns are also found in the synoptic gospels. These include Matt 21:33-44 which correspond to an ancient form of a synagogue address; also Matt 4:1-11. Others correspond to the *Yelemmedenu rabbenu* pattern.

The *Yelemmedenu rabbenu* pattern differs slightly from the "proem" midrash pattern in that it opens by posing a question or problem which is then answered as it progresses. Otherwise it follows the same structure as the "proem" midrash pattern. For instance, Luke 10:25 -37 belongs to this category.

> vs. 25-27 : Dialogue including a question and initial texts, Deut 6:5; Lev 19:18
>
> vs. 28 : A second text, Lev 18:5
>
> vs. 29-36 : Exposition through a parable linked to initial text by the catchwords "neighbour" (vs. 27, 29, 36) and "do" (vs. 28, 37a, 37).
>
> vs. 37 : Concluding allusion to second text ("do likewise")

Matt 1:1-19 is similar, as well as Matt 19:3-8.[18] A more complex statement of problem is found in Matt 22:23-33; Mark 12:18-27.

John 6:31-58 is also one of the extended midrashim in the New Testament. It is a midrash on Ps 78:24. "He gave bread from heaven to eat" (John 6:31). (The Psalms text read "and rained down upon them manna to eat.") Jesus then explains that the "he" of the Psalms is not Moses but God the Father and the "bread from heaven" is interpreted as Jesus himself who came from heaven and was given for the life of the world. Therefore, those who eat this "bread" (i.e. his flesh) are not the ancestors in the desert who ate manna and died but those who hear Jesus. If they eat his flesh and drink his blood, i.e. if they believe in him and receive His Spirit, they would never die.[19]

Rom 4:3-25 is a midrash on Gen 15:6 "Abraham believed God and it was counted to him for righteousness." Paul cites this quotation at the beginning (vs. 3) and in the conclusion (vs. 22). Using Hillel's second rule of interpretation, verbal analogy, Paul brings a second text (Ps 32:1-2) as a basis of his argument linked by the word "counted" or "reckoned" and argues that it should be understood as

---

[18] For a thorough analysis of the *midrashic* technique in these texts, see *ibid.*, p. 206.

[19] See a full discussion of this *midrash* in Dunn, *Unity and Diversity*, p. 87.

implying a "favor" rather than a "reward." In vs. 9-12 he gives an exposition of the term "believed," and using three arguments (vs. 9-12; 13-17a; 17b-21) Paul concludes that it should be understood in the sense he discusses and not in the sense of faithfulness as understood in rabbinic sense. Similarly, Gal 3:8-14 (or 8-29) is a midrash on Gen 12:3; 18:18. The speeches in Acts especially chapters 2 and 13 are also instances of Christian midrash.[20]

The random samples of the Jewish exegetical technique of midrash[21] demonstrate to us that the New Testament writers were at home with it.

Pesher

The word "pesher" simply means interpretation. As I have already hinted elsewhere (see footnote no. 131 above) the pesher technique is a narrower form of midrash and it is more precise in its comments. Dunn observes that while midrash widens the "relevance" of a biblical text pesher explains the "meaning" of such a text "with one to one correspondence."[22] There are certain features which distinguish pesher from general midrash. But there are also certain features that are common to both.

One of the most outstanding features of pesher that distinguishes it from other forms of midrash is the use of a special formula: "The interpretation is," "This is," "This refers to" or "the statement refers to." This feature is clearly demonstrated in Dan 5:25-28. "And this was the writing that was inscribed: MENE MENE TEKEL PARSIN. This is the interpretation of the matter: MENE, God has numbered the days of your kingdom and brought it to an end; TEKEL, you have been weighed in the balances and found wanting; PARSIN, your kingdom is divided and given to the Medes and Persians."

Other examples of Pesher illustrating the special formula are also found in the Habakkuk commentary of the Qumran community:

'For behold, I arouse the Chaldeans, that cruel and hasty nation.' The explanation (pesher) of this concerns the Kittim" (i.e. Romans) (1 Qp Hab 1:6a).

'O traitors, why do you look on and keep silent when the wicked swallow up the man more righteous than he?' The explanation of this concerns the House of Absalom and

---

[20] For a full discussion see J.W. Bowker, "Speeches in Acts: A Study of Proem and Yellemmedenu Form", *New Testament Studies*, Vol. 14 (1967-68), pp. 96-111.

[21] For a similar exposition to the New Testament "*proem*" midrash see W.G. Braude, *Pesikta Rabbat'* (2 vols). New Haven: 1968, who gives, among others, Pesikta Rabbat 37:7. Here we have a text (Isa. 51:12) a second text (Hos 6:1) and an exposition (with parable and application, linked verbally to second text), an additional text (Lam 1:13) and a concluding text, (Isa. 51:12). Also *Pesikta Rabba.t* 44:7. (Quoted in Ellis, "How the New Uses the Old", p. 215, footnote number 35)

[22] Dunn, *Unity and Diversity*, p. 84.

the members of their council who were silent at the time of chastisement of the Teacher of Righteousness..." (1 Qp Hab 1:13b)

'But the righteous will live by the faith'. The explanation concerns all those who observe the Law in the House of Judah. God will deliver them from the House of Judgment because of their application and their faith in the Teacher of Righteousness (1 Qp Hab 2:4b)

A second characteristic is its use or creation of Old Testament textual variants. This character is shared with general midrash. It is this common feature that has led Ellis to discuss pesher under the heading "Midrash pesher" where he suggests either an *ad hoc* rendering or an interpretive selection from various known texts in the citations of Rom 10:11; 12:19; 11:26f; 1 Cor 15:54; Gal 3:8.[23] Stendahl also finds variants in the Matthean special formula quotations and understands this as Matthew's application of the pesher technique to his Old Testament quotations.[24]

A third character of the pesher technique is its practice of linking text and commentary by the use of catchwords. This aspect is also shared by the general midrashic practice as we noted above.

A fourth distinctive feature of pesher not shared with rabbinic midrash but with the early Christian practice is its eschatological and charismatic perspective. Its eschatological view has led scholars to see pesher technique as an eschatological exegesis. The Old Testament prophecies and promises are seen as being fulfilled in the writers' own time and community.

This contemporary fulfilment of prophecy and the promises of God inaugurates the New Covenant of the "last days" (Jer 31:31). This was the view of the Qumran community (1 Qp Hab 2:3-6; CD 6:19; 8:21) and the early Church (1 Cor 11:25; Heb 8:7-13). The community of the writer and their contemporaries constitute the "last generation" just before the coming of the Messiah and the breaking in of the Kingdom.[25] The pesher formula, "This is" and its variants with an eschatological perspective is found in some New Testament quotations: Rom 9:7-9 quoting Deut 30:12 in relation to the problem of the Jews; Eph 5:31 quoting Gen 2:24; Gal 4:22-24 quoting Gen 21 referring to the two wives of Abraham as an "allegory" of the

---

[23] For a thorough discussion on the variants that Paul introduces in these references to adapt the quotations to his present argument, see Ellis, *Paul's Use,* p. 140. For Paul's variants where LXX and Hebrew agree, that is quotations that Paul has deliberately adapted to the New Testament context, see especially his Appendix I, pp. 150-152.

[24] For a summary of Standal's comparative treatment of the variants in the Gospel of Matthew – he compares the variants against the readings in Habbakuk Qumran commentary, the Hebrew Text, the Targum, the LXX, the Peshita and the Vulgate, see *Ibid.*, pp 141-143.

[25] For a discussion of the eschatological views of the Qumran community, see the previous chapter.

two covenants, and 1 Cor 10:1-5,6 where he refers to the events of the Exodus as types of the Christian community, quoting Exodus 13, 16; Num 20:14 among other Old Testament texts.

The charismatic element is also found in the Qumran community as well as in the early Church. The Scriptures are considered as a mystery that can only be properly interpreted by inspired persons: the Teacher of Righteousness and the "maskilim." The community is already experiencing the outpouring of the Holy Spirit in the Messianic era of which it is said:

> God will then purify every deed of man with his truth; he will refine for Himself the human frame by rooting out all spirit of falsehood from the bounds of his flesh. He will cleanse him of all wicked deeds with the spirit of holiness; like purifying waters He will shed upon Him the spirit of truth. (IQs iv, 20, 21).[26]

However, there is a significant difference between the concept of spirit between the Qumran community and the New Testament community. At Qumran the spirit is impersonal and lacks the dynamic eschatological power associated with the Holy Spirit in both the Old and the New Testament where he is personal and a third member of the Godhead.[27] This view is further strengthened by the fact that the text in IQS iv, 20, 21 is the only place in Qumran literature where the Holy Spirit is mentioned in an eschatological context.[28]

Similarly, in the New Testament, Paul, inspired by the Spirit can interpret the mystery embodied in Scripture (Gen 2:24) that speaks of man and woman becoming one flesh in holy matrimony as referring to the divine intimacy of the Church with Christ so that the Church really becomes "one flesh" with Christ, that it becomes the body of Christ (Eph 5:30-32). The disciples in the Upper Room are filled by the Spirit who equips them with the gift of speaking in unstudied languages as a tool for witnessing the Christ event and its implications to the nations gathered around them (Acts 2:1-11).

The Spirit himself bears witness to believers concerning their divine sonship (Rom 8:16) and searches all the things that God reveals to believers through him (1 Cor 2:10). Thus both communities are already experiencing the charismatic and eschatological blessings which in Old Testament promises and prophecies are directly linked with the Messianic age. The Kingdom of God is already becoming an experienced reality. Other examples of pesher exegesis in the New Testament are found in Heb 10:5-10, an interpretation of LXX Ps 40:6-8 which is itself an interpretative paraphrase of the Hebrew text; Rom 9:7; 1 Cor 15:54-56; 2 Cor 6:2; Eph 4:8-11; Heb 2:6-9; 3:7-19.

---

[26] G. Vermes, *The Dead Sea Scrolls in English,* 3rd ed, London: 1987, p. 66.
[27] See my discussion on language and thought at Qumran in chapter two above.
[28] *ibid.*

Dunn has discussed certain targumic interpretations under what he calls the "pesher quote."[29] These are characterized by the incorporation of the interpretive comments or variants into the text itself. I have already discussed similar aspects under "midrash" above. I shall, therefore, note only important aspects of the pesher quotation in a summary fashion. Dunn observes that incorporation of interpretation within the text in some cases leaves the text verbally unaltered, but that usually it involves some modification in the text-form: Matt 2:6; Rom 12:19; Gal 3:10; Acts 1:20; 4:11. There are other citations where the sense of the text is significantly modified through the alteration of the text-form. For instance, 2 Cor 3:16; Eph 4:8. The clearest example of a pesher quote is Matt 27:9-10 (quoting Zech 11:13 and Jer 18-19,32). Others include Matt 21:5; Rom 9:33; 11:8; 2 Cor 6:16-18; Gal 3:8; Heb 10:37; 13:5. Lindars[30] finds examples of modification of a cited text for the sake of interpretation in the formula quotations of Matthew and John where the following Old Testament texts are cited: Ps 34:21; 68:19; 78:2; 118:22; Isa 6:9f; 7:14; 8:23-9:1; 8:14; 28:16; 42:1; 53:4; Micah 5:1; Zech 9:9; 11:13; 12:10; 13:7.

The final type of the "pesher quote" that Dunn finds is that where the citation involves the development of a text which has no real parallel. He finds this in the citation of Matt 2:23. Other citations formed by combinations of references and allusions but without real parallel in the Old Testament include Luke 11:49; John 7:38; 1 Cor 2:9; James 4:5 (Eph 5:14).

It is probably significant to note that pesher exegesis is found in various types of commentary patterns like other forms of midrashic exegesis which include anthology (e.g. 4 Q flor.), single citations (e.g. CD 4:14) and consecutive commentary (e.g. 1 Qp Hab).

These instances of the pesher exegetical technique indicate that the New Testament writers were at home with it.

Allegory

Major Characteristics of an Allegory

In attempting to understand allegory as a technique for interpreting Scriptures in the New Testament era we are again faced with the problem of definition. The ways in which Paul, Philo, Origen and the modern critics understand allegory appear to be quite different. The problem of what really constitutes an allegory and whether it appears in the New Testament is still a matter of scholarly debate. As was seen in the case of midrash above, what makes an allegory depends on how one defines it in

---

[29] For a thorough discussion of the "pesher quotation" see Dunn, *Unity and Diversity*, p. 91-93.
[30] Lindars, *New Testament Apologetic*, p. 284.

terms of emphasis on those features of allegory he considers to be more significant. Here I shall first look at the main characteristics of allegory before I consider its use in the New Testament. A number of scholars have indicated that the following features are characteristics of an allegorical interpretation:

i. The use of Gematria and Onomatology

This is an exegetical technique using letter-number equivalents and symbolic etymology. For instance, the word "Babel" (Gen 11:9) is allegorically understood as meaning "confusion," while the figure 31/2 (that is the 42 months or 1,260 days) of Rev 13:5 is similarly understood as a reference to persecution.[31] Following a similar scheme Abraham's servant is named Eliezer because Gen 14:14 speaks of 318 trained men belonging to Abraham. The letter-number equivalent of the Hebrew letters in the name Eliezer is 318.[32]

ii. The use of symbols without any sense of the historicity of the object being interpreted.

Thus in contrast to typology, the subject of my discussion in the next section, there is no historical correspondence related to allegorical interpretation.

iii. A close attachment to the letter of Scripture while allowing a free range of imagination in search for a spiritual meaning.

For instance, in rabbinic theology, the idea that man is controlled by two urges—one evil and one good, features prominently. In the rabbinic interpretation of Eccles iv:13 the idea of both impulses is allegorically read into it:

> 'Better a poor and wise child than an old and foolish king,' The first clause refers to the good impulse. Why is it called a child? Because it does not attach itself to a person until the age of thirteen and upward. Why is it called poor? Because all do not hearken to it. Why is it called wise? Because it teaches creatures the right path. The second clause refers to evil impulse. Why does he call it a king? Because all hearken to it. Why does he call it old? Because it attaches itself to a person from youth to old age. Why does he call it a fool? Because it teaches man the wrong path" (*Eccles. Rabba* ad loc).[33]

---

[31] See Henri Crouzel, *Origen*, Edinburgh: T&T Clark, 1989, p. 65.
[32] See Ellis, *Paul's Use*, pp. 53, footnote number 1. This is a rabbinic interpretation.
[33] See Cohen, *Everyman's Talmund*, p. 88. For the interesting idea that the two impulses are deduced from Deut 6:5 because the word for heart, there, is written with two "v's", i. e. lebab instead of leb' see Berakoth 9:5, in Herbert Danby, The *Mishnah*, London: Oxford University

iv. It is concerned with the hidden meaning other than the literal one.

Origen, probably the greatest allegorist in the early Church, asserts that the Old Testament passages lack any valid literal meaning and that their real meaning must be sought at the spiritual level. The Holy Spirit is said to have allowed this deliberately as a stumbling block to people's understanding of Scripture so that they can rise to the spiritual level where alone the texts become coherent.[34] Origen proceeds by developing a theory of triple scriptural meaning: literal, moral and mystical or spiritual, although in practice he simply moves from the literal to the spiritual which he considers the most significant.[35] Even in this view of interpretation, this literal meaning is not completely abandoned but that it becomes relatively insignificant.

Origen's allegorical exegesis is rooted in Philo's presuppositions and practice. For instance, both men found in allegorical exegesis a means for avoiding literal anthropomorphism with regard to God; for avoiding trivial, unintelligible or incredible meaning when interpreted literally, a means for handling historical difficulties, and for reaching out of the Old Testament conclusions that are compatible with Greek philosophy and in that way show validity of the Old Testament to the Greek community.[36] It is, therefore, clear that allegorical interpretation existed in the New Testament era and that its presence in the New Testament is worth investigating.

The search for a deeper meaning in every text other than the literal one naturally leads to the attribution to the text of a meaning or meanings that are extrinsic to it and quite different from the apparent meaning that the writer and the original readers or hearers could have. The hidden meanings could derive from elsewhere including the interpreter's fertile mind, independent revelation or a particular theological tradition. Such an "unbridled freedom" of interpretation means that there can be no limit to the range of meanings that can possibly be assigned to a particular text. This

---

Press, 1933, p. 10, footnote number 3; Cf. von Rad, "Typological Interpretation of the OT", in Westermann (ed), *Essays*, p. 21

[34] See Crouzel, *Origen*, p. 62.

[35] Later a theory of quadruple meaning was developed. Although it is also attributed to Origen and fits his practice well, it was initially developed as a theory by Cassian and was current throughout the Middle Ages. First was the literal meaning. Then was the allegorical meaning centred on Christ as key to the Old Testament and centre of history. After this were two corollaries, the moral or tropological meaning which guided the moral life of the Church in the period between the first coming of Christ and the second advent. And the last was anagogical meaning which gave a foretaste of the eschatological realities; see *ibid.*, pp. 79, 80.

[36] See Dunn, *Unity and Diversity*, p. 87.

argument becomes weighty when it is recognized that historical correspondence does not have any meaningful influence on this method although the literal meaning usually serves as a stepping stone toward any subsequent meaning. The original context is simply irrelevant in this scheme.[37]

v. The technique of allegory as a means of interpretation is rooted in Greek philosophy of time which sees time as cyclical.

In this theory events repeat themselves. Graphically, time can be presented as a series of closed circles.[38] Bultmann subscribes to this theory and approaches his study of Christian typology (which he calls "allegorizing") from that perspective:

"If the New Testament in the first instance, i.e., in the understanding of the prophecies ... as referring to the eschatological age of salvation, follows the Jewish tradition of the Old Testament, in the second instance it follows the Stoic tradition of Hellenistic culture. This last developed the tradition on investigating old texts vested with authoritative value for truths, which were far from the minds of the authors of these texts themselves and were actually not contained in the texts at all, but must be read out to them! — by more or less artificial or forced interpretation, by allegorizing. This method was taken over by Hellenistic Jewry and applied to the Old Testament."[39]

But the Christian philosophy of time is different. For Christians, time does not progress in a series of circles and events do not repeat themselves. Time progresses in a linear fashion going into one direction moving from the first advent of Christ to the second advent. "Every expression answering to this scheme is called 'typological' and would belong to the essence of the Christian revelation,[40] and not allegory."

vi. The use of "vertical" symbolism and exemplarism

This is a distinctive feature of the Alexandrian (Greek) scheme. In this scheme the vertical breaks into the horizontal, and what is hoped for a climax in the horizontal scheme is already experienced in its fullness in this scheme. The scheme assumes that there is another world above this perceptible world which is divine, perfect and spiritual and that these two worlds are in a constant interaction in the present so that

---

[37] Crouzel, *Origen*, p. 61. Cf. Goldingay, *Approaches*, p. 103.
[38] See Crouzel, *Origen*, p. 80; Cf. Dodd, *The Bible Today*, Cambridge University Press, 1968, p. 16.
[39] See Rudolph Bultmann, "Prophecy and Fulfillment", in Westerman (ed), *Essays*, p. 51, Cf. Von Rad, "Typological Interpretation", *ibid.*, pp. 19, 20.
[40] See Crouzel, *Origen*, p. 80.

what is here in this perceptible world is in fact a copy of that which is in the world above. The relationship is that of a heavenly reality to an earthly shadow.

This view of the relationship of the two worlds is definitely unchristian in terms of origin: "Wherever, on the contrary, there is assumed to be a world of supernatural beings whose doings have their reflection in our terrestrial universe, we are outside the Christian tradition, confronted with a Hellenization or at best, with an influence drawn from apocalyptic."[41]

The problem here is that this very kind of symbolism and exemplarism appears to be the one we find in certain books of the New Testament. For instance, the whole idea of sacramentalism in the Gospel of John: Jesus as bread of life; the idea of a higher world where the Word was with God from the beginning (John 1:8), from which Christ came and to which he returns (John 8:21-23) of which the Jews have no knowledge (John 8:42); where the Father's house with many rooms is and to which Jesus goes to prepare (John 14:2-5). Similarly, the whole concept of shadows-reality relationship of the two testaments in the letter to the Hebrews is based on this scheme.

Are we to see allegory in these and similar instances? At this point we may just note that the vertical-horizontal tension which exists in this scheme is in fact a characteristic feature of the Kingdom of God itself which breaks into history in the present and at the same time remains future.[42] It therefore appears to me that the traditional view of time as a single horizontal line does not sufficiently account for the sacramentalism and the anticipated realization of eschatological blessings in the temporal Gospel. These can only be accounted for if both the vertical and horizontal schemes are incorporated into the Christian concept of time.

---

[41] *Ibid.*, p. 81. Cf. Gerhard Kittel (ed), *Theological Dictionary of the New Testament*, Vol. 1.; Grand Rapids: Eerdmans, 1964, pp. 260-263 for a thorough treatment.

[42] For a thorough discussion of the present-future tension of the Kingdom of God, see Joachim Jeremias, *New Testament Theology*, London: SCM, 1971, pp. 96-108. For Bultmann the Kingdom is more future than present. Jesus through his presence, his deeds and message, is no more than the "signs" of the Kingdom; "All that does not mean that God's Reign is already here, but it does mean that it is dawning." Bultmann rejects any idea of "a gradual development of the 'Kingdom of God' in history." See Rudolf Bultmann, *Theology of the New Testament*, Vol. One, London: SCM, 1952, pp. 7, 8. Cf. G.E. Ladd, *A Theology of the New Testament*, London: and Gidford: Lutterworh, 1975 pp. 103-4; Dodd, *The Bible Today*, pp. 16-18.

vii. The use of an extended metaphor or an illustrative use of the Old Testament

It is partly under this feature of allegory that the passage which refers to Christ as the Rock which followed the Israelites in the wilderness is classified by some as such (1 Cor 10:4).[43]

viii. The unhistorical nature of allegory

Although this has already been hinted at especially in characteristic number four (iv) above, it deserves special mention. One reason Philo and Origen after him resorted to allegorical interpretation was their view of the Old Testament. To them the Old Testament had too many inconsistencies and discrepancies to be considered as primarily historical. Allegorical interpretation for them provided a means to go around these problems without simply discarding the difficult passages as nonsense.

Allegory in the New Testament

Whether there is any allegory in the New Testament that would meet all the characteristics I have outlined above is still a matter of debate. On the one hand there are scholars who see allegory in the New Testament. For example, Bultmann, who views the Old Testament (if not completely) as unhistorical (at least in the language that has come down to us) sees the whole approach to Old Testament interpretation in the New Testament as allegorical. Consequently, among other places, he finds allegory in Matthew's fulfillment quotations[44] of the Old Testament (Matt 1:22,23; 2:17) in the reference to Isa 54:4 as foretelling Jesus' healing miracles (Matt 8:17); in reference to Ps 78:2 as foretelling Jesus' method of teaching in parables (Matt 13:35); also in the foretelling of his entry into Jerusalem and Judas' betrayal (Matt 21:5; 27:9). He finds further allegory in Paul's reference to Ps 19:5 as foretelling the mission to the Gentiles (Rom 10:18) and to Ps 8:7 as a prophecy of the consummation of the eschatological Lordship of Christ (1 Cor 15:27). Also allegory is found in Paul's reference to Deut 30:11-14 as a prophecy of justification by faith as well as the reference to the crossing of the Red Sea, the marching under a cloud, and the manna, as foretelling the Christian baptism and the

---

[43] See Ellis, *Paul's Use*, p. 51. Goldingay thinks it is not the essence of allegory to be "unhistorical", but accepts that the essence of typology is to be "historical." See Goldigay, *Approaches*, p. 105.

[44] For a thorough discussion of these Matthean quotations in light of their Old Testament context, see my *The Use of Fulfilment Quotations in the Gospel according to Matthew*, Zomba: Kachere Series; Mzuzu: Mzuni Press 2005..

Lord's Supper (1 Cor 10:1-4), as well as the fate of Israel in the wilderness as foreshadowing the experiences of the Christian community.[45]

Obviously, our characteristic number eight (viii) above concerning unhistoricity is one of the major influential factors in Bultmann's discovery of allegory in the New Testament. Similarly, Crouzel, applying primarily our characteristic number six (vi) concerning the use of "vertical" symbolism and exemplarism finds allegorical interpretation in the references to a higher divine world to which Jesus comes from and then goes back to (John 1:1; 8:21-23, 42; 14:2-5); in Paul's reference to the "Jerusalem above" (Gal 4:22-31); his reference to the heavenly citizenship of the believer (Phil 3:20) and to the references to the New Jerusalem "coming down out of heaven from God" (Rev 21:10). Crouzel would no doubt find allegorical interpretation in the Letter to the Hebrews where the theme of heavenly-reality and earthly-shadow is a prominent one.[46]

Dunn, applying the same principle as Crouzel, also finds allegory in the New Testament where symbolism of the shadow-reality type and the use of an extended metaphor are present. Like Crouzel, he finds allegory in 1 Cor 10:1-4; Gal 4:22-31. The former text concerns Israel's experience in the wilderness and the latter is a reference to the Sarah-Hagar "allegory." Similarly in 2 Cor 3:7-18 about the veil on Moses' face (he doubts this reference) and 1 Cor 9:8-10 about not to muzzle an ox. Although he thinks the exegesis in 1 Cor 10:1-4 is based on "typological correspondence" between the experiences of Israel in the wilderness and that of the Church he concludes that there are "clear cut allegory features" and classifies it as such. He also sees allegory in 1 Cor 5:7; John 19:36 which refer to the Pascal lamb; 1 Cor 12:13 about baptism into the body of Christ and Rev 11:8 about the eschatological city which is "allegorically called Sodom and Egypt" (RSV).[47]

On the other hand there are scholars who reject almost any existence of allegory in the New Testament. Such scholars as Ellis and France are in this category. Where Ellis comes closest to seeing allegory in the New Testament is in the case of Gal 4:21-31. He argues rather convincingly that it is not allegory in the general sense of the word. Specifically, Ellis, like Lightfoot long before him (*Galatians*, p. 193)

---

[45] For a thorough discussion, see Bultmann, "Prophecy and Fulfillment", p. 50-55.

[46] See Crouzel, *Origen*, pp. 64-69, 81-82. It is not clear whether Crouzel would find allegory in the other or all references in which Origen finds it. For the sake of completeness, some of the references, according to Crouzel, where Origen finds justification for the use of allegory (hence allegorical themselves) include 1 Cor 10:1-11; 2 Cor 3:6-8; Heb 10:1; Rom 7:14; 1 Cor 2:13; Rev 14:6. Other examples of allegory are Gal 4:21-31; 1 Cor 9:9; 1 Tim 5:18; Gal 3:15; Col 2:16-17; Heb 8:3; Matt 21:61; John 2:19-21; Matt 12:39-14; Luke 24:26-27; John 3:14; John 1:1; 8:21-23, 42; 14:2-5; Rev 21:22; Phil 3:20.

[47] For a thorough discussion see Dunn, *Unity and Diversity*, pp. 90-91.

questions the textual character of Gal 4:25. He also argues that the alleged similarity between allegory and what he sees to be Paul's typology is only apparent for he finds that the charges of alleged use of Gematria in the text was conjectural and that the passage may as well be merely a columnar arrangement of elements in the narrative which Dodd finds to be acceptable practice in the New Testament era.[48] Besides this reference Ellis does not inform us of any other examples of allegory in the New Testament. For Ellis, the principle of historicity or non-historicity becomes prominent. Since allegory presupposes non-historicity, a presupposition which is in complete contrast with his view of the Old Testament as basically historical, he sees no allegory in the New Testament. Rather he sees typological interpretation in it. France shares a similar position.

Typology is not allegory. It is grounded in history, and does not lose sight of the actual historical character of the events with which it is concerned. Typology may be described as 'the theological interpretation of the Old Testament history'. Allegory, on the other hand, has little concern with the historical character of the Old Testament text. Words, names, events, etc. are used, with little regard for their context, and invested with a significance drawn more from the allegorist's own ideas than from the intended sense of the Old Testament.[49]

Viewing allegory as a technique of interpretation from the perspective that sees the Old Testament as embodying historical experiences forces France to see no allegory in the New Testament, especially in the manner Jesus uses Old Testament in the synoptic gospels. This could be understandable when one reflects on the features of allegory that are more determinative for him. In his case it is the historical nature of the Old Testament which is determinative. In the middle position is Goldingay who notes the difference in meaning between allegory, which emphasizes meaning brought to text from elsewhere, and typology which interprets texts literary and then sees analogy between this literal meaning and what comes in Christ. But following this observation on their distinction Goldingay quickly adds that this distinction is "more apparent than real" because of the similarities he finds in the two concepts. For example, Goldingay mentions Heb 2:5-9; Matt 2:15; 1 Cor 9:9.

To us, however, it appears that if the historical understanding of the Old Testament is accepted then we can rightly speak of typological use of the Old Testament as the primary if not the only approach to New Testament interpretation of the Old. Whether we speak of vertical symbolism, extended metaphors, hidden meanings, or any other known feature of allegory, behind the text of any Old Testament quotation on which these tools are brought to bear lies some historical

---

[48] Ellis, *Paul's Use*, p. 126.
[49] France, *Matthew*, p. 40.

background. This view could further be supported by the fact that New Testament writers themselves viewed the Old Testament as history. To neglect this factor is to misunderstand the New Testament approach to the Old Testament interpretation.

If, however, this view is not accepted, then we may speak of allegory in the New Testament; but of a quite different kind. If there is any allegory in the New Testament it is a special type of allegory, quite distinctive from both Jewish and Greek forms of it primarily for the same reason: its unique relationship to the historical character of the Old Testament. New Testament allegory, if it exists, is so typological compared to other types of allegory that the gap between it and typology diminishes to almost a vanishing point.

Typology

The term implies "the imprint made by a blow and from this several New Testament meanings arise – imprint (John 20:25) image (Acts 7:43), pattern or example (e.g. 1 Cor 10:6; Heb 8:5)"[50] As it applies to the New Testament application of the Old, a type could be:

> The recognition of a correspondence between New and Old Testament events (persons, institutions, experiences) based on conviction of unchanging character of the principles of God's working, and a consequent understanding and description of the New Testament event in terms of the Old Testament model.[51]

As it is the case with allegory, there is no consensus on what should be considered typological interpretation. Similarly, there is no agreement on the borderline between what could be considered typological interpretation and what should be understood as allegory. A classical text in this controversy is Paul's use of "allegory" in Gal 4:25. As I noted earlier in the case of both midrash and allegory above, the meaning of what constitutes typological interpretation depends on the relative significance one attaches to certain typological features. It is, therefore, in order that we first look at the major characteristics of typology.

Characteristics of Typological Interpretation

i. The Unchanging Nature of the Outworkings of God.

The typological understanding of the Old Testament arises from the conviction that the principles of God's salvific activities are constant so that the outworkings of his salvific power could be seen forming a pattern of redemptive activities across the Old Testament history of redemption as France puts it:

> [New Testament typology is] the tracing of the constant principles of God working in

---

[50] Ellis, *Paul's Use*, p. 126.
[51] See France, *Matthew*, p 40. Cf. also France, *Jesus*, p. 40.

history, recurring rhythm in past history is taken up more fully and perfectly in the Gospel events.[52]

This concept of unchanging divine principles underlying the idea of typology is probably the most fundamental principle that guided the New Testament writers in their typological application of the Old Testament in the New Testament. In the salvific events of the New Testament they saw an "advance presentation"[53] of corresponding redemptive acts of God that form a pattern across the whole of redemptive history. This correspondence does not merely or primarily consist in external similarities between the events but it is mainly in the essential similarity in God's acts.[54] The God who acted redemptively under the Old Covenant has again acted redemptively through Jesus, the inaugurator of the New Covenant.

ii. The Historical Character of Typological Interpretation

Typological interpretation views the events recorded in the Old Testament as historical in their literal meaning. It is only after acknowledging this historical and literal value that an analogy is made with some aspect of the Christ-event.[55] Dodd observes that "the writers of the New Testament, then, by their attitude to the older scriptures, authorize an historical understanding of them as an indispensable element in their interpretations and application to contemporary situations."[56]

iii. Divine Intention

Some have maintained that the historical factuality is all that matters in the relationship of a type to history and that the divine aspect does not count in the historical factor.[57] But for the New Testament writers history is not a mere collection of past events be they political, social or economic. History for them was essentially religious. It was primarily a record of the dealings of God with his people, Israel, as recorded in the Old Testament. The historical occurrences become especially significant not primarily for their objective value but rather for their being the outworkings of God in history. Hence, these historical events become very important because of their locus in redemptive history. This concept of history as

---

[52] See France, *Jesus*, p. 38. Cf. Goldingay, *Approaches*, p. 99.

[53] Gerhard Friedrich (ed), *Theological Dictionary of the New Testament*, Vol. VIII, Grand Rapids: Eerdmans, 1972, p. 252

[54] *Ibid.*, p. 251.

[55] France, *Jesus*, p. 40. Cf. Gerhard von Rad, "Typological Interpretation of the Old Testament," p. 21.

[56] Dodd, "A Problem of Interpretation", p. 17, quoted in Ellis, *Paul's Use*, p. 127, footnote number 1.

[57] This is the view of Davidson, *Prophecy*, p. 235ff, quoted in Ellis, *Paul's Use*, p 127.

being under the lordship of God is important for typological interpretation.[58] The historical events in the life of Israel as recorded in the Old Testament bear "valuable testimony to the divine governance of history."[59]

iv. Intensification

In the discussion of the first feature of typology above I have already hinted at the analogous feature of typology when I made reference to a pattern of corresponding acts of God distributed throughout the history of redemption and suggested that these acts of redemption are a type of the Christ-event. The correspondence of these Old Testament types to the Christ-event is no mere analogy. There is an element of intensification. In the antitype of the Christ-event the progressive character of the types reaches its finality so that we can speak of attaining their fulfillment in this unique event.[60] All the eschatological hopes and even fears that Israel anticipated find their embodiment in Christ and His Advent:

> We have similar patterns in the New Testament and the Old. Yet the new pattern is never a mere repetition of the Old. It is on a new level, or in terms of new conditions, and it brings a new message and a new power.[61]

v. Christ-Centered

Typology looks at earlier events in the light of what has happened in Christ. It always begins from the Christ-event and then reaches out to the Old Testament persons, events, institutions, experiences in search of types that would help explain the new event, not vice-versa.[62]

vi. Symbolism and Metaphor

Symbolism can be considered as indispensable from typology since by definition a "type" is essentially a symbol. For instance, while the original exodus was a literal exodus, it became a symbol of divine deliverance. It is in this symbolic sense that

---

[58] See Ellis, *Paul's Use*, p. 127.
[59] Walter Eichrodt, "Is Typological Exegesis an Appropriate Method?" in Westermann (ed), *Essays*, p. 226.
[60] See my *The Use of Fulfiment Quotations in the Gospel according to Matthew*.
[61] See H.H. Rowley, *The Unity of the Bible*, New York: Meridian Books, 1957, p. 94. Cf. Eichrodt, "Is Typological Exegesis an Appropriate Method?" Westermann (ed), *Essays*, p. 226. France, *Jesus*, p. 40; Ellis, *Paul's Use*, p. 99f.
[62] In contrast, allegory interprets the text in the light of other concerns including Greek philosophy in the case of Philo, and as a means of explaining the textual problems of the Old Testament in the case of Origen. See Goldingay, *Approaches*, p. 106. Cf. Kittel (ed), *Theological Dictionary*, p. 260.

the return from Babylonian exile is seen as an exodus and is described in language that reflects the original and literal exodus. The same applies to David who was a literal king but later developed into a Messianic symbol. We can, therefore, view all typology as symbolic because its interpretation goes beyond the literal one.[63]

I have already referred to horizontal and vertical symbolism. It is sufficient at this point only to note that the presence of symbolism and the departure from literal meaning as aspects of both typology and allegory, have contributed to the confusion in current scholarship with regard to whether certain passages be regarded as allegory or typology. However, the difference and the degree of similarity where the two forms of interpretation resemble appear to be reasonably clear to allow for some measure of distinctiveness between the two. Those who see these differences as more "apparent than real" tend to see more allegory in the New Testament.[64] However, if symbolism, especially vertical symbolism is accepted as a legitimate feature of New Testament typology, regardless of its Hellenistic background, almost all cases of New Testament interpretation of the Old Testament that are considered as allegorical are capable of being explained in terms of typological interpretation. This could be the case especially with the passages in the Gospel of John, the Letter to the Hebrews and the Book of Revelation.[65]

---

[63] Goldingay, *Approaches,* pp. 100-102, 103.

[64] Goldingay is himself a case in point. He sees the differences as merely apparent but not substantial. He consequently sees much more allegory in the New Testament. He even attempts further classifications, e.g. Christian allegory, Christian typology, typological allegory, non-typological allegory. His classification becomes unnecessarily more complicated. For instance, he suggests that typological allegory is concerned with the link between "subjects referred to in the texts" while non-typological allegory is concerned with the "words of the text", and thinks that Philo's allegorical interpretation is neither exegesis nor eisegesis but "metagesis." See *ibid.,* 103-107.

[65] This is on the assumption that predictive prophecy/fulfilment and *sensus plenior,* which are viewed as alternative methods of New Testament interpretation of the Old operate under the same presuppositions as typology. *Sensus plenior* assumes that there is a deeper meaning to a text which was divinely intended but was not seen by the original author. This divinely intended meaning to a text is said to come to the surface to later readers in the light of further revelation. Since it appears to us that New Testament writers believed to be employing a meaning of a text that was known to the original author, any further discussion of *sensus plenior* lies outside our concern. See Goldingay, *Approaches,* pp 108f. Cf. Henning Graf Reventlow, *Problems of Biblical Theology in the Twentieth Century,* London: SCM, 1986 pp. 37-47. For a thorough treatment see R.E. Brown, *The Sensus Plenior of Sacred Scripture*: Baltimore, 1955.

Other features of typological interpretation include the fact that it is not systematically applied as a method of interpretation in the New Testament. There is no catalogue of "types" that can be made since certain aspects of the Old Testament that we could clearly consider as types are not identified as such in the New Testament while types less obvious to us are employed as such. Passages that to us may be of a doubtful historical value like the story of Jonah, the flood, the creation, and Melchizedek are the ones mostly employed. Typological interpretation is also selective. It only applies those elements in an Old Testament passage that are relevant and applicable to the new situation (e.g. Matt 1:15, Isa 7:14). While texts may be modified in the process, it does not manufacture texts. There is also a "givenness" in the Old Testament passage that leads to the writer's treatment of it as type. For instance, the Servant figure of the Old Testament obviously influenced Jesus' view of it as a type of himself.[66]

The similarities between the type and the antitype are not in details but in key features.[67] France similarly observes that: "This correspondence must be both historical (i.e. a correspondence of situation and event) and theological (i.e. an embodiment of the same principles of God's working). On the one hand, the lack of a real historical correspondence reduces typology to allegory, as when the scarlet thread hung in the window by Rahab is taken as a pre-figuration of the blood of Christ (1 Clem 12:7); both may be concerned with deliverance, but the situation and events are utterly dissimilar. On the other hand, the lack of a real theological correspondence destroys what we have seen as the very basis of typology, the perception of a constant principle in the working of God."[68] France observes that "This is not ... to demand a correspondence in every detail of the two persons or events, but simply that the same theological principle should be seen operating in the two persons or events which presents a recognizable analogy to each other in terms of the actual historical situation." Only where there is both a historical and a theological correspondence is a typological use of the Old Testament justified.[69]

---

[66] See Goldingay, *Approaches*, p. 109. For a contrary view, see Morna D. Hooker, *The Son of Man in Mark: A Study of the Background of the term 'Son of Man' and its Use in St Mark's Gospel*, London: SPCK, 1967, pp. 187-188: "The popular belief that Jesus regarded himself as Messiah ... and reinterpreted the whole concept in terms of the Suffering Servant, is a singularly tortuous but unsatisfying explanation."

[67] See Eichrodt, "Is Typological Exegesis an Appropriate Method?" p. 226.

[68] For a discussion on the distinction between "parallel situation" and "typology", see A.T. Hanson, *Jesus Christ in the Old Testament*, London: SPCK, 1965, p. 162.

[69] See France, *Jesus*, p. 41. Cf. Reventlow, *Problems*, pp. 14-37.

Typology in the New Testament

Typological interpretation as an approach to understanding scriptures has pre-Christian roots and goes back to the Old Testament prophets themselves. The prophets "came to shape their anticipation of the great eschatological situation through the Messiah according to the pattern of the historical exodus under Moses."[70] Similarly, in Ps 67 (68), the Psalmist sees a greater Messianic deliverance prefigured in the Exodus from Egypt. That the Exodus motif was a very significant type of the great Messianic deliverance that the Jews anticipated is clearly evident in the many references to it in subsequent books of the Old Testament. Even in the celebrations of the Passover Jews re-lived the Exodus experience as the ritual required each Jewish "believer" to identify himself with it. "This is what the Lord did unto me when I came forth out of Egypt (Ex 13:8, cf. Pesahim 116b)."[71] The Rabbis also drew a parallel between Moses, the first deliverer and the Messiah the last deliverer.[72] Typological interpretation was, therefore, not a Christian invention.

But typological application of the Christ-event can be traced back to Christ himself.[73] Jesus finds types of himself in certain Old Testament personalities

---

[70] Ellis, *Paul's Use*, p. 131, Cf. H. Sahlin, "The New Exodus of Salvation According to St Paul", in A. Fridrichsen (ed), *Theological Dictionary*, p. 81.

[71] *Ibid.*, p. 132.

[72] For Jewish references to this typological theme, see *ibid.*, especially footnote numbers 5 and 6.

[73] This claim raises the question whether we can indeed trace anything back to Jesus. The interpretive approach, represented by Rudolf Bultmann and his followers concluded that this is almost impossible although some of his followers now think it is probable. I cannot enter into the whole debate here. It is sufficient to note that this position is beset with its own serious difficulties. In the first place the interpretive school approaches the Gospel traditions with a skeptical mind-set as to the historicity of the events narrated. Thus before any investigation begins the presupposition is that the material is a construction of the early Church and therefore basically unhistorical. From that position the school embarks on a recovery program so that if possible certain aspects can be proven authentic and hence open up the possibility of tracing them to Jesus himself.

To help in this recovery a criterion of authenticity is established and is adopted by Bultmann himself and his school. In what is later called the "criterion of dissimilarity" two basic principles are summarized:

a) If an aspect of Gospel material reflects faith of the Church after resurrection; it is a construction of the early Church;

b) If there is a parallel aspect attributed to a Rabbi, i.e. Jewish tradition, it is also a community construction. But if it is clearly distinct from the faith of the Church and from Judaism, then it can safely be accepted as authentic, and hence, going back to Jesus.

However, the application of this criterion of authenticity only creates a Jesus who was in direct contrast to both contemporary Judaism and the Church, a Jesus who never endorsed anything from his Jewish heritage and a Church too unfaithful to preserve anything from him. The assessment of the genuineness of a piece of Gospel material is then determined by its coherence to the picture of Jesus created after the application of this criterion of dissimilarity. The practical application of this criterion has been developed into a second criterion of authenticity which Perrin calls "the criterion of coherence." Obviously much Gospel material would come out of these very badly. But that such criteria could really lead to a genuine discovery of authentic material that paints a complete picture of Jesus is itself difficult to believe. Probably the historicist approach which assumes that the Gospel record is a fair historical representation of the Christ-event is more commendable and that authenticity be doubted only where there is sufficient evidence to prove the contrary. It is from this perspective that we approach the Gospel material with regard to Jesus' use of the Old Testament. Taking a similar approach, Stanton observes that:

The Gospel traditions which the Church retained and used were intended, as one of their purposes, to sketch out the life and character of Jesus .... the Kerygmatic role of the traditions has not smothered interest in the life and character of Jesus. The dual perspective of the Gospel traditions is inescapable; they are Kerygmatic and they intend to sketch out the life and character of Jesus. To by-pass or minimize either aspect is to miss the finely-held balance of the traditions themselves: they are neither purely 'historical' nor 'biographical', nor does their Kerygmatic perspective exclude concern with more than the mere *Dass* of the historical existence of Jesus.

See G.N Stanton, *Jesus of Nazareth in New Testament Preaching*, Society for New Testament Studies, Monograph Series No. 27, Cambridge University Press, 1974, pp. 137, 172. Cf. Bultmann, *The History of the Synoptic Tradition*, Oxford: Basil Blackwell, 1963, p. 295; N. Perrin, *Rediscovering the Teaching of Jesus*, London; SCM, 1967, pp. 34, 43; J.M. Robinson, *A New Quest of the Historical Jesus*, London: SCM, 1959, pp. 12-19, 37-39; France, *Jesus*, pp. 15-24; McKnight, *Interpreting the Synoptic Gospels*, p. 57. Moreover, recent anthropological research in orality, literacy and social memory reveal that most form-critical assumptions have little basis in reality. See, for example, Stephen E. Fowl, "The gospels and 'the historical Jesus'", in *The Cambridge Companion to the Gospels*, ed., Stephen C. Burton, Cambridge: CUP, 2006, p. 80; Richard A. Horsley, "Jesus and Galilee: The Contingencies of a Reformed Movement", in *Galilee through the Centuries, Confluence of Cultures*, ed., Eric M. Meyers, Winona Lake: Eisenbrauns, 1999, p. 68; Werner H. Kelber, "The Verbal Art in Q and Thomas: A Question of Epistemology", in *Oral Performance, Popular Tradition, and Hidden Transcript in Q*, ed., Richard A Horsley, Leiden and Boston: Brill, 2006, pp. 26-27.

including Jonah (Mat 12:39-41 and parallels,) Solomon (Mat 12:42 and parallels), the priesthood (Mark 12:5-6), Elisha (Mark 6:35ff and parallels), Isaiah (Mark 4:12 and parallels). While these texts may represent typological interpretation at various levels of clarity, the principle of a basic pattern essential to genuine typology underlies them all.[74]

Israel, itself, also becomes a type for Jesus. In the temptation narrative, Jesus sees himself as Israel, tested and prepared in the wilderness as a "son" of God (Mat 4:1-11; Lk 4:1-13). As reflected also in his prediction of resurrection, Jesus applies the concept of resurrection after three days to himself. Most likely this concept applied to Israel originally, but Jesus sees in it a reference to his own experience (Jonah 2:1; 11 Kings 20:5; Hosea 6:2 are probably the texts to which Jesus appeals). He also finds a pre-figuration of his passion in the experience of the Psalmist (Ps 22, 41, 42-43 and 118).[75] Jesus also sees types in the Old Testament of his own disciples and the subsequent Church. He also sees types of Jewish unbelief and the divine judgment it receives.[76]

Paul also finds types in the Old Testament which he applies to the Christ-event. Paul draws his typological material primarily from three sources: the creation narrative, the patriarchal period and the exodus experience.[77] From the creation narrative, Paul draws out the Adam-Christ typology with its implications to cosmic redemption. Just as in Adam we all sin and die, in Christ we are made righteous and live. In Christ, we die to our past sinfulness and rise again with him in his resurrection so that we become a new creation (2 Cor 5:17; Gal 6:15; Eph 2:10, 15; Col 1:5-18; Rom 1:4; Rev 3:14; 1 Cor 15, Rom 8, 5). This typology offers a rationale for the justification and resurrection of those who are in Christ to a new life. The Eve—Church typology (Eph 5:31; 2 Cor 11:2ff) is also based on Adam-Christ typology.

The second source for Paul's typological use of the Old Testament is the patriarchal period. The concept of faith and that of true Israel as the seed of Abraham are all developed in the light of this basic typology of Abrahamic covenant. The third source of Pauline typology is the exodus experience. From the exodus event as a type comes the rationale for understanding such concepts as baptism, the Lord's Supper, the Church and other antitypes (1 Cor 5:7; 11:25ff; 1 Cor 10:31; Rom 6:3; 1 Cor 1:30; Gal 3:27; Eph 1:14; 4 30; 1 Cor 10:4; Jn 6:31f;

---

[74] For this section I am gratefully indebted to France, *Jesus*, p. 44-80.

[75] For a thorough treatment of the use of these Psalms in the New Testament, see Hans-Joachim Kraus, *Theology of the Psalms*, E.T. Minneapolis: Fortress, 1986, pp. 180-203; Cf. France, *Jesus*, pp. 56-60.

[76] For a full discussion, see France, *Jesus*, pp. 61-75.

[77] For this section, I am gratefully indebted to Ellis, *Paul's Use*, especially pp. 129-134.

Rom 11:8; Gal 4:25).[78] Similarly, typology of a slightly different type (mainly using vertical symbolism) is found in the Gospel of John, the Letter to the Hebrews and the Book of Revelation.

Fulfilment of Predictive Prophecy

Besides typological interpretations and closely associated with it is another form of scriptural interpretation: fulfilment of prediction. Since this form of biblical interpretation presupposes most of the principles that underlie typological interpretation, I shall also look at this form of interpretation.

Just as the other forms of interpretation I have discussed, prediction as a method of interpretation has also received its share of criticism. This is the case with such eschatological and Messianic predictions claimed to be fulfilled in Jesus Christ (e.g. Mat 1:22-23; 2:25, 17, 18; 3:3) among other notable examples. From the perspective of the History of Religion School, the prophets must be viewed as forth tellers of the will of God in the present rather than foretellers of the future. In this view predictive prophecy is just beside the point.[79] This is the case not because of any real evidence to prove that foretelling was not part of prophecy but rather because it is humanly impossible to foretell. Bultmann sees the New Testament claim to the fulfilment of predictive prophecy as New Testament's "allegorizing" of Old Testament prophecy with the intention of demonstrating that the present events are based and hence determined in God's plan of salvation in the hope of:

> "Taking from these events any offensiveness that might be theirs, and indeed turning the offense into its opposite, into a confirmation of the certainty of salvation.

Then Bultmann asks:

> "But is that theologically tenable? Can the offense of the cross of Jesus be overcome by recognizing it as long prophesied and decided upon by God—or only by grasping its meaning and significance?"[80]

Obviously, here, Bultmann has a very low opinion of predictive prophecy; even its historical value is in the first place doubted as shown by Bultmann's choice of the word "allegory" to designate the method of the New Testament writers' application. He sees the New Testament's appeal to predictive prophecy as a desperate attempt by the New Testament writers to defend the claims of the Gospel from "any offensiveness" which he thinks might even "be theirs." Bultmann then asks whether this apologetic approach is really meaningful. To put it simply, Bultmann suggests that the writers not only base their arguments on wrong Old Testament passages but

---

[78] See *ibid.*, pp. 129-135.
[79] See Goldingay, *Approaches,* pp. 115, 166.
[80] See Bultmann, "Prophecy and Fulfillment", pp. 51, 55.

also use these basically unhistorical material, and therefore, inappropriate passages, to defend the undefendable, the "offence" of the cross. For Bultmann, predictive prophecy is not only non-existent (if it does it has simply failed to materialize) but also unsuitable to apply to so formidable a task, the defense of the Christ-event.[81]

From the perspective of philosophy the whole idea of predictive prophecy is questionable and viewed as an "archaic metaphor and a notion lacking coherence."[82] Obviously, these conclusions are more determined by the presuppositions that govern them than any textual evidence would support.

That the New Testament writers claim fulfillment of certain aspects of Old Testament prophecy seems obvious to me. France further observes that:

> The idea of fulfillment inherent in New Testament typology derives not from a belief that the events so understood were explicitly predicted, but from the conviction that in the coming and work of Jesus the principles of God's working, already imperfectly embodied in the Old Testament, were more perfectly re-embodied, and thus brought to completion.[83]

Consequently, the New Testament writers do not restrict the idea of fulfilment to explicitly predictive prophecy. They include passages of Scripture which to us do not appear to be prophetic. A prediction "demands a future fulfilment. To claim that prediction is fulfilled is not simply to affirm a discernible correspondence, but to assert that the Old Testament passage concerned whether expressed in the future tense or not, intentionally pointed forward to that which has occurred."[84]

It is in this New Testament sense that we find prediction as a method of biblical interpretation.[85] In the synoptic gospels,[86] predictive interpretation is found in the

---

[81] Goldingay, *Approaches*, p. 117.

[82] *Ibid.*, p. 116.

[83] France, *Jesus*, p. 40.

[84] *Ibid.*, p. 83. Hinson thinks the connection between prophecy and fulfillment is not directly a historical one, but a theological one: "We shall only understand these (Old Testament) quotations alright if we can recognize their theological meaning and distinguish it from their historical associations." Others are of the view that predictive prophecy was concerned with fulfillment of what is prefigured rather than fulfillment of predictions: "The Old Testament in its unity has ever pointed to the Messiah as the fulfillment of Israel's history." See Hinson, *Theology of the Old Testament*, p. 136, and Wenham, *Christ and the Bible*, p. 100 respectively.

[85] For this section I am again gratefully indebted to France, *Jesus*, especially pp. 83-163.

[86] In Paul's epistles we do not find explicit claims to direct fulfillment of predictive prophecy. Rather we find an application of principles developed in the Old Testament. These principles are then viewed as realized in the Messianic age in which the New Testament Writers are. See Ellis, *Paul's Use*, p. 126.

material which relates eschatological hopes and Messianic expectations. In the area of eschatological hopes we find predictions of salvation and judgment closely knit. The sense of judgment is stronger in some passages (Luke 21:22; Mark 13:19; Matt 24:30; Mark 9:48, 12-13; Matt 11:10,14). The sense of salvation is stronger in others (Mark 11:15-16, 17; Matt 6:8, 8:11-12, 11:5; Luke 19:10, 24:49). Some possible Messianic predictions are found in the stone references (Luke 20:18); the branch citations (Mark 14:58 and parallels); the question of whether the Messiah is David's Lord (Mark 12:36) and in the declaration before the Sanhedrin (Mark 14:62).[87] Predictive prophecy is also found in Zechariah 9-14 in relation to the three figures: king (Mark 11:1ff), martyr (Matt 24:30) and shepherd (Mark 14:27). It is also present in the references to the Servant of Yahweh (Luke 22:37; Mark 10:45, 14:24).

In relation to the suffering of the Messiah there are allusions in Mark 9:12; Matt 3:15; Luke 11:22.[88] In addition, in Mark 8:31, 9:31, 10:33-34, there are formal announcements of his passion. Jesus' consciousness concerning the inevitability of his passion is also reflected in Mark 2:10, 9:12, 10:38, 21:1, 14:8, 21, 22-23, 25, 49; Matt 26:54; Luke 9:31, 12:50, 13:32-33, 17:25. These are general references to the Old Testament. In some cases it is emphasized that he must suffer (Mark 8:31; Matt 26:54; Luke 13:33, 17:25, 22:22). It appears that Jesus finds allusions to his suffering not only in Isaiah 53, although it might have a central position in his mind but also in certain areas of Zechariah 9-14.[89] The references to the Anointed Deliverer (Isa 61:1-3, 42:1-7) in Luke 4:17-21; Matt 11:5 and possibly in Matt 5:3-4 also belong to this category of Old Testament interpretation.

While Daniel 7 may not be a source for the allusions to the suffering Servant,[90] it is the basis for the references to the Messiah as 'Son of Man' (Mark 8:38, 13:26, 14:62; Matt 10:23; 28:18; 19:28; 25:31).[91]. Finally, predictive prophecy as a means of interpretation can be observed where Jesus himself assumes the role of Yahweh. These passages mainly relate to his future work of judgment (Mark 9:12-13; Luke 19:10; Matt 11:10,14; 13:41, 19:28, 25:31-32). The predictions that Jesus employed almost always were eschatological in nature.[92] The logical conclusion from this

---

[87] For a thorough discussion of these predictive citations, see France, *Jesus*, p. 89-103.
[88] For a critical discussion of these references see *Ibid.*, pp. 123-125.
[89] France finds the suggestion that Daniel 7 is one of the sources of these allusions less convincing. See *ibid.*, pp 127-130.
[90] Hooker, *The Son of Man in Mark*, p. 132, argues that Dan 7 is the source for the allusions to suffering. See idem, *Jesus and the Servant*, London: SCM, 1959, pp. 93-97.
[91] For the view that Jesus used the title "Son of Man" in reference to himself, see Jeremias, pp. 257-276. Cf. France, *Jesus*, pp. 13-138.
[92] France, *Jesus*, p. 160. Cf. Reventlow, *Problems*, pp. 47-54.

observation is that in Jesus' view the process of fulfillment had began with his coming but consummation of the Kingdom of God was still yet to come.

New Testament Presuppositions in Old Testament Interpretation

In the preceding section I have attempted an analysis of various methods in which the Old Testament was interpreted by the New Testament writers, and how these practices affected textual forms of the passages being interpreted. I have, at various points, discussed certain hermeneutical principles that lie behind specific methods of biblical interpretation in the first century AD. The task before me now is, simply, to outline those principles that appear to underlie most of these methods of interpretation and are sufficiently crucial for our understanding of these methods of interpretation.

The Prediction of the Prophets Referred to the Day of the Messiah

New Testament writers along with other Jewish groups presupposed that what the prophets predicted referred to the Messiah who would one day appear to lead the people of God. The distinctive feature of the New Testament writers was, however, that for them the Messiah had already come. The other Jewish groups[93] still looked forward to the coming of the Messiah in fulfillment of what the prophets had prophesied long before.

The "Givenness" of the Old Testament Texts

The Old Testament passage was itself suggestive of its use by the New Testament writers.[94] They did not employ Old Testament citations randomly nor did they use them arbitrarily. At an earlier period, as we have seen above, right from the days of Jesus' earthly ministry, certain Old Testament texts were considered to be eschatological and messianic and were viewed as being fulfilled in Jesus and the New Covenant community as exemplified by Jesus' own use of them. After the resurrection the texts formed the basis of a "testimonial" to which other texts were added in order to clarify the theological significance of the Christ-event,[95] first to the

---

[93] For a discussion on the Messianic expectations of the Qumran Community, see the first chapter in this book. Cf. C.H. Dodd, *The Apostolic Preaching and its Developments,* New York and Evanston: Harper & Row, 1964, p. 21.

[94] Dunn, *Unity and Diversity*, p. 94.

[95] Dodd has convincingly argued that New Testament writers were working with a pre-canonical tradition in which certain passages of the Old Testament were used as testimonia that witnessed to the theological significance of the Christ-event as having taken place in accordance with the "determinate counsel of God." Throughout his work, Dodd labours to identify these Old Testament passages and finally concludes that the method was selective in

members of the New Covenant community itself and then to the non-believing community which was predominantly Jewish.

The Situation of the Interpreter

The Old Testament texts in common use were often interpreted differently by different New Testament writers. A classical passage is found in the interpretation of Hab 2:4 "but the righteous shall live by his faith," by Paul and James (Gal 3:11; James 2:14) who *prima facie* reach contradictory conclusions.[96] Probably these differences in interpretation arise because the writers were using the well-known texts to address specific needs in their situation.[97] Lindars has explained these differences in interpretation of the same Old Testament passages as necessitated by the need to address particular situations that developed in the early Church with the passage of time:

> The shift of application shows the logical sequence in the development of thought

The context with its Christian integration has already defined the meaning of them. It is with this definite meaning that they are found to be useful at a particular stage in argument or discussion.[98]

In the rest of this book Lindars argues his point that the different interpretations arose at different periods of the early church to serve specific apologetic interests in relation to the problems that arose in a specific period of the early church. "Time" is a governing factor in Lindars' thesis. He assumes a standard interpretation of a given text for any period which only changes when another period sets in with new apologetic demands. An obvious implication of this approach is to allow for a sufficiently long period to give room for sequential development of the various interpretations that are given by different authors to certain common passages.[99]

---

choosing these texts, that the context in which such a text falls was taken into consideration, that these selected texts are employed by almost all New Testament writers, and that these testimonia passages were primarily applied in an oral form and found written expression only sporadically. See Dodd, *Scriptures*, pp. 12ff, 57, 60, 126-129.

[96] For a thorough discussion of Paul's and James' use of this prophecy, see John Drane, *Introducing the New Testament,* Oxford: Lion, 1986, pp. 418, 420, 421.

[97] Dodd has argued that these differences in interpretation of the same Old Testament writers show that they were "independently following a pre-canonical tradition", see Dodd, *Scriptures,* pp. 65, 75.

[98] Lindars, *New Testament Apologetic*, pp. 18, 19.

[99] This affects significantly one's idea of the dating of the New Testament books. It is probably this line of thought that led Lindars to think that Matthew (whoever it was) wrote his Gospel so late that he could not even know the background to the formula quotations which he alone of the New Testament writers employs in a very special way. For a thorough

While this might be true, it appears that Lindars has neglected an equally important dimension in his thesis, namely that of "place" as a governing factor. It is equally possible that these developments could take place simultaneously depending on the place-situation of the writer.[100] It appears to me, therefore, that not all cases need to be explained in the manner Lindars suggests. If my observation is correct, then there is no need to posit periods and tie to each of them standard Christian interpretations of a given text. The differences could as well arise in the same period of the early Church, namely its earliest period . In fact the striking similarity in the way New Testament writers make use of this common pre-canonical tradition appears to be better explained by positing more or less a common period in which they wrote and attribute variations in interpretation to differences in situations, purposes, etc, than categorizing the writers into periods which necessarily need to be wide apart in order to account for the differences. This is not to suggest that the New Testament books were written at the same time, but rather to suggest that they were written at times close enough to each other to allow for their use of the common pre-canonical material.

Jesus is the representation and embodiment of Israel and of true humanity

This presupposition is basic to any understanding of the biblical concept of salvation. The relationship of the one and the many is crucial here. Just as sin entered into the world through one man salvation also enters it through one man. This is the basis of the Adam-Christ typological interpretation of the Old Testament redemptive history. Similarly, Israel is elected through the election of a single man, Abraham. The concept of "true Israel" which by implication is the Church of Christ also finds its biblical basis in this principle. The relationship of man to God is always in relationship to this corporate solidarity. Either one is "in Adam" or "in Christ." There is no third option.[101]

A Perception of a constant principle in the outworkings of God in redemptive history

The Exodus-event from Egypt did not only lead to the birth of a national history for Israel but also provided a pattern for the redemptive acts of God. It was hoped, ever since, that God would redeem Israel from her enemies and sufferings as he did with

---

discussion of formula or fulfillment quotations, see my book, *The Use of Fulfillment Quotations in the Gospel according to Matthew*.

[100] See Jonathan Nkhoma, *The Use of Fulfilment Quotations in the Gospel according Matthew*, Zomba: Kachere Series, Mzuzu: Mzuni Press, 2005, p. 255.

[101] See Ellis, "How the New Uses the Old", p. 210. Cf. Ellis. *Paul's Use,* p. 136; Goldingay, *Approaches*, p. 104.

them when they came out of Egypt. "The Day of Yahweh" was the day of a new Exodus. From this hope in the Day of the Lord developed the Messianic hope and other eschatological expectations. The prophets frequently looked forward to a "repetition of the acts of God."[102]

Thus in God's redemptive acts during the Old Covenant era a divine principle was seen constantly at work. In the Christ-event, the same principle of God's redemptive act was seen at work and in order to understand the new redemptive activity the New Testament writers searched scriptures to find similar but lower cases in which the same principle was at work and then understand these as pointing toward the present event. This principle then contributed greatly to their interpretation of the scriptures, particularly to what we have discussed as typological method of interpretation.[103]

Old Testament Interpretation in the Light of Christ

Probably the most significant principle for their interpretation was the conviction that the whole Old Testament pointed to Christ. This is clearly indicated by Luke who reports to us concerning the risen Lord: "And beginning with Moses and all the prophets, he interpreted to them in all the scriptures the things concerning himself" (Luke 24:27). Since all scriptures concerned Jesus Christ himself then these scriptures could only be properly understood in the light of the new event. All New Testament writers appear to have shared this conviction as their interpretation of the Old Testament indicates.[104]

The Charismatic Nature of their Interpretation

New Testament writers believed that they were guided by the Spirit in their interpretation. Consequently, it was their understanding and interpretation of Scriptures that was "correct" as over against Jewish interpretation which was not Spirit-led but letter-tied, and hence the latter's interpretation only degenerated into traditions that were even burdensome to keep.[105] In view of this understanding of Scriptures the New Testament writers were convinced that they were the true Israel. Thus they did not view themselves as a mere sect within larger 'Israel'. They

---

[102] France, *Jesus*, p. 39.

[103] Cf. Ibid.

[104] Goldingay, *Approaches*, p. 94. Cf. McCartney, "The NT's Use of the OT," in Conn (ed), *Inerrancy and Hermeneutic*, p. 102.

[105] Recent research in ancient Jewish traditions reveal that Jewish interpretations were far more dynamic and diverse than this perspective allows for. See George W.E. Nickelsburg, *Ancient Judaism and Christian Origins. Diversity, Continuity and Transformation*, Mineapolis: Fortress, 2003, pp. 1-3.

claimed exclusively all the eschatological blessings foretold in the Old Covenant and applied terms commonly reserved for Gentile groups even to non-believing Jews.[106] Without the Spirit, Jews were no better than Gentiles.

Conclusion

I would conclude by observing, in the light of the foregoing discussion, that the New Testament interpretation was not based on a single principle. Rather it resulted from an interaction of several factors. While their Jewish literary background provided the means of expression, the content of that expression was firmly determined by their Christian orientation. As Christians they were guided by certain presuppositions in their work. It is this complex combination of resources at their disposal for the task of interpretation that makes it difficult to classify their method in simplistic terms.

However, their approach to interpretation is generally "grammatical-historical exegesis plus."[107] The "plus" consists in their claim to find specific references to the Christ-event in scriptures where a non-Christian could naturally have a different understanding. It is this "plus" which makes their approach specifically Christian. I have attempted to outline, in this study, certain presuppositions which helped them to focus on their hermeneutical goal, namely, Jesus and his redemptive work.

Although we may not agree with every aspect in their interpretative methodology and the presuppositions they held, an appreciation of their approach to exegesis does provide new insights that would sharpen our own efforts as we interpret scriptures. Their grammatical-historical emphasis, as well as their focus on Jesus and his redemptive work in their methodology, are issues which no sound Christian exegesis would afford to neglect.

---

[106] Ellis, "How the New Uses the Old", p. 124. Cf. Ellis, *Paul's Use*, p. 136-139
[107] For a similar observation, see McCartney, "*The NT's Use of the OT*", Conn (ed), *Inerrancy and Hermeneutic*, p. 102.

Chapter Five
Discipleship in Matthew:
A Redaction - Critical Study

Introduction

Matthew has used his sources to construct a broad portrayal of discipleship. His idea of a disciple is not limited to the twelve historical disciples of Jesus. It extends to include other followers of Jesus who together form the Matthean community of disciples. Redaction–critical studies have shed much light on this view of discipleship in Matthew's gospel. This chapter is an attempt to highlight some of the issues that have led to such an understanding of the concept of discipleship in Matthew. Scholars have debated whether Matthew "historicizes" Mark's gospel in his treatment of the theme of discipleship. Streeter, for example, has argued that the disciples in Matthew are to be historically identified with the twelve disciples of Jesus.[232] Against this position most scholars argue that Matthew does not limit the concept of discipleship to the eyewitnesses.[233] It is true that there is an element of historicizing. For example, according to Matthew, Jesus is sent to Israel, and so are the disciples (10:5-6; 15:24; 9:35; 10:17,23). Also, just as Jesus has power to heal (4:24; 9:35) the disciples acquire the same ability (10:1,4,8).[234] In this chapter we will show that Matthew's concept of discipleship is broader and is not limited to the historical setting of Jesus' ministry.

Sermon on the Mount

A study of the audience to the Sermon indicates that the followers of Jesus at this point are both the disciples and the crowds. Clearly, these are two different groups of people. However, a closer study of the Sermon reveals that for the purpose of this Sermon, and therefore for the teaching of Jesus, the two groups constitute a single audience.[235] Matthew's source at this point (Q-Source) only mentions "his disciples"

---

[232] Quoted in John K. Riches, *Conflicting Mythologies, Identity Formation in the Gospel of Mark and Matthew*, Edinburgh: T & T Clark, 2000, p.182, footnote number 1.

[233] Examples here include Riches, *Conflicting Mythologies*, and Ulrich Luz, *Studies in Matthew*, Grand Rapids, MI and Cambridge, UK: Eerdmans, 2005.

[234] Luz, *Studies in Matthew*, p. 117-18.

[235] Michael J. Wilkins, *The Concept of Disciple in Matthew's Gospel, As Reflected in the Use of the Term μαθητης*, Leiden, New York Kobenhavn and Koln: E.J. Brill, 1988, pp. 148-49.

(cf. Luke 6:20). Matthew has altered the tradition by adding "the crowds."[236] Although the pronoun "them" of Matt 5:1 who constitute the audience is ambiguous, a clue for understanding its referents is found in Matt 7:28-29 where Matthew informs us that the crowds responded to the Sermon with astonishment.[237] We can conclude from this observation that Matthew sees the crowds as worth of receiving the teaching of Jesus directly as the named disciples do. Thus Jesus is presented as the great teacher whose teaching is not limited to the named few disciples but extends to the other members of society who now constitute a new people, a new community under the great teacher, who, like Moses, gives a teaching from the mountain.

The Mission Discourse

Consistent with the idea that Matthew widens the concept of discipleship to include followers other than the Twelve is the notion that Matthew includes the followers of Jesus in the Matthean community itself and the generations of followers that were yet to come in the future into the circle of disciples. This interest in the community's own experience of the historical incident being narrated is an important feature in Matthew. A close study of the mission discourse reveals that Matthew introduces material that would suit the time of the Matthean community or its future more than it does the historical setting of Jesus' mission.

> This is reflected in the mission charge. As in the other traditions, Matthew informs us that the disciples did receive specific instructions (Matt 10:5/Mark 3:8/Luke 6:2) for their mission. What is unique in Matthew, however, is that the disciples do receive the instructions but there is no hint in this discourse that they actually went on their mission.[238] Throughout the discourse, Jesus speaks to the disciples and at the end of the discourse Matthew tells us: "And when Jesus had finished instructing his twelve disciples, he went on from there to teach and preach in their cities "(Matt 11:1).

This verse is a special Matthean tradition material.[239] A natural understanding of this verse would lead us to think that immediately after giving the instructions, Jesus does not sent them away into the mission field but rather goes with them on a renewed itinerant ministry as a way of training them how to conduct such a

---

[236] Kurt Aland (ed.), *Synopsis of the Four Gospels, Greek-English Edition of the Synopsis Quattuor Evangeliorum*, Stuttgart: United Bible Societies, 1976, p. 49.
[237] See ibid. p. 64. Also Wilkins, *The Concept of Disciple in Matthew's Gospel*, p. 149.
[238] Luz, *Studies in Matthew*, p. 118.
[239] Aland (ed.), *Synopsis of the Four Gospels*, p. 97.

ministry.²⁴⁰ What is important for our purpose is to note that Matthew's comment does not provide for an immediate independent missionary activity following the charge. In Mark and Q-Source, by contrast, the disciples are expressly absent, away to the mission field.²⁴¹ The content of the instruction, however, especially the second half of the chapter, does clearly suggest that these instructions will be fulfilled in the post-Easter period when the disciples are delivered to synagogue councils, governors and kings (10:17-18), a time when the mission is no longer limited to Israel but becomes open to the Gentiles (10:18; 24:9-14).²⁴² The reference here to kings and Gentiles is also a Matthean redaction, lacking in the Q-Source (cf. Luke 12:11-12).²⁴³

In this way, Matthew shows that Jesus' commands must be understood as relevant for the present and that the authority given to the disciples to perform miracles is also an authority given to the Matthean community. Hence, the Matthean community is invited to participate in the exercise of the missionary charge since as members of the Matthean community they are also disciples of Jesus.

The broader understanding of the concept of discipleship is also shown by the manner in which the word μαθητης in this discourse is used. In Matt 10:24,25 and 42 the word is used with reference to a wider circle of disciples. Since in Matthew Jesus is not only the Teacher of the Twelve disciples but also of the other followers, it would follow that anyone who receives the teaching of Jesus is his disciple. The general application of this concept here also suggests the Matthean broader understanding of the term, going beyond both the spatial and the temporal setting of Jesus' ministry.²⁴⁴

Matthean Redaction of the Central Markan Discipleship Section

The way in which Matthew has reworked the central Markan discipleship material (Mark 8:22-10:52) also reflects his understanding of discipleship. In Mark the disciples do not understand Jesus. Their lack of understanding concerns the person and the suffering of Jesus as the Son of Man.²⁴⁵ The Markan section is framed by

---

[240] John Nolland, *The Gospel of Matthew, A Commentary on the Greek Text*, Grand Rapids, MI,/Cambridge,UK: William B. Eerdmans and Bletchley: Paternoster, 2005, p. 447.
[241] Luz, *Studies in Matthew*, p. 118.
[242] *Ibid.*
[243] Aland (ed.), *Synopsis of the Four Gospels*, p. 92.
[244] Luz, *Studies in Matthew*, p. 119; Wilkins, *The Concept of Disciple in Matthew's Gospel*, p.167. For a fuller treatment see Benno Przyabylski, *Righteousness in Matthew and his World of Thought*, Cambridge: Cambridge University Press, 1980, pp. 108-10.
[245] Luz, *Studies in Matthew*, p. 123.

two narratives of the healing of the blind men. Matthew omits the healing of the blind men of Bethsaida, although he is closely following Mark as a source at this point, since Q-Source also did not have this narrative.[246] Matthew, then, introduces a new section. In the first part of this section Matthew presents Peter's confession as its climax, renaming Peter and investing him with the power to hold the keys to the entrance into the kingdom of God. In the second part of the section Matthew introduces a community discourse that discusses matters of discipline and relations within the church.[247] By making these modifications, Matthew has transformed Mark's figurative use of the blind men's stories which, in Mark, shows that true discipleship involves "seeing" and recognizing the person of Jesus as the Messiah. Discipleship, which for Mark involves a transition from darkness to light, becomes, through Matthew's modifications, a call to membership in a community of disciples who understand and follow Jesus' teaching.[248] For Matthew, understanding presupposes both Christian life and Christian teaching and the living out of one's life guided by the new ethic which Jesus teaches.

> The shift toward discipleship as a call to live by the ethic that Jesus teaches is further reflected in the way Matthew uses the Markan narrative of the call of the disciples (Matt 4:18-22/Mark 1:16-20). Matthew follows Mark to 1:20. He omits 1:21-38 but adapts the Markan summary in vs 39. At this point, Matthew inserts the three chapters of the Sermon on the Mount, and thereafter returns to Mark 1:40, where the narrative of the healing of the leper begins.[249] By juxtaposing the Sermon on the Mount to the call of disciples, Matthew is providing an interpretation of what it means to be a disciple, that is to belong to a community that lives by the ethic that Jesus teaches. In addition, by linking the crowds with the Sermon on the Mount, Matthew sees this teaching of Jesus as being provided not only to the Twelve disciples but also to the Matthean community as a whole, and by implication to all who hear Jesus' teaching.[250]

The Healing Miracles

The authoritative nature of the teaching of Jesus is further demonstrated through the miracles he performs. Matthew interprets these miracles as fulfillment of Old

---

[246] Aland (ed.), *Synopsis of the Four Gospels*, p. 148.
[247] Riches, *Conflicting Mythologies*, p. 183.
[248] *Ibid.* p. 185.
[249] *Ibid.*
[250] *Ibid.* p. 185, footnote 5.

Testament prophecy (Matt 8:17; 11:5-6; 12:18-21).[251] These do indicate that Matthew sees the mission of Jesus as fulfilling a specific messianic mission to the people of Israel. Matthew presents these miracles as historical in the ministry of Jesus. However, at another level, Matthew has shaped his sources so as to address the community of disciples of his own day.

In the stories of the stilling the storm in Matt 8:22-27 and 14:23-33, Matthew is not simply interested in the miracles as they happened in history. He is also interested in his own community's experience of the continuing presence of the Lord. In the disciples' following Jesus into the boat, an act which Matthew highlights by having Jesus enter the boat first and then have the disciples "follow,"[252] in the "swamp(ing)" of the storm, and in the cry "Lord Save," in the anxiety of the disciples and in their being men of "little faith," the experiences and concerns of the Matthean community are reflected.[253] Thus the experiences of the original disciples find further expression in the experiences of the Matthean community, in this way broadening the concept of discipleship in terms that are both spatial and temporal.

It can similarly be argued that Matthew also sees the authority of Jesus transferred to the Matthean community of disciples.[254] Matthew sees the authority that Jesus gave to the original disciples (Matt 10:3-6; Mark 6:7; Luke 9:1) being exercised by his own community of disciples. The special authority that Jesus gave to Peter continues in the work of the Matthean community. This becomes more evident in the Matthean discourse of Matt 18, and the Matthean addition of the clause "for the forgiveness of sins" to the Last Supper account. Peter has become a "type" of the Matthean community. The authority to bind and loose (16:19) given to him is now understood as being possessed by the community itself.

---

[251] For a thorough discussion see Jonathan Nkhoma, *The Use of Fulfilment Quotations in the Gospel according to Matthew*, Zomba: Kachere Series; Mzuzu: Mzuni Press, 2005, pp. 162ff., 199ff.

[252] Matthew is very clear in his depiction of Jesus first entering the boat and then have the disciples follow. In Mark, it is the disciples who "took" Jesus with them into the boat. Q-Source only has Jesus get into the boat "with" the disciples. The idea of "following" Jesus into the boat is not clearly expressed. Matthew has, in this way, turned this miracle story into a story of discipleship. See Aland (ed.), *Synopsis of the Four Gospels*, p. 77.

[253] Luz, *Studies in Matthew*, p. 126.

[254] The eschatological cry of some disciples, asking Jesus to admit them into the kingdom on the basis of the miracles they performed in his name in Matt 7:22 presupposes the existence of charismatic activity in Matthean community. The cry is a Matthean redaction. See Aland (ed.), *Synopsis of the Four Gospels*, p. 63.

The Great Commission

The use of the word "to disciple" in the commission for mission that Jesus makes is probably the most outstanding illustration of the broadness of meaning that Matthew attaches to the concept of discipleship. The word occurs three times, and it is probable that all the three occurrences are redactions.[255] In Matt 13:52, the word μαθητεύω describes "every scribe" who is made "a disciple" for the kingdom. In Matthew 27:57, it describes a rich man from Arimathea, Joseph, who suddenly appears on the scene on the day of Jesus' crucifixion, and in the commission itself, it describes any one who believes in Jesus. In the commission, it is made clear that the believer must be taught the ethic of the kingdom as had been delivered in the teaching of Jesus. These three uses show the inclusive character of Matthew's understanding of the concept of discipleship. It includes a scribe, a group that basically opposed Jesus; Joseph of Arimathea who appears suddenly on the day of Jesus' crucifixion, and finally everyone who accepts the gospel of Jesus. At this point it becomes clear that Matthew has framed his gospel narrative as commentary on what it means to be a follower and, therefore, a disciple of Jesus. The significance of the teaching of Jesus comes into sharp relief, for in Matthew's understanding "all new disciples were to be taught what Jesus had previously taught" (Matt 28:18-20).[256]

Conclusion

We would conclude by observing that discipleship is probably the most significant theme in Matthew. To understand the Matthean emphasis on Jesus as a Teacher of the kingdom ethic, it is important to be aware that this teaching is central in the process of discipleship. Every disciple of Jesus will have to learn this teaching and then live out his or her life on its basis. The whole gospel turns out, in a way, to be a commentary on true discipleship. His broad understanding of the concept of discipleship is in keeping with its centrality in his gospel and generally provides key to our understanding of his gospel as a whole.

---

[255] The sources Mark and Q-Source agree in their recognition of the authority that Jesus gave to his disciples. See Aland (ed.), *Synopsis of the Four Gospels*, p. 90.
[256] Wilkins, *The Concept of Disciple in Matthew's Gospel*, p. 221.

Chapter Six
"Love Your Enemies": A Study of Luke 6:27-36

Introduction

Jesus' teaching about loving enemies forms a climactic statement in the new teaching he brings about the kingdom of God. It clearly indicates that the new ethic and the life it presupposes are grounded in the love and mercy of God. Life in the kingdom is to be governed by being merciful even to the undeserving, just as God is merciful to all. This chapter examines the love command in light of its Old Testament context, suggests its role in shaping Christian identity over the centuries, and highlights the tension between particularity and universality in Christian teaching on salvation.

Textual Context

The command to love enemies falls within the Sermon on the Plain. It would seem that the sermon forms a literary, sociological, historical and theological context for understanding the command to love enemies. Various aspects of the sermon, therefore, do shed light on this command and in turn the command provides a climactic point in the ethical teaching of Jesus which the sermon in general embodies.

The sermon falls under a series of episodes that are inserted into Markan material. This series, generally known as the "little interpolation,"[1] runs from 6:20-8:3. Luke has inserted material mainly from Q,[2] from L and from his own redaction. Comparison with the Sermon on the Mount in Matthew shows both similarities and differences in content and general structure. Both sermons teach about the expected conduct of disciples, have the beatitudes and woes, have parallel sayings, teach about love for one's neighbour, love for one's enemies, and both conclude with short parables.

The similarities seem to suggest that this sermon is based on a sermon or series of sermons originally delivered by Jesus in the early period of his ministry. Some of the differences may be accounted for by Luke's elimination of material that he

---

[1] Joseph A. Fitzmyer, *The Gospel according to Luke (I-IX)*, The Anchor Bible, New York and London: Doubleday, 1970, p. 627.

[2] For suggested material from Q, see Ibid.

would find too Jewish for his Gentile readership, and his preference to reserve some of its material for his travel narrative account. Luke, however, seems to have preserved the original order,[3] and his structure appears relatively loose when compared to that of Matthew.[4]

Within the sermon itself the command to love enemies (vv 27-36) has a central significance. Structurally, it overturns the Golden Rule by the manner in which Jesus speaks immediately after it, and by stating the command to love enemies (vv 31-35) soon after:

And as you wish that men would do to you, do so to them

> If you love those who love you, what credit is that to you?
>
>> For even sinners love those who love them.
>
> And if you do good to those who do good to you, what credit is that to you?
>
>> For even sinners do the same.
>
> And if you lend to those from whom you hope to receive, what credit is that for you?
>
>> Even sinners lend to sinners, to receive as much gain.

But love your enemies, and do good, and lend, expecting nothing in return (RSV).

In the concentric structure above, the two commands frame the three conditional statements, and the command to love enemies forms a climactic point[5] giving a new interpretation to the Golden Rule itself.[6]

This new interpretation of the Golden Rule embodied in the command to love enemies is further explicated by the poetic structure that the command itself takes. The Greek text brings this out more clearly:

v. 27   αγαπατε τους εχθρους ὑμων
         καλως ποιειτε τοις μισουσιν ὑμας
         ευλογειτε τους καταρωμενους ὑμας
         προσευχεσθε περι των επηρεαζοντων ὑμας.

---

[3] Cf. ibid., p. 628
[4] Ibid., p. 629.
[5] Cf. Paul Ricoeur, "The Golden Rule, Exegetical and Theological Perplexities", *New Testament Studies*, Vol. 36 (1990): p. 392.
[6] Ibid., p. 397.

The parallelism provides us with ideas that interpret key concepts within it. For example, αγαπατε is defined as καλως ποιειτε. Εχθρους is explained as τοις μισουσιν ,ὑμας, τους καταρωμενους ὑμας. Therefore, according to the poetic structure of this verse, "love" is defined as "doing good," "blessing," and even "praying" for those who abuse you. "Enemies" are defined as those who "hate" you, those who "curse" you, and those who "abuse" or "speak scornfully" about you.[7]

To fully appreciate the significance of the command to love enemies, we need to understand the concepts of "love" and "enemy" as understood in the history of Israel. To this we now turn.

"Love" and "Enemy" in the History of Ancient Israel

Who is the enemy in the ancient history of Israel? The Hebrew word for "enemy" *'oyev* refers to both personal and national enemies. The root usage refers to the Gentiles as enemies of Israel.[8] It expresses not merely the varying and unstable political enmity which would shift from friend to foe; it also expresses the constant opposition expressed in various forms of enmity between Israel and the Gentiles. For the Gentiles, by virtue of being enemies of Israel, they are also enemies of God.[9] The redemption of Israel is, therefore, understood, not only in terms of liberation from the oppressive Gentiles, but also in terms of complete destruction of these constantly opposing forces.[10]

In the LXX, *'oyev* is translated as εχθρος and still maintains the basic meaning of a national enemy. This is further reflected in Zechariah's prophetic utterance (Luke 1:71-74) at the beginning of the New Testament period. It is also found in the prophetic sayings of Jesus about the fall of Jerusalem (Luke 19:43) from the special Lukan source.[11] In the New Testament, however, the main connotation of εχθρος is a personal enemy with reference to various aspects of daily life. This is the basic meaning that it has in the command to love enemies.

The next question we need to ask is: What is this love, and how did it function in the Old Testament, in the context of the various relationships including the relationship between Israel and her enemies? The Hebrew word for "love," *'ehavah* stands for the three different Greek words for it, αγαπη, φιλεω and ηρος. Stauffer defines love in the Old Testament as a "spontaneous feeling which impels to self-

---

[7] Cf. O.J.F. Seits, "Love your Enemies", *New Testament Studies* 16 (1969), p. 44.
[8] Forster, "εχθρος", *Theological Dictionary of the New Testament*, ed., Gerhard Kittel, transl. & ed. Geoffrey W. Bromiley, Vol. II, Δ-H, Grand Rapids: Eerdmans, 1964, p. 812.
[9] Ibid.
[10] Ibid.
[11] Ibid.

giving."[12] The most distinctive aspects of the love of God in the Old Testament understanding are its spontaneity[13] and its preference. The love of God which is spontaneous is also a love that "makes distinctions, chooses, prefers, overlooks."[14] The idea of preference is best conveyed by the word αγαπαν in pre-biblical Greek. Although it lacks the emotional power of εραν and the brotherly warmth of φιλειν, it preserves the original Hebrew sense of preference, a love that makes distinctions, choosing and keeping its object. It is a love that denotes the freedom and decisiveness of action determined by its subject.[15]

The idea of preference in the love of God reflected in 'ehavah, and preserved in αγαπητος, stands in sharp contrast with the root meaning of the Greek word ερος which, apart from its emotional quality, emphasizes the idea of a love that is universal, generous, unbound and non-selective, equally applying to all without distinctions.[16]

The spontaneous and preferential love of God is the basis on which the election of Israel and the subsequent covenant that God made with her is founded. The practical effect of Israel's covenant relationship with God is that Israel adopts the preferential quality of divine love in the application of the love commandment. As a result, Israel, in its interpretive framework of the commandment to love sets limits and boundaries, moving into the direction of particularity, so that the application of the command becomes limited and restricted to fellow nationals who are members of the divine covenant that Israel has with God. It is significant here to notice that the spontaneous quality of the divine love is lost while its preferential character is emphasized. Divine preferential love becomes definitive in Israel's understanding of God's love, and in her adoption and application of the divine commandment.

Israel recognizes her obligation to love the neighbour as one loves himself or herself. Neighbour, however, is understood in covenantal terms and restricted to fellow nationals. This raises for Israel the question of whether the command to love be extended in its application to non-members of the covenant, and to its active enemies.

In Deut 30 we find both blessings and curses which God sets up for Israel as a prophetic warning to her in order to challenge her to a life of obedience to the law. Within the context of blessings and curses, there is a promise that the Lord God of Israel will lay curses on her enemies and on those who hate her and persecute her.

---

[12] Stauffer, "αγαπητος," *Theological Dictionary of the New Testament*, Vol. I, A-Γ, p. 22.
[13] Cf. Stauffer's observation in his basic definition of the love of God in the Old Testament quoted above.
[14] Stauffer, "αγαπητος", *Theological Dictionary of the New Testament*, Vol. I, A-Γ, p. 38.
[15] Ibid., p. 36.
[16] Ibid., p. 38.

For our purpose, we would note here that divine anger is to be directed to enemies of Israel who are essentially the enemies of Yahweh, the God of Israel. It would seem that the commandment to love enemies is an allusive reference[17] to this text that reverses lack of goodwill for and the spirit of hatred toward the enemy.

Although Lev 19:17-18 concludes with an injunction to love one's neighbour, the context suggests that the neighbour implied is a fellow Israelite, a brother, sister and member of the covenant community. It excludes the enemy from participating in this loving relationship, or at least it encourages such an interpretation. The extent and scope of obligation to love one's neighbour remained a live issue in legal debates.

Various Jewish sources which grapple with this debate do not offer conclusive evidence for the love of enemies. Neither the Palestinian *Tannaim*, the writings of the Dead Sea community (DSS) nor the teaching of specifically, famous rabbis like Hillel suggest an unconditional love for the enemy. Thus both the Old Testament and later Jewish literature do indicate limits of love toward enemies.[18] Such a background throws into sharp relief the command to love enemies once it appears in the Gospel tradition as represented by the Lukan text.

Love and Enemy in the New Testament Context

In the New Testament, the command to love enemies creates a new situation in which God's mercy and unlimited love is seen not as a divine disposition that has already been there, but as an event which expresses itself in the person and work of Jesus. It is an event which establishes a new relationship among men.[19] The beatitudes and the woes which are both prophetic[20] and eschatological[21] suggest a radical reversal in the social, ethical and spiritual situation. In this new situation love of the enemy becomes a touchstone for new ethics.[22]

The command to love enemies is a call for a new kind of reciprocity among the new people and in their relationship with humanity in general. It is a new attitude for

---

[17] Cf. Seitz, "Love your Enemies", p. 45.

[18] Ibid., pp. 42-43, 49. Also Stauffer, "αγαπητος', *Theological Dictionary of the New Testament*, Vol. I, A-Γ, p. 27.

[19] Stauffer, "αγαπητος", *Theological Dictionary of the New Testament*, Vol. I. A-Γ, p. 47.

[20] For a discussion of the beatitudes and woes as prophetic declarations, see Robert C. Tannehill, *The Narrative Unity of Luke-Acts, A Literary Interpretation, Vol. 1: The Gospel according to Luke,* Philadelphia: Fortress, 1986, pp. 207-08.

[21] For a discussion of the eschatological function of the beatitudes and woes, see Charles H. Talbert, *Reading Luke. A Literary and Theological Commentary on the Third Gospel*, New York: Crossroads, 1982, p. 20.

[22] Ricoeur, "The Golden Rule, Exegetical and Theological Perplexities", p. 394.

a new people, an attitude that does not expect anything in return. It is a call for compassion grounded in the unlimited love and mercy of God. Among the divine qualities, Luke chooses compassion instead of holiness as a foundation for Christian character and behaviour.[23]

Through the command to love enemies, Jesus overturns, re-interprets and fulfills the Golden Rule. Coupled with his re-interpretation of neighbour to include everyone in need of love and mercy, this command abolishes the limits and boundaries that controlled the application of the Golden Rule within its Old Testament interpretational framework. The call to love enemies points to the ultimate and boundless love and mercy of God, and therefore acts as a corrective on the earlier Old Testament and Jewish views regarding the extent and scope of divine love.

In the context of the Lukan Gospel, the command to love enemies is given in the midst of ethical controversies in which people respond variously to enemies. These include collaboration, separation of political and religious spheres, withdrawal into radical apocalypticism, and deep hatred for the enemy.[24] In such a confused ethical situation, the command to love enemies defines Christian ethics and shapes Christian identity throughout the early decades of the Christian church.[25]

The association of the command about giving with the command to love enemies can best be understood within the context of the Lukan community itself in light of the Old Testament background. In the Lukan community Jewish persecution is no longer a major threat. People of means and high status have joined the church and these in turn influence attitude toward fellow Christians.[26] In the Old Testament, interest on loans was prohibited. This made acquisition of a loan extremely difficult. Lending, therefore, became a virtue, like love and doing good works.[27] The idea of lending without expecting return or profit, however, must have been shocking to Luke's audience. In the Lukan social context, therefore, giving becomes one way in which love of enemies is to be expressed, along with "doing good" and "not judging."

---

[23] For a thorough discussion of compassion as the ground for Christian behaviour, see François Bovon, *Luke 1, A Commentary on the Gospel of Luke 1:1 – 9:50*, Hermeneia – A Critical and Historical Commentary on the Bible, Minneapolis: Fortress, 2002, p. 241. For a discussion on how mercy as theme is emphasized in Luke, see Ibid. Also see Tannehill, *The Narrative Unity of Luke-Acts*, p. 209.

[24] Bovon, *Luke 1*, p. 234.

[25] Ibid.

[26] Ibid., p. 236.

[27] Burton Scott Easton, *The Gospel according to St. Luke, A Critical and Exegetical Commentary*, New York: Charles Scribner's, 1926, p. 87.

The Command to Love Enemies in the History of Interpretation

The way in which the command to love enemies has been interpreted over the ages reflects its function as a basis for Christian ethics. The ethical emphasis can be traced even in the writings of the early church fathers. Saint Ambrose views the commandment to love enemies as a climactic point in the teaching of Christian ethics and emphasizes that "one who follows a loftier calling" is to be bound by this commandment.[28] It has to be noted here that the main reason for having the command binding on those in ministerial positions is that they do serve as examples for Christian living. Ambrose further appeals to Christ himself as the example of loving enemies.[29]

The same emphasis on its role in Christian living is found in Saint Benaventure's writings. He calls it a commandment of "perfect benevolence," and suggests that it is binding especially to "the perfect," by reason of their official positions in order to give "a good example."[30] Benaventure particularly observes that the command to love enemies does not prevent lay people from defending themselves.[31] The subject of need to defend themselves, and the problem of just war, as ethical themes, are further discussed in the writings of other writers like Saint Augustine, John Calvin, and Thomas Aquinas.[32] In more recent times, the command to love enemies has been interpreted in support of non-violent political resistance in many places including the United States of America.

Conclusion

In conclusion, we would only emphasize that the command to love enemies has been central in the formation of Christian identity from the earliest times. It has also guided Christian response and action both at personal and social-political levels in various ways and at different times. The call to love enemies will continue to resound in history as the only true basis for genuine forgiveness and reconciliation at all levels of human existence whether personal, social, political or spiritual. The

---

[28] Saint Ambrose of Milan, *Exposition of the Holy Gospel according to St Luke*, transl., Theodosia Tomkinson, Erna, CA: Center for Traditionalist Orthodox Studies, 1998, p. 174.

[29] Ibid., p. 175.

[30] Saint Bonaventure, *Commentary on the Gospel of Luke Chapters 1-8*, introd., transl., and notes, Robert J. Karris, New York: Saint Bonaventure University Franciscan Institute Publications, 2001, p. 525.

[31] Ibid., p. 526.

[32] For a brief discussion of the history of interpretation, see Bovon, *Luke 1*, p. 243.

challenge lies with Christians who must take the initiative and make the first step toward action.[33]

From a theological perspective, the command to love enemies stands in tension with divine preferential love which forms the basis for election and the covenant. The commandment suggests that this preferential love is at the same time boundless and unlimited. Do the "enemies" who are loved and receive divine mercies, become by that virtue, beneficiaries of the divine elective preferential love? Here, the problem of particularity and universalism comes into sharp relief, giving expression to the paradox or mystery of salvation in Christian teaching.

---

[33] The challenge to make the first step is also noted by Bovon. See Ibid., p. 245.

Chapter Seven
Table Fellowship in the Gospel of Luke

Introduction

Meals play a central role in the Lukan narrative of the gospel. Much of previous Lukan studies approached the question of the role of meals in Luke's gospel from a historical-theological perspective. It is not until recently that the social dimension of table fellowship in Luke's contemporary world began to receive much scholarly attention. Information derived from the social-anthropological approach can in turn be used to enrich our historical-theological perspective of the meals. This chapter is a brief attempt to look at the meals in the Lukan gospel, especially those meals that are very similar to the Hellenistic symposium banquet, in order to see how Luke uses this social context in his presentation of Jesus' *kerygma*.

Meals in the Greco-Roman World

Meals or table fellowship played a great role in the Greco-Roman world with which Luke was familiar. The meal traditions were often associated with the "symposium"[1] A symposium was a social institution where the host and his guests traditionally gathered for philosophical, moral or religious debates, spiced by meals provided by the host. These banquets provided not only entertainment but also a relaxed background for enlightened debates.

> "The symposium as a social institution was, of course, the second course of the traditional banquet, or the drinking part that followed the meal proper. It was during the drinking part that the entertainment of the evening was traditionally presented. In the philosophical tradition, this tended to consist of elevated conversation on a topic of interest to all in the group."[2]

Apart from "symposium," a serious discussion of issues, the banquet scene also provided a context for satire, a related literary genre that discussed or presented important people, events or institutions in a way that expressed or illustrated the ills of society in amusing and entertaining ways. Satire could, for example, depict such characters as the drunken stupor, the pretentious rich man or the boring philosopher.[3]

---

[1] Denis E. Smith, "Table Fellowship as a Literary Motif in the Gospel of Luke", *Journal of Biblical Literature* 106/4 (1984), p. 614.
[2] *Ibid.*, p. 614.
[3] *Ibib.*, p. 616.

Smith has ably summarized the functions of table fellowship as symbol of status, mode of teaching, symbol of luxury, symbol of community service and as symbol of community fellowship in the Gospel of Luke[4]

There are several references to meals or table fellowship in Luke. For our purpose we shall only discuss four meals. These are the meal at the house of Levi, Luke 5:27-32; Jesus' first meal with a Pharisee, Luke 7:36- 50; Jesus' second meal with a Pharisee Luke 11:37- 54 and Jesus' third meal with a Pharisee, Luke 14:1-24. There are two reasons limiting our discussion to these four meals. First, these meals in Luke bear the closest resemblance to the requirements of a Greco-Roman symposium banquet. The requirements for a Hellenistic symposium genus included a host, a guest of honour, other guests, an invitation, an unfolding of the host's identity and of the other guests and a *fait divers* or an action that sparks the speech of the guest of honour. These meals do fulfill these requirements.[5] The second reason is simply the limited scope of the present study.

Luke 5:27-32: The Meal at the House of Levi

Table fellowship signified acceptance of the other's social values. To eat together was a symbol of friendship. The etiquette of table fellowship established social boundaries in which only some could be included while others were excluded. Only the like-minded would partake in a table fellowship.[6]

Levi was an agent employed by a chief tax collector. The chief tax collector could lease the taxes of a particular city or region by paying the Roman Government a specified sum to represent that particular city's or region's tax revenue. The chief tax collector would then be allowed to collect the same amount but with profit from the city or region leased, for example, Galilee. The system was open to abuse as the chief tax collectors inflated tax to make maximum profit. They would then hire tax agents, like Levi, to collect various forms of tax like tolls, tariffs, duties and customs. The agents could be stationed along borders, at bridges, in harbours and in cities.[7] Most tax agents became notoriously corrupt and dishonest as they attempted to create profit for themselves. This attracted moral accusations from the Pharisees

---

[4] A discussion of these themes forms the essence of Smith's paper.
[5] Stewart Love, "Women and Men at Hellenistic Symposia Meals in Luke", in Philip F. Esler (ed.), *Modelling Early Christianity, Social-Scientific Studies of the New Testament in its Context*, London and New York: Routledge, 1995, pp. 201-202.
[6] James R. Resseguie, *Spiritual Landscape, Images of the Spiritual Life in the Gospel of Luke*, Peabody, MA: Hendrickson, 2004, p. 70.
[7] Francois Bovon, *Luke 1, Hermeneia, A Critical and Historical Commentary on the Bible*, Mminneapolis: Fortress, 2002, p.189; Also John P. Heil, *The Meal Scenes in Luke Acts, An Audience-Oriented Approach*, Atlanta, GA: Society for Biblical Literature, 1999, pp. 21-22.

who ranked them among "sinners," and general hatred from the Jewish society.[8] The call of Levi, therefore, and his repentant response to Jesus represents a radical repentance comparable to that of the disciples who also "left everything" and followed Jesus.

In appreciation for Jesus' call and forgiveness, Levi prepares a banquet. As host he extends hospitality and meal fellowship to Jesus whom he invites as guest of honour. The meal fellowship that follows underlines the close bond of unity, friendship, hospitality and peace with God which result when social boundaries collapse as "the other" becomes acceptable and welcomed. It is important to note that at this banquet there are three traditionally opposed groups, namely, Jesus and possibly his disciples, the Pharisees and "the crowd of tax collectors." While some are reclining on coaches at table the many tax collectors and Jesus' disciples who may probably not receive a place of honour at the table at this point, find their own places in the banquet room. Table fellowship establishes a close religious and social bond among participants.[9] In this banquet, boundaries between the "sinners" as tax collectors were classified and the "righteous" as the Pharisees understood themselves to be are broken. The "others" who were outside the realm of traditional religious purity have been included.[10] The banquet raises as a topic for the symposium the question of social and religious borders, boundaries and barricades. The Pharisees do not understand why Jesus, as guest of honour and probably as a prophet, would tolerate the unclean sinners to a table fellowship with the righteous. They therefore understandably ask Jesus, "Why do you eat and drink with tax collectors and sinners?"[11] For them it is against God's will to share such table fellowship with publicly recognized sinners.

In response Jesus classifies the "sinners" along with the sick, who the Pharisees have seen him heal before, and declares that his mission is to bring healing to the sick who need a physician. Jesus therefore sees the sharing of table fellowship with tax collectors and sinners as part of his ministry of bringing God's healing and forgiveness to those who are sick and sinful. Earlier Jesus had declared his mission at the Nazareth synagogue in terms of being sent in the Spirit of the Lord, to declare freedom to captives, forgiveness, and the year of the Lord (Luke 4:16-21). Thus for Jesus table fellowship becomes, as Resseguie observes, an occasion to receive "the other," not just a gathering of like-minded people to the exclusion of "the other."[12]

---

[8] Bovon, *Luke 1*, p. 189; Heil, *The Meal Scenes in Luke Acts*, pp. 21-22.
[9] Heil, *The Meal Scenes in Luke Acts*, p. 24.
[10] Resseguie, *Spiritual Landscape*, p. 70.
[11] Luke 5: 30.
[12] Resseguie, *Spiritual Landscape*, p. 70.

Jesus' First Meal at a Pharisee's Invitation, Luke 7:36-50

Jesus now accepts an invitation to a table fellowship from Simon the Pharisee. The incident that provide topic for this meal and the subsequent debate in the symposium that follows illustrates the pitfalls of a spirituality that is based the observation of external boundaries and how it restricts a proper vision of how God works.

Although Simon has invited Jesus as his guest, he receives him as a total stranger, denying Jesus traditional hospitality etiquette. Simon does not provide water to Jesus to wash his feet, does not kiss him and does not anoint his head with oil.[13] A sinful woman however enters the banquet room. She stands behind Jesus, weeping, with tears falling on Jesus' feet. She wipes them with her hair. She kisses Jesus' feet and anoints his head with prepared oil.

According to Heil, the woman's "standing behind" Jesus "at his feet" rather than directly facing him indicated her "extremely humble, shameful, and loving gestures of unconventional and extraordinary hospitality."[14] This incident provides topic for the subsequent debate. While Jesus sees a true expression of repentance in the woman's action, Simon the Pharisee only sees a contaminating touch of a sinner and wonders why Jesus tolerates her behaviour. A spirituality that focusses on external boundaries that are totally exclusive to others leads to Simon's failure from noticing how God works in searching and including the excluded in a fellowship that anticipates the final messianic banquet at the end of time.

We find in this incident a dramatic reversal between the woman and Simon. On the one hand, it is the woman who accords Jesus genuine hospitality. It is the woman who sees her need for repentance and forgiveness. On the other hand, Simon is sure that he is righteous and does not see any compelling need for Jesus. For him, to be righteous is to observe the external, almost ritual, requirements of purity laws. Thus we find in this incident, the excluded being included while the included get excluded from fellowship with Jesus.

In an attempt to bring Simon to an understanding of the nature of repentance and forgiveness, Jesus narrates the parable of the creditor and shows him that only those who feel the need for God's repentance and forgiveness would truly appreciate the

---

[13] Although Robert C. Tannehill, *Luke,* Abingdon New Testament Commentaries, Nashville: Abingdon, 1996, p. 136 suggests that we do not have evidence that foot washing, kissing and head anointing were part of the traditional etiquette of hospitality accorded to a guest in Israel, Smith, "Table Fellowship as Literary Motif" p. 629, observes that feet bathing was customarily part of hospitality as a way of preparing the guest or guests for taking their places on the couch. Bovon also observes that anointing the body with oil was part of both the customs of hospitality and daily body care. It would therefore seem to us that Jesus is only referring to a well known hospitality practice which the Pharisee deliberately chose to omit.

[14] *The Meal Scenes in Luke Acts*, p. 45.

salvation that God has brought in him. Jesus then proceeds to demonstrate his divine powers by declaring God's forgiveness of the woman's sins. The woman walks away, experiencing the love and forgiveness that God grants through the ministry of Jesus. The challenge for the audience and the guests is whether they will acknowledge and experience the love and peace of God that comes by repenting, being forgiven and loving Jesus.[15]

A Second Meal at a Pharisee's Invitation, Luke 11:37-54

This is a second time in Luke we hear that Jesus is invited to a table fellowship by a Pharisee. The many references to Jesus' meal fellowship with Pharisees seem to suggest that it was Jesus' practice to dine with them.[16] The Pharisee again functions as a socially respectable host for Jesus who is a prominent guest for the banquet symposium. The topic for the symposium is sparked by Jesus' disregard of ritual washing before a meal. In Jewish understanding, the sharing of food which is a gift of God was to be done in a state of holiness. The ritual washing before partaking in the meal was intended to remove any ritual impurity from the partakers in the meal.[17] Jesus' action seen in this light becomes a serious breach of ritual purity. The Pharisees had drawn what Resseguie calls a "purity map," a system of do's and don'ts, for example prescribing special times, places, what to eat, how to wash hands, how to clean vessels, in order for one to maintain purity.[18]

When Jesus started eating without the ritual washing the Pharisees were naturally displeased and surprised. In response to this surprise, Jesus addresses the Pharisees criticizing them for being more concerned with external purity to the neglect of inward spirituality. The Pharisees focus meticulously on external rules and are more selfishly interested in what they would gain for themselves. Jesus uses very strong language, accusing them of being full of greed (αρπαγης) and wickedness (πονηρίας), calling them foolish men (αφρονες), and then follows this up with a series of woes addressed both to the Pharisees and the scribes.

Thus the spirituality of inward purity that Jesus teaches stands in sharp contrast with the spirituality of the Pharisees with its focus on external purity, a self-righteous attitude and love for material things and honour. The spirituality that Jesus advocates instead is summarized in his demand for alms giving (δοτε ελεημοσυνην, literary "give alms"). Jesus is not simply talking about giving to charity. "Alms giving" for Jesus is an expression of genuine social solidarity that embraces all who

---

[15] *Ibid.*, p. 51.
[16] For a similar view, see Robert J. Karris, *Eating Your Way through Luke's Gospel*, Collegeville, MN: Liturgical Press, 2006, p. 44.
[17] Heil, *The Meal Scenes in Luke Acts*, p. 100.
[18] Resseguie, *Spiritual Landscape*, pp. 74-5.

are in need, destroying all boundaries of the "purity map" turning greed and excessive grasping to generous and excessive giving.[19] It is this radical reversal in spirituality Jesus is calling for. The new spirituality becomes a genuine expression of God's love and forgiveness. It is not surprising, therefore, that after such a strong denunciation, Luke tells us that the Pharisees began to plot against him, looking for issues in his teaching that would serve as ground for his betrayal (v 54).

Jesus' Third Meal with a Pharisee, Luke 14:1- 24

This is the third time Jesus dines with a Pharisee in the Lukan narrative. The *fait divers*, that initiates debate or controversy, for this banquet is the sudden appearance of a man suffering from dropsy. In the Roman world, dropsy was believed to be a consequence of gluttonous behaviour. A person suffering from dropsy has his body filled with excessive fluid. Yet he craves for more drink which when given makes his condition worse. The disease served as a metaphor for insatiable greed or desire.[20]

Hence the sick man in need of help functions as a subtle metaphor characterizing the morally dropsical Pharisees who are ironically in need of healing by repenting of their greed and selfish desires for which Jesus accuses them. When Jesus asks whether it is lawful to heal on the Sabbath the scribes and Pharisees remain silent. For them any healing constitutes work and therefore should not be done on the Sabbath. For Jesus, restoring health on the Sabbath perfectly accords with its nature and purpose as a sacred time of rest and restoration that prefigures God's final restoration of all things at the end of time. It also accords with his mission to proclaim the year of freedom to captives and restoration to the blind as announced in the Nazareth synagogue (4:16-18).

By remaining silent the lawyers and the Pharisees refuse to acknowledge Jesus' authority as lord of the Sabbath to heal the man lawfully on the Sabbath. Jesus argues that if the religious leaders do approve of releasing animals on the Sabbath, then the "son of Abraham" as a fellow human being, is much more deserving of receiving healing on the Sabbath. In proceeding to heal the man, Jesus is not only asserting his divine authority even on the Sabbath but also challenging the social and religious exclusivism that was officially acceptable.[21]

---

[19] *Ibid.*
[20] Heil, *The Meal Scenes in Luke Acts*, p. 100.
[21] Reta Halteman Finger, *Of Widows and Meals, Common Meals in the Book of Acts*, Grand Rapids, Michigan and Cambridge, UK: Eerdmans, 2007, p. 131, suggests that Jesus' open table fellowship was a strategy he deliberately used to challenge social and religious exclusivism wherever it was officially endorsed and treated as normal. For the view that such symposium banquets could not be a feature of Galilean village life, see Horsley, "Jesus and Galilee", p. 71.

Taking places of honour for oneself is another *fait divers* in this banquet symposium. Jesus observes that as guests come into the banquet hall they choose places of honour for themselves. This observation sparks Jesus' accusation of the scribes and Pharisees. The Pharisees' love of honour for self-glorification is part of their moral "dropsy." Jesus then teaches that honour is a gift of God and that God exalts those who humble themselves. Craving for honour and self-gratification only leads to shame. He, therefore, challenges the Pharisees to get "healed" of their spiritual and moral "dropsy" by seeking repentance and forgiveness. He teaches the guests not to recline on the place of honour before they are assigned to, and advises the host to invite to the banquet hall people who will not be able to reciprocate hospitality.[22]

The parable of the great dinner, which Jesus narrates immediately after his teaching on the need for compassion for those in need, the need for religious leaders to repent and the need to open up table fellowship to those who would not reciprocate hospitality, needs to be understood in light of this teaching. Thus Jesus depicts the eschatological fellowship with God in terms of table fellowship where social and spiritual boundaries no longer hold; where "the other" finds a place, and where a spirit of grasping gives way to a spirit of giving. Table fellowship becomes an essential metaphor for the nature and character of the kingdom of God. As we noted earlier, meals in Luke function at double levels: at the social level as a challenge to discriminatory social and religious practice, and at the spiritual level as a symbol of the eschatological kingdom of God.[23]

Conclusion

It could now be concluded that table fellowship in Luke generally takes the form of the Hellenistic symposium banquet. These function as a springboard for theological debates and offer Jesus an opportunity to engage with the Pharisees at their own social level. Through the symbol of table fellowship and other meal narratives not covered in this chapter, Jesus presents his teaching on the nature and character of the kingdom of God, the very essence of his *kerygma*. Understanding the theological significance of the meals in Luke, therefore, offers one of the keys to an understanding of the kingdom of God itself as the Lukan Jesus presents it.

---

[22] Heil, *The Meal Scenes in Luke Acts*, p. 101.
[23] Finger, *Of Widows and Meals*, p. 131, observes that there is now a scholarly consensus that Jesus' radical practice of open table fellowship was a key strategy in the process of his announcing and redefining the kingdom of God. For an argument for the historicity of Jesus' practice of table fellowship, see Norman Perrin, *Rediscovering the Teaching of Jesus*, New York: Harper & Row, 1967, pp. 102-108.

Chapter Eight
Acts as History in Ancient Historiography

Introduction

The genre of the Book of Acts has been a subject for scholarly debate for a long time. There are still divergent views on the subject. Proposals range from ancient lives, through Hellenistic and Jewish historiography, to historical fiction. In this chapter I argue that Acts of the Apostles is a standard ancient historiography with a strong Jewish apologetic motif.

Acts in Current Debate

Pervo is probably the most critical scholar, in recent times, against the view that the Book of Acts can best be understood as a form of ancient historiography. Pervo acknowledges that the preface in the Book of Acts, the use of speeches and the manner in which events are narrated, with occasional references to secular history, do provide a strong case for historiography.[1] For him, however, the form of the preface does not necessarily suggest historiography because prefaces were also used by other writers including astrologers, dream interpreters and novelists.[2] He asserts that a comparison of Acts with the major works of Flavius Josephus reveals "vast differences."[3] He also finds the chronology "so thin."[4] He further asserts that Acts does not reflect unity of style, vocabulary, syntax, proportion and balance, elements that are important for historiography. He suggests that a good number of incidents were invented by the writer, that good sources were not utilized even if they were available, and that characterization of both people and events seems "highly improbable or contrary to known facts."[5]

Pervo, then, states his thesis that "the canonical Acts [is] best explained as an example of one type of historical novel."[6] Pervo's argument is clearly forceful. However, most of his claims are not sufficiently substantiated, and he appears to

---

[1] Richard I. Pervo, *Profit and Delight. The Literary Genre of the Acts of the Apostles*, Philadelphia: Fortress, 1987, p. 4.
[2] Ibid.
[3] Ibid., p. 5.
[4] Ibid.
[5] Ibid., p. 8.
[6] Ibid., p. 122.

exaggerate the differences between Acts and Hellenistic or Jewish historiography to create room for his theory of "historical fiction."[7]

Most scholars have reckoned with the historiographical features and have sought to understand how these relate to the genre of ancient historiography. The dominant view is that it belongs to the *Gattung* of history. Within this broad genre, some have sought to demonstrate that it fits Hellenistic historiography, while others have advocated for a Jewish historiography. Yet others have observed that both Hellenistic and Jewish historiographical elements are found in Acts. Dibelius considered Acts a historical work in the Hellenistic historiographical tradition, and explained what he saw as a deficiency in style by suggesting that early Christian writers hard not yet become *literati* and that the Christian audience would not mind matters of literary style.[8]

Thus despite the literary style, Dibelius acknowledges the historical character of the content and the manner in which that content was collected:

"It is quite probable that communities did preserve stories of individual events stories of healings, conversions, and martyrdoms ... but an author [who] wished to write history ... could not be content with collecting, sifting, and linking together such fragments of narrative ... He had to mould them into a significant sequence ... to bring to light a certain 'meaning' indicated in the events. But here too, he was dependant upon the material that was at his disposal."[9]

Thus, to write history one needs well researched data that can then be interpreted and presented in a consecutive narrative. Dibelius suggests that the writer has used "memoirs," itinerary documents, and has also composed the speeches which he inserted into the outline.[10]

Cadbury also shares a high regard for the historical character of Luke's sources. He observes that "all ancient history and biography rested in the last resort on material much like Luke's,"[11] the raw material of facts.[12] He further observes that such material could sometimes have the advantage of greater completeness, a closer

---

[7] Ibid., pp. 119-120.

[8] Martin Dibelius, *The Book of Acts, Form, Style, and Theology*, ed., K.C. Hanson, Minneapolis: Fortress, 2004, pp. 6, 53.

[9] Ibid., p. 6. It is however, difficult to understand what Dibelius means when he maintains that the Book of Acts is "historical" in light of his essay on the speeches which will be discussed below. For a similar view, see W. Ward Gasque, *History of the Interpretation of the Acts of the Apostles*, Peabody, MA: Hendrickson, 1989, p. 233.

[10] Dibelius, *The Book of Acts*, p. 7.

[11] Henry J. Cadbury, *The Making of Luke-Acts, With a New Introduction* by Paul N. Anderson, Peabody, MA: Hendrickson, 1927, 1958, p. 138.

[12] Ibid., p. 131.

relation to eyewitness and a more historical connection and order.[13] Cadbury, however, notes that the problems of incompleteness in historical sources, lack of historical connection and the influence of popular traditions are common features underlying most of ancient formal histories and biographies.[14] He concludes: "No doubt, Luke's work is nearer to history than to any other familiar classification. In the Book of Acts particularly we have enough variation from concentration on persons to suggest that we are getting the history of a group – the church."[15]

Like Dibelius, Cadbury also notes the deficiency in Luke's style, "[Luke's] efforts at literary form only bring into sharper outline the incurably unliterary character of his materials."[16] In a study based on the preface, speeches and the emphasis on autopsy, van Unnik also concluded that Acts is a historical work.[17] Dibelius, in some sense, Cadbury and van Unnik see Acts as Hellenistic historiography. Drury and Schmidt have both argued that Luke and Acts are Jewish rather than Hellenistic historiography. "Luke is Jewish in the story-telling traditions of Genesis, Judges, Samuel and Kings, and the tales in the apocrypha, a tradition still alive in Josephus' *Antiquities* and in *Joseph and Asenath*."[18] Talbert has argued that Luke-Acts follows lives in Diogenes Laertios in terms of content, form and function. He argues that these lives were intended to define the specific way of life for each philosophical school.[19]

Fitzmyer seeks a middle position to the historical problem of Acts. While granting that sometimes Luke's information is incorrect, he insists that the Lucan story in Acts is a good illustration of Hellenistic historiography: "Consequently, we have to admit that the Lucan story in Acts is a good example of a Hellenistic historical monograph."[20] Marguerat sees Acts of the Apostles as both Hellenistic and

---

[13] Ibid., p. 138.
[14] Ibid.
[15] Ibid., p. 133.
[16] Ibid., p. 134.
[17] W.C. van Unnik, "Luke's Second Book and the Rules of Hellenistic Historiography", in *Les Actes des Apôtres: Tradition, Redaction, Theologie*, ed., Jacob Kremer, Leuven: University Press, 1979, pp. 37-60.
[18] John Drury, *Tradition and Design in Luke's Gospel*, pp. 3-8. See also Darly Schmidt, "The Historiography of Acts: Deuteronomistic or Hellenistic?" in *Society of Biblical Literature 1985 Seminar Papers*, ed., Kent Harlod Richards, Atlanta: Scholars Press, 1985, pp. 417-427.
[19] Charles Talbert, *Reading Luke: A Literary and Theological Commentary on the Third Gospel*, New York: Crossroads, 1982, pp. 2-6.
[20] Joseph A. Fitzmyer, *The Acts of the Apostles, A New Translation with Introduction and Commentary*, New York: Doubleday, 1998, pp. 124, 127.

Jewish historiography, and emphasizes the meticulous character of Luke's research process: ""[21] Sterling has also emphasized the dual character of the historiography of the Book of Acts, with special focus on its apologetic quality as a central feature in Jewish historiography.[22]

This brief survey shows that except for the "literary style" of his presentation, which some scholars consider unpolished, most scholars reckon with the historiographical character of the Book of Acts. As it will be shown in the rest of this chapter, the Book of Acts shares both the features of Hellenistic historiography and the characteristics of Jewish historiography.

Historiography in Antiquity

Historiography in general has its background in Greek ethnography. Ethnography studied land, history, wonders and customs of a people.[23] Greek ethnographers collected data on various nationalities in the Hellenistic world in an attempt to better understand such peoples. It is, however, Herodotus (ca 484-420 BC) who pioneered the study of the past as a scientific activity[24] and is primarily responsible for joining history to ethnography.[25] Herodotus developed a practice of making careful distinction between accounts of various groups and historical truth. He considered historical only that which he could personally verify in his research.[26] He applied these principles in his research on the major events of the Greek and the non-Greek world.[27]

Thucydides (ca 460-400 BC) also formulated principles of evidence in order to accurately present the past. He insisted on the use of living witnesses as sources where possible and on meticulous comparison of varying accounts in order to establish the truth.[28] Polybius (ca 200-115 BC) employed the principles outlined by

---

[21] Daniel Marguerat, *Les Actes des Apôtres (1-12)*, Commentaire du Nouveau Testament Va, Genève: Labor et Fides, 2007, p. 26 ("Très exactement, notre auteur se situe au confluent des historiographies greco-romaine et juive. Comme les historiens hellenistiques, il recolte ses données par enquête personnelle, recomposé par la fiction ce que ne lui livrent pas ses sources et soigné la qualité litteraire du texte.")

[22] Gregory E. Sterling, *Historiography and Self Definition, Josephus, Luke-Acts and Apologetic Historiography*, Leiden, New York: E.J. Brill, 1992, p. 17.

[23] Ibid., p. 53.

[24] Steve Mason, *Josephus and the New Testament*, Peabody: Hendrickson, 1992, p. 186.

[25] Sterling, *Historiography and Self Definition*, p. 51.

[26] Mason, *Josephus and the New Testament*, p. 186.

[27] John Marincola (ed.), *A Companion to Greek, and Roman Historiography*, Vol. 1, Malden/Oxford: Blackwell, 2007, p. 4.

[28] Mason, *Josephus and the New Testament*, p. 186. See Marincola (ed.), *A Companion*, p. 5.

both Herodotus and Thucydides. By the time of Josephus and the New Testament, Hellenistic historiography was an established field of inquiry.[29] Jewish historiography has its background in national responses to Greek ethnographical studies. The tendency to assess Near Eastern cultures by Greek standards became offensive to the sensibilities of the Near Eastern peoples.[30] In response to this tendency, natives, usually priests, offered counter interpretations of their fellow countrymen and women, rejecting Greek ethnographical representations, and using their own national records to reconstruct a superior image of their own cultures and civilizations.[31] Hekataios' *Aigyptiaka*, Megasthenes' *Indika* and Berossos' *Babylonia* represent such nationalistic responses to Hellenism.[32]

The work of Josephus provides an historiographical model that is both Hellenistic and Jewish in its character. Attridge has emphasized Josephus' similarities with Dionysios of Halicarnassus, a rhetor and historian in the Augustan period.[33] Luke-Acts shares a common historiographical tradition and perspective with Josephus.[34] To understand the historical nature of Luke-Acts, therefore, it is important to compare these elements in order to demonstrate our thesis that Luke-Acts is a standard ancient historiography with an apologetic motif.

Luke-Acts, Josephus and Historiography

A full discussion of all the similarities is beyond the scope of the present study. For our purpose, therefore, we will look at a few key elements of both Hellenistic and Jewish historiography in order to see how Luke-Acts fits into the mode of ancient historiography. It is probably significant to note at this point how history as a discipline was viewed in the ancient world. History was not considered as a discipline that led to exact knowledge. The results of historical research formed part of δοχα (opinion). It did not lead to truth in the philosophical sense of the term.

---

[29] For a brief discussion on mythography, ethnography, chronography, horography and contemporary history as subgenres, see Marincola (ed.,), *A Companion*, pp. 5-6.
[30] Sterling, *Historiography and Self Definition*, p. 103.
[31] Ibid., pp. 135-136.
[32] Ibid., pp. 73, 100, 115, 135.
[33] For a thorough treatment of similarities, see Harold W. Attridge, *The Interpretation of Biblical History in the Antiquitates Judaicae Flavius Josephus*, Missoula, Montana: Scholars Press, 1976, pp. 43-60.
[34] Sterling, *Historiography and Self Definition*, pp. 366-367. See also Louis H. Fieldman, "A Selective Critical Bibliography of Josephus." In *Josephus, the Bible and History*, (eds.) Fieldman, Louis, H. and Gohei Hata, Leiden: Brill, 1989, p. 351, who also observes that Josephus "employs the methods used by the great Greek historians, especially Dionysius of Halicarnassus, and also follows the Hellenistic Jewish authors who preceded him."

Philosophers of the 4th Century BC and the Hellenistic age did not devote themselves to historiography.[35] It is also significant to observe that ancient historiography was intended to educate citizens in the values of the city-state by providing role models for imitation.[36] It provided a means for advancing political, civic and cultural goals of the city-state. To achieve this, therefore, there was a deliberate attempt in historiography to portray the city-state as an ideal, mythical and immortal entity.[37] This suggests that even Hellenistic historiography had an apologetic function although this is not often recognized.

It is within the context of these assumptions that ancient historiography perceived truth. The ancient world assessed historiographical speeches, for example, in terms of their plausibility rather than as a word-for-word connection with what was actually said. In other words, ancient historiography employed speeches to communicate "facts" or "truths" about an historical event.[38] Among the most important characteristics of Hellenistic historiography are: the use of prefaces to introduce the work, the use of speeches, appeal to the miraculous, and a meticulous research procedure to ascertain the historical value of the sources.

The Preface in Luke-Acts and Josephus

Although prefaces were used by other categories of writers in antiquity,[39] they were an indispensable feature of Hellenistic historiography. In contrast to the Hebrew Scriptures which begin by an immediate narration of events, Hellenistic historiography required that a work should have a clear beginning, middle and end in conformity with the Greek sense of order.[40] A preface served to lay out the aim, the scope and the thesis of the work in a manner that would convince the reader that the subject under discussion is of utmost significance. A typical preface included a statement on: "(a) the subject and its importance; (b) the inadequacy of previous histories of this period; (c) the author's circumstances and reasons for writing; (d) the author's complete impartiality and concern for the truth; (d) the author's

---

[35] Roberto Nicolai, "The Place of History in the Ancient World," in Marincola (ed.), *A Companion*, p.17. Also Sterling, *Historiography and Self Definition*, pp. 3-4 who adds that prose did not enjoy a place of honour in antiquity, and that the ancients preferred poetry.

[36] Todd Penner, "Civilizing Discourse: Acts, Declamation, and the Rhetoric of the Polis," in Todd Penner and Caroline Vander Stichele (eds.), *Contextualizing Acts, Lukan Narrative and Greco-Roman Discourse*, Atlanta: SBL, 2003, p. 73.

[37] Ibid., p. 37.

[38] Ibid., p. 38.

[39] Porvo, *Profit and Delight*, p. 5.

[40] Mason, *Josephus and the New Testament*, p. 187.

strenuous research efforts and access to eyewitness testimony ... (e) the author's thesis ... and (f) a brief outline of the work's contents."[41]

In his preface to the first volume, Luke follows this pattern: (1) 'Επειδηπερ πολλοι επεχειρησα αναταξασθαι διήγησιν περι των πεπληροφορημένων εν ημιν πραγματων (2) καθως παρεδοσαν ημιν οι οπ̓η αρχης αυτοπται και υπηρεται γενόμενοι του λογου (3) εδοξ καιμοι παρηκολουθηκοτι ανωθεν πασιν ακριβως καθεξης σοι Υράψαι κρατιστε Θεοφιλε (4) ινα επιγνως περι ων κατηχηθης λογων τήν ασφαλειαν (Luke 1:1-4). In this single sentence, Luke outlines his historiographical statement. He refers to the "many" who undertook to write an account of the events he is about to narrate. The significance of the topic is underscored by reference to the fact that the events are "fully accomplished." He therefore finds it a good idea to prepare a fresh account based on "eyewitness" reports that are "carefully investigated" to establish their "certainty or truth." The words επεχειρησα, πραγματων, παρεδοσαν and παρηκολουθηκοτι, or their forms, do appear in Josephus' *Contra Apionem* (1.53), suggesting a similarity in their historiographical approach.

Similarly, in a preface to his *War,* Josephus states the significance of his subject as "the greatest of all" wars in their time (*War* 1.1). He also mentions some who have written accounts on the war using inferior sources and misrepresenting facts, demonstrating the greatness of the Romans, while diminishing the role of the Jews. He, therefore, sets out to write an accurate account, as one who himself participated in that war (*War* 1.1-3). He promises to give a balanced treatment of the two sides, and to begin his account from where "the histories of our ancestors ... break off" (*War* 1.4-6).

Luke introduces his second volume (Acts 1:1-3) in a similar way. His historiographical statement here is again similar to Josephus' preface in his *Contra Apionem* (1.1-2). Both make reference to their first books, address the patron, provide a summary of the first book and introduce the second.

Thus in this aspect, both Josephus and Luke-Acts situate themselves in the literary tradition of ancient historiography.

Speeches in Luke-Acts and Josephus

One of the most contested aspects of ancient historiography is the nature and role of speeches in a historical work. As we saw earlier, at the beginning of this chapter, scholars, with a few exceptions, have reckoned with the historical significance of the narrated account. However, this is not the case with the speeches. In modern scholarship, largely due to the influence of Martin Dibelius, the historical value of the Book of Acts in general and the speeches in particular has diminished. Although

---

[41] Ibid.

Dibelius never wrote a full length monograph on Acts, he published a number of essays that have influenced modern scholarly views. Dibelius argued that while the author of Luke-Acts was controlled by the Gospel traditions he received in the writing of his first volume, he exercised great freedom as a creative author of the second volume.[42] The writer used this freedom to invent the speeches of Acts, and used them as a tool to further his theological purpose.[43] Dibelius argues that invention of speeches was a common practice among ancient historians. "The ancient historian was not aware of any obligation to reproduce ... the text of a speech ... even if the text was known, the historian did not incorporate it."[44] For Dibelius, an actual speech, even if available, would not sufficiently serve the writer's theological goals, and so would simply be left out in favour of a speech specifically invented to serve those theological goals.

To support his theory of speech invention, he cites passages from Thucydides, Dionysius of Halicarnassus, and Polybius, as evidence for the common practice of speech invention among historians in antiquity. Thus Dibelius effectively removes the speeches from any consideration of historical value. As rhetorical devices, the speeches can only be understood within the rhetorical context of the whole book, rather than as an authentic reflection of an historical event or reality.[45] It is important to remember that Dibelius is one of the scholars who founded form-criticism, and that he sought to apply its principles in his studies on Acts. Dibelius was, therefore, already skeptical about Acts' historical value before he started to write his essay.[46]

A critical review, however, reveals that most of his assumptions were not correct. Lack of response to opposing views also weakens his theory of speech invention. Although he may have known the work of W.M. Ramsay, A. von Harnack and A. Wikenhauser, all of whom convincingly argued for the historical value of Acts, Dibelius skipped any discussion of those works and only focused on a synchronic reading of the text of Acts.[47] A closer look at the quotations he draws from Thucydides and Polybius reveal that they actually contradict his theory rather than support it.[48] While there are still scholars who have followed Dibelius, others remain convinced that the Book of Acts is an ancient historiography and that much of its historical information has been vindicated as such through parallel accounts in other ancient literature and archaeological findings. For example, Fitzmyer

---

[42] Cf. Gasque, *A History of the Interpretation*, p. 203.
[43] Dibelius, *The Book of Acts*, pp. 49-50.
[44] Ibid.
[45] Ibid. p. 58.
[46] Gasque, *A History of the Interpretation*, p. 207.
[47] Ibid. pp. 136-7, 154, 158.
[48] For a thorough discussion of Dibelius' work, see ibid., pp. 201-250, especially 224-238.

concludes his observations in this way: "Consequently, we have to admit that the Lucan story in Acts is a good example of a Hellenistic historical monograph ...That does not guarantee, of course, the historicity of every Lucan statement or episode, but it reveals that what is recounted in Acts is substantially more trustworthy from a historical point of view than not."[49] The debate continues and a last word is yet to be said. However, it seems appropriate to look at the speeches as based on some historical facts or events which Luke wants to relate to the reader.

Luke-Acts, Josephus as Jewish Historiography

In addition to the Hellenistic historiographical features that Acts and Josephus share with Hellenistic historians, there are other features which reveal a distinctive apologetic motif that situates them in the context of Jewish historiography. Both the Book of Acts and the works of Josephus tell a story of a people. They rewrite texts from within their group, and seek, through these rewritten texts, to reconstruct a self definition of the subgroup to which they belong. They seek to establish a place of respect within the wider Roman society for their subgroups.[50] Due to widespread antagonism to Judaism in the ancient world, Jewish writers needed to defend their religious tradition by responding to charges that came their way.[51]

Jewish historiography was also propagandistic, and sought to extend the Jewish faith throughout the Greco-Roman world. It attempted to show that its tradition was superior to the Greeks, and that therefore it was worth of acceptance and adoption by everyone. It combined both judicial and deliberative rhetoric. Both Luke-Acts and Josephus share this apologetic quality.[52] They also display the awareness that their traditional records are sacred history. They are both informed by the concept of history that is found in the LXX, especially in Deuteronomic history.[53] Thus Jewish historiography functioned as a means for shaping Jewish identity and situating that identity within the wider Greco-Roman world.[54]

---

[49] Fitzmyer, *The Acts of Apostles*, p. 127.
[50] Sterling, Historiography and Self-Definition, p. 368.
[51] Todd Penner, *In Praise of Christian Origins, Stephen and the Hellenists in Lukan Apologetic Historiography*, New York, London: T & T Clark International, 2004, p. 223. Also Mason, *Josephus and the New Testament*, pp. 197-98.
[52] Ibid. p. 224.
[53] Sterling, *Historiography and Self Definition*, p. 369.
[54] Ibid., p.308. Also Penner, *In Praise of Christian Origins*, p. 228.

Other Historiographical Aspects

There are other historiographical aspects that show through in both Luke-Acts and Josephus which cannot be discussed in detail in this chapter. These include use of secular contemporary history and openness to Hellenistic literature. For example, both Acts and Josephus show interest in Theudas who is mentioned in Gamaliel's speech (Acts 5:36; *Antiquities* 20.97-98), and in the story about Herod Agrippa I's miraculous death in Caesarea (Acts 12:19-23; *Antiquities* 19.343-350). Despite some differences in historical detail, the two common accounts sufficiently show that their reports are based on good research on shared history. Differences of detail would naturally be expected in historical works.

In Acts 5:36 Gamaliel's speech refers to Theudas and Judas as examples of revolutionaries who had followers but nevertheless ended in failure. Despite problems in the order of events, in light of modern knowledge, Josephus keeps the same order in his reporting.[55] Similarly, the accounts of the death of Herod Agrippa I share a basic outline. Both accounts set the incident in Caesarea at a feast, mention Herod's glittering garments, record his acclamation as a god—a factor to which they attribute his death—and describe the death in a similar way.[56]

Another historiographical aspect they share is Atticism, deliberate imitation. In imitating the LXX and archaizing their accounts, they follow both Jewish and Hellenistic traditions as practiced by Dionysius of Halicarnassus, Arrian, Appian, Cassius Dio, Philo and other ancient historians. The final aspect we can mention here are the "we" passages. Along with other eyewitness accounts, these serve to offer credibility to the tradition.

Conclusion

In this chapter I have argued that the Book of Acts is a standard ancient historiography with a strong apologetic motif. It shares both Hellenistic and Jewish historiographical aspects. Although some scholars have argued that the speeches in Acts are creative inventions by the author, it appears more likely that the speeches are based on historical facts or events and, therefore, do provide a more historical perspective than a mere literary one, as Dibelius and Porvo have forcefully argued. Parallels in contemporary literature, and archaeological findings have supported the historical value of much of the information that we find in Acts. I would therefore conclude, as Fitzmyer did, that as long as we are aware that certain statements may not be historically correct, we do have a compelling case in support of the Book of

---

[55] For a more detailed discussion of the problems, see Sterling, *Historiography and Self Definition*, p. 366, footnote 282.

[56] For a detailed discussion, see ibid.

Acts as a historiography and a valid historical source for our reconstruction of the history of early Christianity and its contemporary world.

Chapter Nine
History of the Johannine Community: Its Possibility and Legitimacy

The attempt to reconstruct and write a history of the Johannine community is a legitimate and worthwhile task to undertake. This chapter argues that although the task is a difficult one, a reconstruction of the history of a Johannine community helps us better understand the nature and character of the first recipients of the Gospel and leads to a fresh appreciation of the Gospel's message. It further encourages a new reflection of the significance of that message to our own situation.

Literary Confirmation of a Historical Portrait

Probably, the most critical challenge to the task of reconstructing a history of the Johannine community in recent scholarship has come from scholars who have applied the new approach of literary-critical or narrative criticism to the Gospel, led and represented by Allan Culpepper.[1] As it is typical in this approach, Culpepper rejects the idea of seeing the Fourth Gospel as a window through which one would look at the historical reality of the Johannine community, or of Jesus himself.[2]

Despite his ahistorical approach, however, his analysis of the implied author's role and that of the implied readers actually fit a historical context in which a threatened community gets courage from its perception of its founder in order to face a present threat.[3] In this way, even the literary-critical approach seems to vindicate the historical search for the nature and character of the Johannine community.

Historical Reconstruction of the Johannine Community

Since the publication of J. Louis Martyn's seminal work, *History and Theology in the Fourth Gospel* in 1968, there has been a general recognition that the Johannine

---

[1] Allan Culpepper has applied this new critical model in his study of the Fourth Gospel, especially in his groundbreaking *Anatomy of the Fourth Gospel: A Study in Literary Design*, Philadelphia: Fortress, 1983.

[2] For a similar assessment, see D. Moody Smith, "The Contribution of J. Louis Martyn to the Understanding of the Gospel of John," in J. Louis Martyn, *History and Theology in the Fourth Gospel*, 3rd ed., Louisville and London: Westminster and John Knox, 2003, pp. 13-14.

[3] Ibid., p. 17.

community had a long and rich history.[4] Martyn's assumption was that the hostility between "the Jews" and Jesus in this Gospel presuppose a real historical situation, not necessarily that of Jesus and his actual disciples but rather that of the Johannine community to which the Gospel is addressed. Here, Martyn is simply applying one of the foundational principles of Form Criticism. If the Fourth Gospel bears testimony to the *Sitz-im-Leben* of the Johannine community, then that situation in life was worth investigating. He therefore develops the thesis that the reference to the excommunication of Christians (John 9:22; 12:42; 16:2) and the demand to recite the *Birkath ha-Minim*, that cursed heretics (Berakoth 28 of the *Babylonian Talmud* and Justin Martyr's *Dialogue with Trypho* 16, 110) do reflect a historical situation in the life of the Johannine community when its members were being excommunicated from the synagogue.[5]

Raymond E. Brown extended research from the middle stage of the parting of the ways with the synagogue, backward to the formative period when the tradition was in its formative stage and when Christians still attended the synagogue along with the other Jews. It is generally agreed that this period was a long one in which the Gospel tradition was shaped through teaching and preaching.[6] Brown extends the history of the community further to the period of the Johannine epistles,[7] a time when external conflict with "the Jews" had subsided, and new problems had arisen from within the Johannine community itself. Other scholars like Ashton[8] and Meeks[9] have generally accepted the broad outline of the history of the Johannine community, but have sought to modify certain aspects of the theory.

Textual Evidence for a Johannine Community

The attempt to reconstruct a history of the Johannine community has been fueled by the nature and character of the Johannine Gospel text itself. As we saw above, Martyn based his theory of conflict with "the Jews" on John 9:22; 12:42; and 16:2.

---

[4] For example, see Francis J. Moloney, *The Gospel of John*, Collegeville, Minnesota: Liturgical Press, 1998, pp. 2-3.
[5] Martyn, *History and Theology in the Fourth Gospel*, 3rd ed., pp. 6-7.
[6] For example, see Raymond E. Brown, *The Community of the Beloved Disciple*, New York: Paulist, 1979, p. 59.
[7] Ibid., pp. 93-144, but especially p. 93.
[8] John Ashton, *Understanding the Fourth Gospel*, Oxford: Clarendon, 1991; idem, *Studying John*, Clarendon, 1994.
[9] Wayne Meeks, "Breaking Away: Three New Testament Pictures of Christianity's Separation from the Jewish Communities", in *"To See Ourselves as Others See Us": Christians, Jews, "Others" in Late Antiquity*, eds Jacob Neusner and Ernest S. Frerichs, Studies in the Humanities 9 (1985): 93-115, especially p. 102.

The texts clearly reflect tension between the Johannine community which still exists as a Messianic group within the larger Jewish community and "the Jews." Coupled with the external evidence from the *Babylonian Talmud* and Justin Martyr's *Dialogue with Trypho*, it becomes even more credible that such a situation may have actually existed at some point in the life of the community.

The emphasis on "the Jews" as the community's opponents adds further credibility to the theory. Although it is possible to argue from literary-critical perspective that the term "the Jews" is used symbolically, and that its function in the narrative is simply to advance conflict within the plot of the narrative, it would still call for some kind of explanation why the symbolic representation agrees with the historical picture of the community.

An analysis of the question of authorship of the Gospel also suggests that the text has been worked on by a number of people at different times, and that the final version that comes down to us is a fruit of collective effort. The final version does reveal, to some extent, the various stages of the Gospel text within the life of the community. In 19:34-35, the narrator informs us that the eyewitness who stood beside the cross of Jesus, and saw the soldiers pierce his side out of which blood and water flowed, is the one who bears testimony to the Gospel story that has been narrated and that his testimony is true. In this statement, the narrator effectively attributes authorship of the Gospel to this eyewitness.[10] He is the witness to the events narrated in the Gospel story. Earlier, at 19:26, this eyewitness has been described as the disciple whom Jesus loved. From these verses we can, at least, differentiate two stages in the life of the community: the period during which the Beloved Disciple personally bore witness whether orally or through the first edition of the Gospel. The second stage is that of the narrator who is speaking in these two texts. He is, very likely, speaking to his contemporaries who need assurance that there is eyewitness testimony behind the Gospel text that they have.

At 21:24, we have further testimony that the disciple whom Jesus loved is behind the Gospel story and that it is he who wrote it. The phrase ὁ γράψας ταυτα may not necessary mean the writer who actually puts pen to paper in antiquity as it is the case in modern times. However, it does refer to the one who causes the particular book to be written, the one who dictates information or the one who is in some sense the source of the information being written.[11] Whatever the phrase might mean, it is clear that the narrator is ascribing authorship to the Beloved Disciple in more specific terms than he does at 19:34-35.

---

[10] For a similar view, see, for example, Moloney, *The Gospel of John*, p 6.

[11] For the view that the phrase cannot have a literal meaning, see Raymond E. Brown, *An Introduction to the Gospel of John*, ed., Francis J Moloney, New York: Doubleday, 2003, p. 193.

It is generally accepted that chapter 21 is a later addition to the Gospel text which originally ended at 20:30. A close reading of chapter 21 reveals that the chapter reflects yet another stage in the development of the Johannine community. It appears that the Beloved Disciple is now dead. There also seems to be a deliberate attempt to conform to the Great Church in which the role of Peter is being elevated and the early Christian communities are increasingly getting more organized. The narrator seeks to acknowledge the role of Peter in the early church, without at the same time neglecting the role of the Beloved Disciple who is the founder of the community and the authority behind its gospel.[12] Thus within the Gospel text itself, we can, with Brown, identify at least three figures behind it: the Beloved Disciple who bears eyewitness testimony to the Gospel and who is said to have written it; the "evangelist" who is the narrator at 19:34-35; and the "redactor" who attaches chapter 21 to the rest of the Gospel. Each of these figures represents a period in the life of Johannine community.

The life of the community continues beyond the final edition of the Fourth Gospel to the period of the Johannine epistles.[13] There is sufficient internal evidence within the Johannine epistles that suggests that the epistles represent a distinctive period in the life of the community. The nature of the problems and challenges facing the community has changed. While in the Gospel the main problem comes from outside the community itself, from "the Jews," by the time the letters are written the main problems arise from within. The conflict with the Jews has subsided. The community has grown and divided itself into a number of sub-Johannine communities. The conflicts that arise within the community seem to be rooted in competing interpretations of the Fourth Gospel. The result is that there are Christological[14] and pneumatological misunderstandings[15] which translate into open conflict, and unwarranted sense of spiritual pride among some of the members. The humanity of Jesus is being neglected and spiritual fullness is being equated to a state of sinlessness.[16] There is also an apparent struggle for power and leadership among leaders in the various sub-Johannine communities.[17]

Although the idea of a sudden rise in the levels of conflict between the members of the community and "the Jews," following the introduction of the *Birkath ha-*

---

[12] Sundra M. Schneiders, *Written That You May Believe, Encountering Jesus in the Fourth Gospel*, New York: Crossroad, 1999, p. 40.
[13] Brown, *The Community of the Beloved Desciple*, pp. 93-144.
[14] For a more detailed discussion, see Brown, *The Community of the Beloved Disciple*, pp. 109-122.
[15] Ibid., pp. 138-144.
[16] Ibid., pp. 124-135.
[17] Ibid., pp. 103-109.

Minim Benediction in the synagogues as proposed by Martyn, and taken for granted by most scholars in the past four decades, is now being challenged,[18] the possibility of such a conflict cannot completely be ruled out.

Conclusion

We would therefore conclude by observing that literary, historical and textual evidence seem to be in favour of the historical existence of a Johannine community. A reconstruction of such a community is, therefore, a justified endeavour. While the task is a difficult one, and complete certainty is impossible at many points, such a reconstruction helps us situate the community into a plausible historical context, and this in turn helps us to understand Johannine literature and better appreciate its teaching.

---

[18] For example, see Raimo Hakola, "The Johannine Community as Jewish? Some Problems in Current Scholarly Consensus," in *Jewish Christainity Reconsidered, Rethinking Ancient Groups and Texts,* ed., Matt Jackson-McCabe, Minneapolis: Fortress, 2007, pp. 181-201, especially pp. 181, 183-85.

Chapter Ten
Water as Revelatory Symbol in John 1-12

Introduction

The Fourth Gospel more than any other canonical gospel uses symbolic language as a means to communicate its *kerygma*. In this section of the gospel such themes as life, light, judgment and of course water are woven into the narrative, not in direct progression with each theme developed from beginning to end, but rather in a symphonic way like musical notes. A theme is introduced, developed to some point, and then it is woven with another, sometimes it is dropped, only to be taken up again later.[1]

The theme of water is treated in the same manner. This chapter is based on a close reading of the Johannine text. It is an attempt to outline how the evangelist has used the notion of water as a revelatory symbol to bring out the theological meaning of Jesus and his mission.

Water as Symbol of Transformation by the Spirit

Water is first mentioned in relation to John the Baptist (1:26). He announces to the messengers from the Pharisees that he baptizes with water, but among them stands one who is yet to be identified, and is greater than John himself. Then the next day John identifies Jesus as the Lamb of God who takes away the sin of the world (1:29). Shortly afterward, John sees the Spirit of God descend and rest upon Jesus (1:32). The idea of water here is related to regeneration. It marks transformation through ritual where sinners become holy and outsiders become insiders,[2] creating a new community of God. The baptism with water, however, points to Jesus who baptizes by offering the Holy Spirit of God which leads to forgiveness of sins and a new life in the Spirit. Thus the cleansing that is symbolized by the use of water in baptism is ultimately effected through the Spirit of God which Jesus gives to those who believe and repent.

The next time we come to a mention of water is in the context of the wedding at Cana. Upon request, Jesus commands that jars of water be filled. The jars were used to hold water that was needed for Jewish purification rituals.[3] Jesus transforms this

---

[1] C.H. Dodd, *The Interpretation of the Fourth Gospel*, Cambridge: CUP, 1953, p. 383.
[2] Jerome H. Neyrey, *The Gospel of John*, Cambridge: CUP, 2007, 102.
[3] Francis J. Moloney, *The Gospel of John*, Collegeville, Minnesota: Liturgical Press, 1998, p. 68.

water into wine. The evangelist then says that this was the first sign Jesus did (2:11) and that it manifested his glory (2:12). The transformation of water can here be interpreted variously. For example, one can see in this story a Messianic banquet[4] where God prepares a table for his people. Whatever it means, the evangelist sees in this incident the revelation of Jesus' own glory, demonstrating his creative power, a power that only God holds. The transformation of water to wine therefore shows that Jesus is the one who comes from God to fulfill Old Testament promises of abundance of wine in the Messianic era.[5]

Some have seen, symbolized in this incident, a new kind of religion being inaugurated,[6] replacing the old Jewish religion.[7] The connection between water baptism and the cleansing effected by the Spirit becomes even clearer in the Nicodemus story (3:1-15). Jesus declares before Nicodemus that unless one is born of water and the Spirit, one cannot enter the kingdom of God (3:5). Thus water becomes a powerful symbol of the cleansing that is, ultimately, effected through the Spirit, thus creating a new person out of the old one, a new person who is filled with the Spirit of God. In this way the rebirth which is from above is marked by the ritual of baptism of water in the Johannine community.[8]

Water as Symbol of the Revelatory Truth Embodied in Jesus

The theme of water is greatly heightened in the story about Jesus' encounter with the Samaritan woman (4:7-26). There is an intensive dialogue between Jesus and the woman. We have the more references to water in this periscope than in any other. The symbolic meaning of water is further elaborated in this climactic episode with regard to the use of the notion of water. The previous periscopes in which water is mentioned tend to emphasize its symbolic representation of the transformative power of the Spirit of God, the "washing" aspect and therefore, the creative aspect of the Spirit.

In this episode, the dimension of water as a symbol is extended to the revelation of truth that is embodied in Jesus and his teaching. Therefore, accepting the teaching of Jesus means receiving the truth that is from God. The knowledge of this truth that

---

[4] Reymond E. Brown, *An Introduction to the New Testament*, New York: Doubleday, 1997, p. 340.
[5] Ibid.
[6] Dodd, *The Interpretation of the Fourth Gospel*, p. 314.
[7] Ibid. For the view that the theme of replacement was very significant in the shaping of the Johannine community, see Reymond E. Brown, *An Introduction to the Gospel of John*, (ed. Francis J. Moloney) New York: Doubleday, 2003, pp 76-77, 161. For Moloney's own view on this theme, see p. 237 and footnote 38.
[8] Moloney, *The Gospel of John*, p. 92.

is embodied in Jesus himself, the knowledge that Jesus is the springboard of everlasting life, is what it means to be saved. The woman is slowly led along this path of enlightenment until she recognizes and confesses that Jesus is the Messiah.

While in the previous water periscopes the central focus has been water and the Spirit, and the cleansing that is brought about, here water becomes a symbol not merely of an action of cleansing by the Spirit, but as a symbol of Jesus himself and the totality of revelation that is embodied in his person. The woman therefore rightly confesses that Jesus is the Messiah. Neyrey makes this point well when he observes that the meaning of water here "metamorphoses from the liquid from the well ... to the substance that Jesus himself gives."[9]

Consequently, the water pericopes that follow in this section seek to add more understanding to the notion of this Messiah by closely linking Jesus to God. They show that Jesus is not only the Agent who ushers in the Spirit, but that he is also one with God. In terms of water as theme, from this point there appears to be a clear shift from a pneumatological function to a Christological function in terms of emphasis. There is a reference to water at 4:46, however, it only looks back to an earlier Cana incident and the text surrounding this reference does not deal with the notion of water. The next significant reference to water is at 5:7, where a man who had been ill for thirty eight years complains to Jesus that there is no one to put him into the pool "when the water is troubled." The significance of this reference is not in the notion of water itself, but in Jesus' response to the charges placed against him for healing this man on the Sabbath. Jesus declares that just as his Father is still working, he also continues to work even on the Sabbath. The work of Jesus is equated to the work of God. The Jews understand this as a claim to equality with God, and they resolve to kill him. Thus the water reference in 5:7 with reference to the Pool of *Beth-zatha*, continues to shape the plot, the sequence of events, until the divine prerogative of Christ in 5:17 is made.

The next water pericope is the walking on the water scene in 6:16. Reminiscent of the creation story where there was no order and the Spirit of God hovered upon the waters, the sea rises due to a strong wind causing chaos. Then Jesus walks on the sea, and brings order to the chaotic waters and salvation to the frightened disciples. The Messiah recreates the world and brings salvation. The disciples recognize the mysterious nature of this Messiah and rejoice for their salvation. Thus although the word "water" is not mentioned in the Greek text of this periscope, water is implied in the mention of "the sea," and serves to develop further the Messianic status of Jesus.

The two remaining references to water in this section of Johns' Gospel echo themes related to water that have already been referred to in the earlier references.

---

[9] Neyrey, *The Gospel of John*, pp. 89-90.

At 7:37, in a context of a Jewish feast, Jesus proclaims that he is the drink for those who are thirsty and that those who come to him become sources of living water. Clearly, here Jesus is the "water," although the evangelist comments that the reference is to the Spirit that Jesus gives. We have already noted in our discussion of the earlier periscopes that water and Spirit are closely connected.

The final water reference is found in 9:7 where Jesus plasters the eyes of a blind man with soil and tells him to go and wash in the pool of Siloam. The man goes and washes, and immediately he is able to see (9:15). This emphasizes the revelatory function of water as a symbol. The man sees. He sees not only the things around him but also becomes aware of the revealed truth that is embodied in Jesus. From this point to the end of ch. 12, there are no references to water. Other themes that have been woven into the narrative earlier are taken up again and replace water as a theme for the last time in this section.

Conclusion

Our discussion on water as theme in chs 1-12 shows that water provides a powerful symbol for communicating the nature of the new birth effected by the Spirit of God and the Messianic nature of Jesus himself. True to the evangelist's writing style, the theme is taken up, developed, sometimes dropped for a while, only to be taken up again until it is finally dropped in ch 9 for the last time in this section. A close reading of the text helps us to notice the way a theme is developed and the nuances that get attached to it as the narrative continues. The soteriological, pneumatological and Christological nuances attached to this theme can hardly escape one's eye.

Chapter Eleven
Ignatius: Martyrdom or Suicide? A Study in Light of His Letter to the Romans

Introduction

At first glance, one would easily conclude that Ignatius' death is a suicide case. His willingness to die and the manner in which he arranges and conducts his journey to Rome, refusing to have anyone prevent his impending death through the beasts in the arena would seem to support such a preliminary view. A careful study of Ignatius' letters and the times in which he lived, however, does not lead to such a conclusion. The complexity of the issues that may have shaped Ignatius' understanding of his death in the arena and the symbolic world which his letters construct have always attracted contradictory assessment in terms of meaning and significance of his death.

In this chapter, I will argue that at the time of Ignatius the concept of martyr was fluid and that the traditions that seem to lie behind Ignatius' understanding of martyrdom are ambiguous. I will also argue that Ignatius blends Greco-Roman and Christian ritual language, thus creating a new synthesis of ritual meaning which he then applies to the martyr procession that his writings construct. In Ignatius' construction of meaning for his martyr procession, his *Letter to the Romans* is central since it focuses on Ignatius himself, the martyr procession he creates and the meaning of his death in the arena he constructs.

The Idea of Martyrdom

At the beginning of their book, Droge and Tabor ask: "When does a martyr become a suicide?"[1] The rest of the book is an attempt to answer this question by looking at Greek, Jewish, Roman and Christian attitudes and responses to various forms of voluntary death in antiquity. Probably before we look at a martyr becoming a suicide, we need to know what it means to be a martyr in the first place. If we begin by assuming that to be a martyr involves voluntary death then we need to inquire how such death is perceived in antiquity. Droge and Tabor have suggested that a voluntary death can be viewed as martyrdom with connotations of being noble,

---

[1] Arthur J. Droge and James D. Tabor, *A Noble Death, Suicide and Martyrdom among Christians and Jews in Antiquity*, New York: Harper Collins, 1992, p. 3.

sacrificial or heroic, or it can be viewed as suicide with implications of being sinful, self-centered and irrational.[2]

This clear demarcation between "martyrdom" and "suicide" is, however, modern and anachronistic to the time of Ignatius. There is no comprehensive term in the ancient world that denotes "suicide" with its associated negative implications. The closest we come to nominal expression for suicide in general is the second century AD. The rule that one should not seek martyrdom but rather if challenged to submit to it rather than sacrifice to the Roman gods was not in place until the time of Clement of Alexandria and Cyprian in the late 2nd Century and early 3rd Century AD, about a century after Ignatius.[3] This suggests that there is absence of a clear terminology in antiquity to denote suicide in its negative sense.[4]

This conceptual deficit is not in conflict with the general attitude to voluntary death in the Jewish and Greco-Roman world. Here we find an action-thought dichotomy. The act of dying a voluntary death is seen as a neutral event such that it rarely becomes a subject for debate. What becomes a topic for discussion, however, are the reasons brought forward to justify such an action. The theoretical justification becomes more important that the act itself.[5]

In the Greco-Roman world voluntary death was not only viewed as neutral but also praised by philosophers, poets and other writers. It was admired in antiquity. Seneca viewed it as a "great triumph" over evil. For Homer it was natural and usually considered heroic. Sophocles held that one must live or die nobly.[6] But why should voluntary death be praised? This question calls for justification. Plato advanced three reasons that justify voluntary death. For him, a voluntary death was not only acceptable but also honourable if it was ordered by government, if the person was experiencing devastating misfortune or if he or she was or about to face intolerable shame.[7]

There is however, an ambiguity in the positions of both Plato and Aristotle. Socrates repudiates voluntary death on the one hand, looking at it as a usurpation of the privileges of the gods who alone must determine when someone is to die. On the other hand, Socrates sees death as a release from earthly troubles and entry into the

---

[2] Allen Brent, *Ignatius of Antioch, A Martyr Bishop and the Origin of Episcopacy*, London and New York: T&T Clark, 2007, p. 19.
[3] Ibid., p. 19.
[4] Arthur J. Droge and James D. Tabor, *A Noble Death, Suicide and Martyrdom among Christians and Jews in Antiquity*, New York: Harper Collins, 1992, p. 3.
[5] Ibid. p. 17.
[6] Ibid. pp. 17-18.
[7] Ibid. p. 21.

perfect world for which this earthly world is only a shadow.[8] Perhaps the most difficult aspect in Socrates' view on voluntary death is the element of divine will that he introduces: "Perhaps from this point of view it is not unreasonable to say that a person must not kill himself until god sends some necessity upon him, such as now has come upon me."[9]

Socrates here suggests that voluntary death is acceptable or even necessary when the time and circumstances appointed by the gods for one to die have come. In his own "voluntary" death, Socrates sees his death penalty as a divine sign that his time to die has come, and finds justification in it for taking away his own life by drinking poison. However, the interpretation of what constitutes a "divine sign" that would justify voluntary death remained an unresolved problem in antiquity. Aristotle's ambiguity arises from his suggestion that a person who takes his own life away does injustice to the state although he is not unjust to himself.[10] It would appear, therefore, that no philosophical school completely condemned the practice of voluntary death, except for the Pythagoreans who viewed it as "irrational."[11]

Generally, however, four arguments were used to moderate the practice. First, there was the religious argument that taking away one's life is an act of rebellion against the gods, second the civil argument that voluntary death is an act against the state, third was the counsel to persevere in difficult circumstances and fourth was the argument that such a decision would never be rational.[12]

A similar view toward voluntary death occurs in Jewish traditions. As early as the period of the early monarchy, voluntary death was understood as being honourable, given proper circumstances. Reasons for the justification for such deaths were similar to those found in the Greco-Roman society. They include God's will, avoidance of persecution and shame, and patriotism.[13]

It is again interesting to note that there is no verbal Hebrew expression for voluntary death in the modern negative sense of suicide until Talmudic times, and that a noun does not appear in Hebrew, corresponding to "suicide," until the 19th Century AD. There is also lack of standard verbal expression for the concept of suicide.[14]

---

[8] Ibid. pp. 21, 42.
[9] Quoted in Ibid. p. 21. Cf. Garrison, *The Graeco-Roman Context of Early Christian Literature*, p. 73.
[10] Ibid. p. 23.
[11] Ibid. pp. 40, 43.
[12] Ibid. pp. 43-44.
[13] For a full discussion, see ibid., pp. 54-57.
[14] Ibid. p. 58.

Voluntary death in Jewish tradition became particularly appealing in the Hellenistic period, from about 300 BC when the finality of death was transformed to become a way to immortality, or reversed through the resurrection to a heavenly life. With the vindication of the righteous suffering in Isaiah 53 and Daniel 7, willingness to die rather than submit to practices that violated their faith became a common feature, especially during the Maccabean struggles.[15] The tradition also reflects common elements: first, that most voluntary deaths occur in situations of conflict and persecution. Second, that the choice of death in such circumstances is seen as a noble and heroic recourse; third, a vicarious benefit is said to accrue from the suffering and the death, and fourth, there is an expectation of reward and vindication in the other world, beyond present death.[16] Again we do not find a complete condemnation of voluntary death in the earlier Jewish traditions, just as was the case with the Greco-Roman traditions discussed above.

Similar views are found during the New Testament period. Josephus holds a positive attitude towards voluntary death provided the circumstances are justifiable. In the right circumstances, the choice to die is for Josephus a noble act of freedom.[17] Philo can also say that "the wise would most gladly choose death rather than slavery."[18]

Thus we see that both the Greco-Roman and Jewish traditions do not condemn voluntary death but rather seek to justify it in light of the circumstances leading to it.. We also note that the concept of suicide with its negative implications does not arise in the period before Ignatius. The word "martyr" as found in the New Testament does not seem to add anything to the idea of voluntary death. Wherever the term or its associations appear in the New Testament[19] it simply means bearing faithful witness to the Lord Jesus.[20] Accordingly, the New Testament seems to be silent on voluntary death.

We would therefore conclude from this background that Ignatius' willingness to die is not in conflict with the Greco-Roman and Jewish traditions concerning voluntary death that might have been influential in his day.[21] The problem for us is to understand the "why?" of his willingness to die.

---

[15] Ibid, pp. 69-75
[16] Ibid., p. 75.
[17] Ibid. pp. 86-89.
[18] Quoted in ibid. p. 17.
[19] For example, μαρτυρες μαρτυς (Acts 7:58; Rev 1:5; 3:14).
[20] G. W. Bowersock, *Martyrdom and Rome*, Cambridge: Cambridge University Press, 1995, 2002, p. 75.
[21] The Rabbinic tradition of his day, although complex and contradictory in many respects, is generally in line with the earlier Greco-Roman views discussed above. See Droge and

The Martyr Procession as a Greco-Roman Ritual

To understand Ignatius' martyrdom it is not sufficient to simply look at the voluntary death tradition that undeniably forms an important background for him. Rather, it is crucial to view Ignatius as creating a martyr procession ritual.[22] In this process, Ignatius blends Greco-Roman and Christian ritual language and thus creates a new synthesis of ritual meaning which he then applies to the martyr procession that he constructs in his writings.[23] The grounds for Ignatius' condemnation are unclear[24] although Christian unity[25], false teaching,[26] and external persecution[27] have all been suggested. What is clear, however, is that we see him condemned and *en route* to Rome to be persecuted in the arena by being thrown to the beasts.

A careful reading of his *Letter to the Romans* reveals that Ignatius is constructing a splendid martyr procession comparable to imperial and other processions that were conducted in the ancient world. Ignatius adopts the secular political concept of *homonoia* and uses it to construct a martyr procession that ritually creates cosmic

---

Tabor, *A Noble Death*, pp. 97-106. For the view that suffering constituted a locus for the encounter between "self" and the divine in Ignatius' contemporary world, see Judith Perkins, *The Suffering Self, Pain and Narrative Representation in the Early Christian Era*, London and New York: Routledge, 1995, pp. 188-92.

[22] Although Catherine Bell's theory of ritualization and the ritualized body offers significant insights for understanding a ritual process, the theory focuses on ritual as an activity and does not explain sufficiently how that ritual activity relates to its symbolic meaning. For her, "symbols and symbolic action ... fail to communicate clear and shared understandings." See her *Ritual Theory, Ritual Practice*, New York and Oxford: Oxford University Press, 1992, p. 184.

[23] For the view that Ignatius' language cannot simply be dismissed as "neurotic" in modern psychology terms, see L.W. Bernard, *Studies in the Apostolic Fathers and their Background*, Oxford: Basil Blackwell, 1966, p. 19.

[24] Allen Brent, *Ignatius of Antioch, A Martyr Bishop and the Origin of Episcopacy*, London and New York: T & T Clark, 2007, p. 12.

[25] Karen L. King, *What Is Gnosticism?* Cambridge, MA: and London: Harvard University Press, 2003, p. 44, observes that "For Ignatius the issue at stake was Christian unity."

[26] Ibid. Also Robin D. Young, *In Procession Before the World, Martyrdom as Public Liturgy in Early Christianity*, Milwaukee WI: Marquette University Press, 2007, p. 17. For a more detailed discussion of background issues at the Church in Antioch which give rise to Ignatius's situation, see C. H. Hammond Bammel, "Ignatian Problems" in Everret Ferguson et al (eds.), *Studies in Early Christianity, A Collection of Scholarly Essays*, New York and London: Garland, 1993, pp. 75-97.

[27] Brend, *Ignatius of Antioch, A Martyr Bishop*, pp. 19-22.

unity for the Church. In Romans 2:2, Ignatius uses a characteristically pagan word for sacrifice, the word *thusia* (θυσια) which literally refers to a slain animal that is offered as a sacrifice.[28] With reference to the teeth of the wild beasts, Ignatius pleads with the Roman Christians: "Petition Christ on my behalf, that I may be found a sacrifice (θυσια) through these instruments of God."[29] *Homonoia* and *thusia* were important concepts in relation to the unity and wellbeing of the Hellenistic states. When a dispute arose between equal and autonomous states, such disputes were resolved through ambassadors, who, once an agreement had been reached, would celebrate the *homonoia* between the two cities. Sometimes the cities could mint coins jointly that showed the deities of the two cities. The treaty could finally be concluded with offering a joint sacrifice, a *sunthusia* (συνθυσια).[30]

Thus the *thusia* used in the *sunthusia* created peace and sealed the unity between the quarrelling cities or states. Once peace and unity or *homonoia* was secured, the function of the ambassadors was both to celebrate it in a joint sacrifice and to proclaim it in their own cities.[31] In that way peace and unity between the cities was established.

In applying this language of *homonoia* sacrifice ritual to himself, Ignatius sees himself as a sacrifice that will be offered on the alter in order to create cosmic unity for the Church, just as the pagan sacrifice creates peace and unity not only for the cities or states but also for the Roman Empire itself. He visualizes the Roman arena as a temple setting, with an alter, and identifies his persecution with the sacrificial ritual.[32] As he travels to Rome, he invites ambassadors from different churches along the way to join in this martyr procession. By meeting or joining or supporting the procession through their ambassadors, the churches became part of the glorious martyr procession and therefore became partakers in the peace and unity that will be established once he is "poured out"[33] as sacrifice and cosmic Christian unity declared. His sacrificial suffering, as a repetition of the suffering of God, will bring benefits to the churches that support and join the martyr procession.[34]

In this way, Ignatius, through the *Letter to the Romans*, constructs a glorious martyr procession ritual patterned on the Greco-Roman *homonoia* ritual that has the

---

[28] Frederick W. Danker (ed.), *A Greek-English Lexicon of the New Testament and Other Early Christian Literature*, 3rd ed, Chicago: University of Chicago Press, 2000, p. 462.

[29] Ignatius, Romans 4:2, in Bart D. Ehrman, *The Apostolic Fathers*, Vol. 1. The Loeb Classical Library, Cambridge, MA and London, UK: Harvard University Press, 2003, p. 275.

[30] Brent, *Ignatius of Antioch, A Martyr Bishop*, pp. 48, 52.

[31] Ibid., p. 57.

[32] Young, *In Procession before the World*, p. 15.

[33] Ignatius, Romans 2:2.

[34] Young, *In Procession before the World*, p. 18.

effect of establishing peace and unity among the states and in the empire as a whole. He visualizes the result of his martyr procession as being the cosmic unity of the Christian Church that will transcend all strife and divisions that have necessitated his becoming a sacrifice.[35]

The Martyr Procession as a Christian Ritual

Despite the Greco-Roman sacrificial imagery that Ignatius uses, the martyr procession symbolism that he constructs is essentially Christian, modelled on the suffering and death of Christ. He visualizes his martyrdom in the arena as a Eucharist celebration for the Roman church[36] Martyrdom, like Eucharist, is "the pledge of the resurrection."[37] He tells the Roman Church: "But if I suffer, I will become a freed person who belongs to Jesus Christ, and I will rise up, free, in him"[38] He, thus sees his sacrificial death as a way to attain to God and to Christ.[39] In the construction of the martyr procession, Ignatius visualizes it as a "mystery play in which he is re-enacting Christ's suffering and thereby achieving union with God." By his imitation of the suffering of Christ he gets absorbed into the Divine through death and resurrection.

The significance of the procession, however, is not limited to his own union with God. All those who join the mystery drama as the martyr procession moves on, not only become united among themselves, in a context of cosmic unity[40] but also are united with God. It is only when Ignatius is in union with Christ that he can become "a word of God,"[41] that is a word of God's revelation whose effect is far-reaching. If,

---

[35] For a more detailed discussion of the sacrificial concepts employed in the Hellenistic *homonoia* sacrificial ritual, see Allen Brent's larger work, *Ignatius of Antioch and the Second Sophistic, A Study of* an *Early Christian Transformation of Pagan Culture*, Tübingen: Mohr Siebeck, 2006, pp. 230-40.
[36] Young, *In Procession Before the World*, pp. 17-18
[37] Ibid.
[38] Ignatius, Romans 4:3.
[39] Ignatius seems to be using the two terms: "attaining to God" and "attaining to Christ" to mean more or less the same idea. See Romans 1:2; 6:3.
[40] Brent, *Ignatius of Antioch, A Martyr Bishop*, pp. 72-3.
[41] Ignatius, Romans 2:1. To appreciate the revelatory character of Ignatius as "a word of God" one only needs to realize that one of Ignatius' key concepts is "the Silence of God" whose mystery can only be revealed to us through "his word." For a thorough discussion of this concept in Ignatius and other ancient writers, see Barnard, *Studies in the Apostolic Fathers and their Background*, pp. 26-27.

however, his sacrificial death is prevented, Ignatius will not be a word of God. He will simply exist in the flesh as "a mere noise"[42]

The Martyr Procession and the Construction of Meaning

As we suggested at the beginning of our study, a more rewarding approach to understanding Ignatius is to look at his martyr procession as a ritual process in which the action-thought dichotomy is temporarily suspended, as the two binaries merge to create a new synthesis and meaning. Despite the suggestion by some scholars, who study the ritual process, that meaning should not be sought outside its symbolic representations, the assumption remains necessary in order to understand Ignatius. The glorious character of the procession he leads and its meaning must lie outside the activity itself.[43] To be sure, there was nothing "glorious" about Ignatius' journey to Rome. He was a prisoner, in chains, and under guard. It was a fairly common practice for representatives of churches that lie close to highways or harbours to come over to meet Christian leaders who were passing through. To many, he was just another victim of cruel persecution, condemned to die by being thrown to the wild beasts. The meaning of the martyr procession, therefore, has to be sought in the world of symbolism to which the martyr procession activity pointed.

Conclusion

In this chapter I have argued that Ignatius employs both pagan and Christian ritual concepts, creating a new synthesis of religious ideas. It would seem that the main problem facing his church at Antioch, and many other churches too, was disunity. Using both pagan and Christian concepts, he creates a martyr procession ritual which symbolically represents him as a sacrifice for cosmic Christian unity. The Letter to the Romans presents us with a ritual construction that places Ignatius as a sacrifice at the centre. His sacrificial role in the martyr procession, and the rewards that role would bring both to himself and to others seem to provide us with one option for understanding Ignatius' willingness to die.

---

[42] Ignatius, Romans 2:1.
[43] For a very critical objection to the cultural theory that meaning in ritual lies outside its symbolic representations, see, for example, Talal Asad, *Genealogies of Religion, Discipline and Reasons of Power in Christianity and Islam*, Baltimore and London: John Hopkins University Press, 1993, pp. 30-35.

Chapter Twelve
Martyrdom of Perpetua: Public Spaces and the Early Christian Martyrs

Introduction

In the early church martyrdom served a number of functions. Martyrdom was viewed as an embodiment of Christian witness both to Christians themselves and to non-Christians. It also served as a process of self-definition for the church as it struggled with its own theological self-understanding. The texts do generally portray reflection or development of important Christian teachings. Martyrdom also served as a moral and social challenge to Greco-Roman culture and its excesses. This chapter is an attempt to examine the role of public spaces, especially the arena, in martyrdom, and how these public spectacles were viewed by Christians, the Roman administration and society in general.

Background to Christian Martyrdom

Several factors, cultural, social, religious and political seem to have combined to create an environment that would not only allow but also promote martyrdom for centuries in the Roman Empire. First of these is the development of the emperor cult. The Roman emperors began to claim divine powers patterned on the eastern monarchs and the pharaohs of Egypt. The plurality of religions itself did not present any political problem. The local people were simply asked to acknowledge the gods of Rome and to sacrifice to the emperor as a means of confirming loyalty to the state and promoting unity among the people. Once this was done, people were free to worship their own gods.[1] Jews were exempted from observing this imperial requirement because their strict monotheistic stance on religion was acknowledge by the state.[2]

Secondly, the Romans, like the Greeks before them, had special love for games, sports and drama. These were traditionally violent[3] and had religious connotations.

Thirdly, as Christians became more and more distinct and separate from the Israelite religion, their religious practices became more and more suspect.[4] In the

---

[1] Denis C. Duling, *The New Testament, History, Literature and Social Context*, 4th ed., Belmont CA,: Wordsworth/Thomson, 2003, p. 448.
[2] *Ibid*.
[3] Robin D. Young, *In Procession before the World, Martyrdom as Public Liturgy in Early Christianity*, Milwaukee, WI: Marquettte University Press, 2001, p. 12.

view of the non-Christian public mystery surrounded Christian meetings, prompting charges against what they perceived as immoral Christian behaviour. The Agape and the Eucharist, for example, were perceived as particularly scandalous. This earned them scorn, dislike and outright hatred from society, while the political administration viewed them as politically dangerous fanatics. The refusal of Gentile Christians to participate in emperor worship seemed to confirm these fears, and thus exposed Christians everywhere to the possibility of persecution.[5]

Fourthly, the nature of the Roman judicial system was such that it allowed Roman officials to demand that Christians acknowledge Roman gods. The law gave these officials power to determine punishment which could lead to banishment, imprisonment, torture or even execution.[6] Various officials in different provinces used this power to summon Christians to recant or refuse. This seems to account, partly, for the sporadic incidents of Christian martyrdom in the empire before it reached climactic proportions in the reigns of Decius and Diocletian who systematically carried out widespread state-sponsored persecutions of Christians.

The final factor we can mention here is that Christians, on their part, seemed to contribute to the widespread character of martyrdom by sometimes availing themselves for martyrdom in large numbers on grounds that even the state could not understand. We shall be coming to these issues repeatedly in our discussion. Fundamental questions still remain. Why should the Roman emperors demand or at least tolerate deification either of themselves or of past emperors? Why should so many Christians, for so long, voluntarily avail themselves for martyrdom? Why should the public find pleasure in watching fellow human beings humiliated, tortured and executed? What kind of people attended these functions and what interest did they represent? How did these public spectacles in the end affect the church, Roman administration and society in general?

Viewing the Public Arena

In seeking to probe into the complexities that shaped the culture of martyrdom, we will focus on the arena which emerges to be the focal point for the Roman administration, the Roman society and the Christians. The symbolism they drew

---

[4] F. L. Cross and E. A. Livingstone (eds), 2nd ed., *The Oxford Dictionary of the Christian Church*, Oxford: Oxford University Press, 1974, p. 1065.

[5] Ibid. Cf. Elizabeth Castelli, *Martyrdom and Memory, Early Christian Culture Making*, New York: Columbia University Press, 2004, pp.

[6] Duling, *The New Testament, History, Literature and Social Context*, p. 448. Also K.M. Coleman, "Fatal Charades:Roman Executions Staged as Mythological Enactments", *Journal of Roman Studies*, Vol. 80 (1990), p. 57.

from their gaze on the arena seems to provide a key to our understanding of some of the mysteries that surround the power of the gaze.

The Romans and the Power of the Public Gaze

The first clear account of Christian martyrs condemned and executed publicly and *en mass* is the description of the Neronian persecution of Christians in 64 CE. Tacitus, an ancient historian, describes the scene as follows:

> But all human efforts, all the lavish gifts of the emperor, and the propitiations of the gods did not banish the sinister belief that the conflagration was the result of an order. Consequently, to get rid of the report, Nero fastened the guilt and inflicted the most exquisite tortures on a class hated for their abominations, called Christians by the populace ... Accordingly, an arrest was made of all who pleaded guilty; then, upon their information, an immense multitude was convicted, not so much of the crime of firing the city, as of hatred against mankind. Mockery of every sort was added to their death. Covered with the skins of beasts, they were torn by dogs and perished, were nailed to crosses, or were doomed to the flames and burnt, to serve as nightly illumination when daylight expired. Nero offered his gardens for the spectacle, and was exhibiting a show in the circus, while he mingled with the people in the dress of a charioteer or stood aloof on a car. Hence, even for criminals who deserved extreme and exemplary punishment, there arose a feeling of compassion; for it was not, as it seemed, for public good, but to glut one man's cruelty, that they were being destroyed.[7]

We notice from this quotation that Nero has carefully planned for this "spectacle" to coincide with "a show in the circus" and has even offered "his gardens" for this special event to ensure a maximum gaze from the public. We also notice that Nero is setting a precedence with regard to the manner in which the dead bodies of the martyrs are being treated: "Mockery of every sort was added to their death. Covered with the skins of beasts, they were torn by dogs and perished, or were nailed to crosses, or were doomed to the flames and burnt." We should further note that this event is a matter of historical accident rather than a systematic imperial policy against the Christians, and was probably limited to Rome.

Half a century later, a similar precarious situation developed in Asia Minor, about 112 CE and is documented in the correspondence between Pliny, the governor of Bithynia in northern Asia Minor and Trajan, the Roman Emperor. Pliny writes to Trajan:

> It is my custom to refer all my difficulties to you, Sir, for no one is better able to resolve my doubts and to inform my ignorance. I have never been present at an examination of Christians. Consequently, I do not know the nature and extent of the

---

[7] Tacitus, Annals, XV. 44 in C.K. Barrett (ed.), *The New Testament Background: Selected Documents*, London: SPCK, 1956, pp. 15-16.

punishments usually meted out to them, nor the grounds for starting an investigation and how far it should be pressed. Nor am I at all sure whether any distinction should be made between them on the grounds of age, or if young people and adults should be treated alike; whether a pardon ought to be granted to anyone retracting his beliefs, or if he has once professed Christianity he shall gain nothing by renouncing it; and whether it is the mere name of Christian which is punishable, even if innocent of the crime, or rather the crimes associated with the name.

For the moment this is the line I have taken with all persons brought before me on the charge of being Christians. I have asked them in person if they are Christians, and if they admit it, I repeat the question a second and third time, warning of the punishment awaiting them. If they persist, I order them to be led away for execution; for whatever the nature of their admission, I am convinced that their stubbornness and unshakeable obstinacy ought not go unpunished...

Now that I have began to deal with this problem, as so often happens, the charges are becoming more widespread and increasing in variety. An anonymous pamphlet has been circulated which contains the names of a number of accused persons. Among these I consider that I should dismiss any who denied that they were or ever had been Christians when they had repeated after me a formula of invocation to the gods and had made offerings of wine and incense to your statue (which I had ordered to be brought into court for this purpose along with the images of the gods) and furthermore had reviled the name of Christ: none of which things, I understand any genuine Christian can be induced to do. Others whose names were given to me by an informer, first admitted the charge and then denied it ... This made me decide it was all the more necessary to extract the truth by torture from two slave-women, whom they call deaconesses. I found nothing but a degenerate sort of cult carried to extravagant lengths.

I have therefore postponed any further examination and hastened to consult you. The question seems to me to be worthy of your consideration, especially in view of the number of persons endangered; for a great many individuals of every age and class, both men and women, are being brought to trial, and this is likely to continue. It is not only the towns, but villages and rural districts too which are infected through contact with this wretched cult. I think though that it is still possible for it to be checked and be directed to better ends, for there is no doubt that people have began to throng the temples which had been almost entirely deserted for a long time; the sacred rites which had been allowed to lapse are being performed again, and flesh of sacrificial victims is on sale everywhere ... It is easy to infer from this that a great many people could be reformed if they were given an opportunity to repent.[8]

---

[8] Betty Radice (transl. with introd.), *The Letters of the Young Pliny*, New York: Penguin, 1969, pp. 285-91.

In this lengthy quotation, a number of things can be inferred. First, Pliny indicates that he has no personal experience in handling a martyrdom situation, despite probably having worked in a number of provinces previously. This suggests that the escalating martyrdom situation is a recent problem in his province, probably a direct response to a local edict, issued by Pliny himself, banning "all political societies."[9] This collaborates our earlier assertion that local and spontaneous occurrences of martyrdom usually depended on how far the local government officials were willing to evoke their powers to summon Christians for judicial interrogation.

Secondly, we would also infer from this correspondence that, though local and spontaneous, the great numbers of people implicated and condemned to execution provided a steady flow of victims to be used in the spectacles in an attempt to satisfy the insatiable longing for a violent gaze in the arenas of the main cities across the Roman Empire.

Thirdly, we note that Pliny is personally convinced that the "stubbornness and unshakeable obstinacy" of Christians "ought not go unpunished." This is a reflection of how society generally failed to comprehend why Christians could expose themselves to capital charges. Even Marcus Aurelius (161-180 CE), the philosopher Emperor and one of Rome's best rulers saw in them a "vulgar effrontery" with which they faced death.[10] In Trajan's response to Pliny, the Emperor does not answer Pliny's first question regarding "the nature of extent of the punishment usually meted out." Instead, he responds to the second question and advises that those who recant and demonstrate their loyalty by worshiping the imperial cult in the presence of the governor should be exempted from punishment regardless of their past. He further advises that anonymous lists of names of accused persons should not serve as grounds for the legal process and that Christians should not be searched out with an intention of bringing them to court to answer charges. Trajan must have been aware about how Christians were punished in such circumstances but leaves that question to Pliny's own determination: "For it is impossible to lay down a general rule to a fixed formula."[11] Implicitly, Trajan is advising Pliny to proceed with executions of condemned Christians.

---

[9] Pliny claims that his edict "issued on your instructions which banned all political societies" was successfully putting an end to Christian meetings in his province: "For there is no doubt that people have began to throng the temples which had been almost entirely deserted for a long time; the sacred rites which had been allowed to lapse are being performed again." *Ibid.*, p. 291.

[10] Angelo Di Berardino, (ed.), *Encyclopedia of the Early Church*, Vol. 1 (transl. Adriano Walford), New York: Oxford University Press, 1992, p.531.

[11] Radice (transl.), *The Letters of Young Pliny*, p. 291.

Fourthly, it is important to notice how the imperial legal process to which Christians are brought actually transforms into a religious ritual as the magistrate or governor takes upon himself or herself the role of a priest or priestess of the imperial cult. Pliny, for example, as he indicates in the quotation above, would ask Christians to repeat a religious formula of invocation to the Roman gods, make them offer sacrifice to the statue of the emperor and demand that they renounce Christ. Here we observe that the interests of the state machinery are not only political and judicial, but also religious. The public spectacle which was the final destination for condemned Christians served these state interests.

A historical survey of the first three centuries of the Christian church reveals deep-seated contempt and hatred against Christians both by Roman authorities and by society. Tacitus' description of the Christians represents the ordinary Roman perception about them.[12] He described them as "a class hated for their abominations ... by the populace," "a most mischievous superstition," "an evil" from Judea "hideous and shameful."[13] The Roman masses still worshiped the traditional gods. Although there was skepticism about these cults on the part of the educated, their sense of patriotism necessitated their identification with these gods and still held them in high regard.[14] Generally, Roman authorities allowed traditional and national religions to practice their faith provided they operated within the law. New cults were thoroughly investigated before they were formally admitted. Mystery religions were often held suspect since authorities would not be sure that their clandestine meetings were not intended for political subversion.[15] Christian practice itself did attract such contempt and hatred.

At first Christianity was considered as a movement within the Israelite religion, a national religion whose members were exempted from the imperial requirement of worshiping the Roman gods and from the imperial cult. As soon as Christianity began to emerge as a distinctive religious movement, this privilege was lost and its members were now required to participate in the imperial cult. Christians rejected this demand and refused participation in public festivals which had strong religious

---

[12] James Hastings et al. (eds.), *Dictionary of the Apostolic Church*, Vol. II., New York: Charles Scribner and Edinburgh: T & T Clarke, 1918, p.175.

[13] C.K. Barrett, *The New Testament Background*, pp. 15-16.

[14] N.T. Wright, *The New Testament and the People of God*, Minneapolis: Fortress, 1992, p. 154. Also Hastings, *Dictionary of the Apostolic Church*, Vol. II., p.177.

[15] Helmut Koester, *Introduction to the New Testament, History, Culture, and Religion of the Hellenistic Age*, Vol. 1, New York & Berlin: Walter de Grutyer, 1982, p. 365. Also Cross and Livingstone (eds.), *The Oxford Dictionary of the Christian Church*, p. 1065.

connotations.[16] The secrecy that surrounded Christian activities at their religious meetings which were usually conducted at night further fanned suspicion among the Roman authorities.

The Christian religion also introduced divisions not only at society level, for example, through their withdrawal from public functions, but also at family level.[17] Christian converts defied family traditional gods and related traditional practices. Their stubborn obedience to Christ, their Lord, presented a challenge not only to the imperial cult but also to the very unity of the empire which the cult intended to promote. Their refusal to participate in the worship of the other traditional gods also meant a challenge not only to the power of the Roman gods but also to the question of their very existence. Since, as we noted earlier, the masses still held these gods in high regard, Christian refusal to honour them was seen as an act of blasphemy against the very gods in whom the welfare of the empire resided. Thus Christian practice constituted a considerable threat to both the political administration and society, shaking the foundations on which the unity, and indeed, the existence of the empire depended.

Such a challenge could not be taken lightly. As early as 81-96 CE, during the reign of Domitian, Christianity was clearly seen as a danger and formal steps were taken to ensure that its spread among the Roman citizens was suppressed. Although no special laws were passed against Christians, their activities were closely monitored by Roman authorities. They were branded them "atheists" for their refusal to worship the Roman gods, and the authorities classified them as members of a subversive sect.[18] They were collectively charged with "hatred for the human race" (*odium humani generis*).[19] Their rights as citizens of the empire were effectively revoked and could only be restored by a public confession of and sacrifice to the Roman gods.

Within the Roman judicial system Christians were condemned to the worst forms of punishment which were execution by crucifixion, *crematio* (burning) and *damnatio ad bestias* (condemnation to the beasts), or a combination of these.[20]

---

[16] Wright, *The New Testament and the People of God*, pp. 347-48; Koester, *Introduction to the New Testament*, Vol. 1, p. 371; Hastings et al (eds.), *Dictionary of the Apostolic Church*, Vol. II., p. 176.

[17] Hastings et al (eds.) *Dictionary of the Apostolic Church*, Vol. II., p. 17.

[18] Wright, *The New Testament and the People of God*, pp. 347-48; Hastings et al (eds.), *Dictionary of the* Apostolic Church, Vol. II., p. 176. Cf. Helmut Koester, *Introduction to New Testament, History and Literature of Early Christianity*, Vol. 2, New York & Berlin: Walter de Gruyter, 1982, p. 347.

[19] Hastings et al (eds.), *Dictionary of the Apostolic Church*, Vol. II, p. 17.

[20] Coleman, "Fatal Charades", pp. 55-56.

These types of punishment applied to the *humiliores*, a category of people with low status, usually "slaves and other persons without *dignitas*,"[21] like prisoners of war and worst criminals. In preparing for these executions, careful planning, effort and resources were spent to ensure the highest possible sensational gaze from the public. This was especially important for state-sponsored spectacles because the quality and level of sensation in the public gaze was directly related to the decrease or the "increase of status and popularity" of the Emperor himself. It was a symbolic show of Roman imperial power.[22] To ensure that such sensation is cultivated and sustained in the public gaze the victims were humiliated and degraded, on stage, in any possible way, and were subjected to brutal treatment to increase suspense in the gazing public, and thus make the victims' suffering as spectacular, violent and "enjoyable" as possible. It was held that only such a sensational spectacle could sufficiently reflect the glory of the empire and provide public entertainment worthy of the loyal subjects.

Since the legal system created a social gap between the condemned victims of the arena and society, such dehumanizing treatment of the victims did not appear to be offensive to notions of propriety. "So effective was the gulf created between spectacle and spectators that the dominant reaction among the audience was pleasure rather than revulsion."[23]

When we recall that the Roman society attributed every disaster and misfortune to Christian atheism[24] and every fortune to their gods and that they gazed at the Christian martyrs through such lens, we realize that the gulf between them and the Christian martyrs was even wider than it was between them and the common

---

[21] *Ibid.*, p. 57.

[22] *Ibid.* pp. 51, 54. Christopher A. Frilingos, *Spectacles of Empire, Monsters, Martyrs, and the Book of Revelation*, Philadelphia: University of Pennsylvania Press, 2004, p.36 observes that the emperor was the most visible parsonage in the arena and that his name was synonymous with Roman civilization itself. His benevolence was even acknowledged by the gods: " Even the gods, looking down, could not help but be impressed with the emperor." In the arena, just as in the imperial cult, his honour is at stake.

[23] *Ibid.*, p. 49.

[24] This is well reflected in Tertullian's summary of the Roman attitude: " They think the Christians to blame for every public calamity, for every loss that afflicts people. If the Tiber rises to the walls, if the Nile does not rise over the fields, if the sky gives no rain, if the earth quakes, if there is famine or plague, immediately the shout is raised, 'To the lions with the Christians!'" (*Apol.*, 40), quoted in Hastings et al (eds.), *Dictionary of the Apostolic Church*, Vol. II, p. 179. Although Tertullian is writing late in the history of the early church, his sentiments do reflect the Roman view against Christians from early times. Cf. Young , *In Procession before the World*, p. 6.

criminals. Their gaze upon the suffering and dying martyrs is not only a gaze of contempt and hatred. It is also a gaze of total condemnation. It is a gaze that befits a class of people who are not worthy of a place in the empire and its society, and even in life. The question, however, remains. Does this kind of gaze, through its political, social and religious lens, justify the culture of martyrdom which caused untold suffering and persisted for so long?

Christians under the Power of the Public Gaze

Whether by historical accident or political scheming, martyrdom became a reality which Christians had to face, endure and explain in light of their faith and experiences under the Roman public gaze. What did it mean for a Christian to be condemned and to die as a martyr in the arena under the piercing Roman public gaze? A study of early Christian documents indicates that Christians gazed at the arena through their own lens, and interpreted the dramatic end of the martyr's life in their own way. It is the meaning and significance they attached to this dramatic moment, not shared by their Roman counterparts, which explains the manner in which they responded to martyrdom, to the stunning surprise of the Roman society. In our attempt to understand the Christian version of the public gaze, we shall focus on a contemporary text, *The Martyrdom of Perpetua*.

In the preface to the text, Tertullian[25] offers a theological justification for preserving the accounts of the martyrs, arguing that they equally testify to God's grace and are just as edifying as ancient accounts of heroic faith. He indicates that the raising up of martyrs, and the revelations through visions given to them is a sure indication that God raised them "for a testimony to unbelievers, and to believers for a benefit." Tertullian, therefore "declares" the martyr's public testimony so that, in addition to those who personally witnessed the martyr's suffering and death, "you who know them by report may have communion with the blessed martyrs, and through them with the Lord Jesus Christ." The reader of the martyr's story is invited to share in the experience of the martyr.[26]

---

[25] Any discussion of the historical authenticity of the text lies beyond the scope of this study. As literature, however, the text is a fairly accurate reflection of the social, political and religious world in which it was produced. While the historical value of specific points in the text may be doubted, the text presents broadly an outline of a martyr's experience in the social world of the early church in which martyrdom was a living reality.

[26] Elizabeth Castelli has noted this intended function of the martyrdom texts. Castelli observes that there is "a desire to situate contemporary readers/hearers in continuous relation to events of the distant and more recent past in which divine activity has touched human existence directly." Elizabeth Castelli, "Visions and Voyeurism: Holy Women and the Politics of Site in Early Christianity", in Christopher Ocker (ed.), *Protocol of the Colloquy of the*

Young's thesis that there was Christian training for would-be martyrs[27] on how to view the challenge of martyrdom seems to be vindicated by the text. Young has argued that the role of such instruction would be to provide them with a religious understanding of what it meant for a Christian martyr to be under the gaze of the Roman public in the arena. The martyr had to see herself/himself as a "public liturgical sacrifice."[28] They needed to see themselves as a Eucharistic sacrifice whose death would provide testimony to non-believers and communion to believers, and through them experience divine communion with Christ. They understood themselves as possessing the fullness of the Spirit and the power to transmit revelations through visions. They also imagined themselves engaged in a cosmic struggle in which the real enemy was Satan himself, with their persecutors serving only as human instruments. In them was the very manifestation of the presence of God.[29] Martyrdom is turned into an eschatological struggle. They saw their martyrdom as a consummation of their love for God, a passionate love expressed in almost erotic terms.[30] Death in the arena for the martyr was also understood as a second baptism, a baptism of blood, an imagery drawn from the death of Christ and linked to the idea of sacrifice.

These religious ideas effectively prepared the martyr for the Roman gaze. The martyrdom of Perpetua is a clear reflection of these religious views. Soon after the arrest of Perpetua and the other martyrs, according to the narrative, they are taken for a water baptism. Shortly after baptism the Spirit brings a prescription to Perpetua: "In that same interval of a few days we were baptized, and to me the Spirit prescribed that in the water baptism nothing else was to be sought for bodily endurance."[31]

Center for Hermeneutical Studies, 6 December 1992, Berkeley: Center for Hermeneutical Studies, 1994, p. 9.

[27] Young, *In Procession Before the World*, p. 2.

[28] For a more detailed discussion of the idea of sacrifice as key to the understanding of martyrdom to both Christians and Romans, as well as the "manly" participation of early Christian women in the church's struggle with martyrdom, see Castelli, *Martyrdom and Memory*, pp. 50-67.

[29] Young, *In Procession Before the World*, pp. 10-11.

[30] Castelli, "Visions and Voyeurism", pp. 11, 14. Also Daniel Boyarin, *Dying for God, Martyrdom and the Making of Christianity and Judaism*, Stanford, CA: Stanford University Press, 1999, pp. 95, 107. For a discussion of the erotic tendencies associated with the arena and other public spaces among the spectators, see Frilingos, *Spectacles of Empire*, p. 35f.

[31] Tertullian, *The Passsion of the Holy Martyrs, Perpetua and Felicitas*, I.2, trasl. Roberts and Donaldson, earlychristianwritings.com.

About half of the narrative space of this text is a narration of visions, not events in the story. By emphasizing the visions of the martyrs,[32] the narrator is arguing, in a narrative way, that the Spirit of God who provided a prescription to Perpetua soon after her water baptism is present and working through the martyrs. It is the Spirit who enables them to function as channels of divine revelation through the visions. This provides divine authentication to their witness and therefore justifies the telling of the martyrs' story as witness to God's grace in Christ their Lord.

Through the visions, it is revealed that Perpetua as a would-be martyr has powers to intercede, even for the dead. She prays for her long dead brother, Dinocrates, and in a vision sees him "in a state of heavenly bliss" having been "translated from the place of punishment." Through the rest of the visions, the Spirit confirms to them that their arrest will end in martyrdom, that they will be able to face the challenge victoriously to the very end, and that a world of heavenly bliss, where other martyrs are, is awaiting them.[33]

Therefore, equipped with strong religious convictions regarding the meaning and significance of a martyr's death, Perpetua and her friends are prepared for the Roman public gaze in the arena. As they are paraded into the arena, they stage a final act of defiance to the imperial power and its religious systems by refusing to dress in costumes that are symbolic and suggestive of the Roman gods. In a dramatic twist, the young women are stripped and clothed with nets. Exposed as they are, they are led into the arena. As they boldly walk in, "the populace shuddered as they saw one young woman of delicate frame, another with breasts still dropping from her recent childbirth."[34] The mighty piercing gaze of the Roman people can no longer stand the sight. It breaks down. Only the martyrs' gaze remains.[35] The women are called back.

---

[32] Herbert Musurillo (transl.), *The Acts of Christian Martyrs*, Oxford: Clarendon Press, 1972, sees in this emphasis a reflection of the apocalyptic character of the narrative, comparable to the Book of Revelation in the New Testament, a feature he thinks historically suggests an association with the Montanists in the ancient churh of North Africa (p. xxvi).

[33] *Ibid..*, I.3; III. 1-2; IV.1-3.

[34] *Ibid.*, VI.3.

[35] Frilingos sees the reference to the exposure of the women's bodies in the narrative as a weakness, suggesting, "little or no interest in protecting the martyr's body from death and desire" (p. 83). Contrary to this view, it seems to me that it is this very exposure of the bodies to the insatiable gaze of the Roman people that becomes an instrument for breaking it. When we recall that the gaze is a symbol of power in the context of the arena, then we are likely to conclude that rather than being a weakness, the narrator is, at this very point, portraying the victory of the martyr in very strong narrative terms.

Here we have two opposing religious societies, each with its own public gaze. Young describes a similar clash: "The speakers in the ensuing dialogue were utterly at odds, giving voice to opposing religious societies. These voices could only clash because they represent two distinct societies' divergent sacrificial systems ... Each sacrificial system left no room for the other."[36]

Young is describing legal proceedings concerning a group of Christians before the governor, Vigellius Saturninus which took place in 180 CE. If we substitute "viewers" for "speakers", "scene" for "dialogue," and "gaze(s)" for "voice(s)," the description portrays the clash between the Christian and the Roman gaze in the arena in a very perceptive way.

The final scene in the narrative emphasizes further the clash of the opposing gazes. "And when the populace called for them into the midst, that as the sword penetrated into their *body* they might make their *eyes* partners in the murder, they rose up *of their own accord*, and transferred themselves *whither* the people wished."[37]

The language of "body," "eyes" and voluntary relocation here puts further the opposing gazes into sharp relief. Each of the two sides is critically aware of the role of the public gaze and tries to make use of it in accordance with what each side sees depending on the kind of lens they are using as we saw earlier. As the story and the narrative ends, the public gaze lingers on in the minds of both the characters in the story and the reader. It bears witness to both. But what kind of witness is derived from the power of the gaze in the arena? The question takes us back to where we started our discussion, and the answer lies with the one who does the *seeing*.

Conclusion

From our discussion it has become clear that the public gaze in the arena is a central feature in the culture of martyrdom. It has also become clear that each side looks at the public gaze and understands its significance in light of its own symbolic meanings as shaped by the various participating institutions. The question of who sees what in the public gaze depends on who does the seeing and what institution provides the lens for that seeing. Readers may ask themselves what they see in this public gaze and even ponder on the kinds of lens they are putting on as they do the seeing. In the approach we took in our discussion, it was assumed that one way of looking at this public gaze, one type of lens one may put on, so to speak, is to understand the social, political and religious perceptions of the Roman society and the church. These seem to provide the lens through which each of the participating groups in the public gaze does their seeing.

---

[36] Young, *In Procession Before the World*, p. 1.
[37] Tertullian, *The Passion of Holy Martyrs, Perpetua and Felicitas*, VI. 4. Emphasis mine.

Chapter Thirteen
Ritual and Symbolism as a Hermeneutical Approach

Introduction

The study of the New Testament which was previously dominated by philosophical, historical and literary approaches is now coming more and more under the influence of sociological and anthropological methods. New Testament scholars are now turning to the study of the Mediterranean world in search for clues that would enhance our understanding of the world in which Jesus lived.[1] It is now generally understood that the culture of the ancient Mediterranean world would be similar to the cultures of traditional societies who are currently the object of anthropological inquiry. Within the wide range of issues that provide material for this inquiry, the phenomenon of ritual and symbolism takes a central place as a window to the understanding of cultural dynamics in traditional societies.

In this chapter I will focus on the contributions of Victor Turner, Clifford Geertz and Talal Asad. Each of them offers new perspectives through which we can understand ritual and symbolism within the wider context of culture.

---

[1] The need for a sociological approach to Biblical Studies was recognized long ago. Max Weber's *Ancient Judaism*, transl. and ed. by Hans H. Gerth and Don Martindale, New York: The Free Press; London: Collier Macmillan, 1952, 1967, whose chapters first appeared in 1917-1919, is a clear demonstration of this interest. More recently, some members of the Jesus Seminar have turned to anthropological studies of the Mediterranean world of the New Testament era in an attempt to understand the historical Jesus. In a book on the historical Jesus, John Dominic Crossan, a member of the Jesus Seminar, devotes almost half of the study to anthropological issues of the ancient Mediterranean world before moving to an examination of Jesus himself in the last half of his *The Historical Jesus, The Life of a Mediterranean Jewish Peasant*, New York: HarperCollins, 1992, pp. 1-224, 225-466. For a critical review of the Jesus Seminar project see Birger A. Pearson's chapter on the Jesus Seminar in his *The Emergence of Christian Religion, Essays on Early Christianity*, Harrisburg, PA..,: Trinity Press International, 1997, pp. 23-57. For his view on the social science methods as the principal approaches used by the Jesus Seminar, see ibid., especially p. 30.

Turner, Ritual and Symbolism

Turner's work on ritual and symbolism is significant both in terms of the methodology he used and the conceptual contributions he made toward a fresh understanding of this cultural phenomenon.

Turner's Methodology

Methodologically, Turner departs from the general trend of his predecessors like van Gennep, Durkheim and Weber who attempted to arrange cultural practice by making universal generalizations. Turner argued from specific data particularly from his own findings from his research among the Ndembu people.[2] Turner also sought to understand his data in light of the people's own interpretation of the observed phenomenon. In this way Turner attempted to minimize the gap in the meaning attributed to cultural phenomena by traditional performers themselves and the observing theorist.[3] Turner also succeeds in his methodological approach by avoiding overlaying his theoretical constructions with philosophical or "theological" assumptions.[4]

His theoretical positions are mainly supported by empirical data from a research done on a specific people group, the Ndembu. Turner also approaches his task with a recognition of the complexity of any cultural phenomenon, and collapses the divide between the "simple" traditional cultures and the "complex" technologically developed cultures of the developed world.[5] In adopting this perspective, Turner departs from a philosophical assumption which most scholars took for granted. It is, therefore, not surprising to note that his critics accused him of "blurring important differences between simple and complex societies."[6] Turner is further able to relate the findings both to general theory and to wider society. This is particularly clear with his concept of *communitas*. It is generally acknowledged that his development and application of the theoretical concept of *communitas* constitutes a major contribution to the field of anthropology.

Theoretical Contribution

In his development of the concept of *communitas*, Turner builds on the work of earlier scholars, particularly Arnold van Gennep. Van Gennep's seminal

---

[2] Victor Turner, *The Ritual Process, Structure and Anti-structure*, New Brunswick (US) and London (UK): Aldine Transaction, 1969, 1997, p. xi.
[3] Ibid. pp. 9, 11, 86.
[4] Ibid. p., 4.
[5] Ibid. p., 3.
[6] Ibid. p., ix.

contribution is his recognition and discussion of the "rites of passage" which he simply defines as "the ceremonial patterns which accompany a passage from one situation to another or from one cosmic or social world to another."[7] Van Gennep managed to establish that the universal phenomenon of ritual is constituted by three subcategories: the rites of separation, the rites of transition and the rites of incorporation; subcategories also known as preliminal, liminal and postliminal rites of passage.[8] In his concluding chapter, van Gennep observes that "an individual is placed in various sections of society, synchronically and in succession; in order to pass from one category to another and to join individuals in other sections, he must submit, from the day of his birth to that of his death, to ceremonies whose forms often vary but whose function is similar."[9] To argue his case, van Gennep has attempted a classification of these "rites" into three main categories. Although his book is dated in certain respects, his treatment of the subject remains a classical one.

Of the three stages for the rites of passage, it is the liminal stage that provides Turner an entry into his work. Building on van Gennep's work, Turner develops the theory of the liminal stage extensively and from it arises his own concept of *communitas* which is then related to society in general. In this way Turner contributes to anthropological theory. The concept of *communitas* helps us understand certain kinds of social phenomena.

Van Gennep had shown that the first phase of the rites of passage involves symbolic behaviour that emphasizes separation of the neophyte from society. In the second phase the neophyte is in a state in which his or her social position and obligations are suspended or ambiguous. It is a delicate stage in which former social roles are left behind, and the future roles are yet to begin. The third phase involves symbolic behaviour that emphasizes integration. The ritual subject is now restored to society and placed in a new social position with obligations and responsibilities applicable to the new status.

Operating from this theoretical basis, Turner seeks to explore its implications on society and culture. He observes that society has two major models which are structure and *communitas*. He describes *communitas* largely in terms of features of the liminal state. Structure is defined in terms of: "society as a structured, differentiated, and of the hierarchical system of politico-legal-economic positions with many types of evaluation, separating men in terms of 'more' or 'less.'"[10] *Communitas* is defined as: "society as an unstructured or rudimentarily structured and relatively undifferentiated ... community or even communion of equal

---

[7] Arnold van Gennep, *The Rites of Passage*, University of Chicago Press, 1960, p. 10.
[8] Ibid., pp. 10-11.
[9] Ibid., p. 189.
[10] Turner, *The Ritual Process*, p.96.

individuals who submit together to the general authority of the ritual leaders."[11] From this extended understanding of the liminal phase as *communitas*, Turner is now able to explore its implications in wider society.

From the principle of alternating states in the rites of passage, Turner observes that social life is a dialectical process that involves high and low[12] throughout a lifetime as a person passes through this process. Moments of power and moments of powerlessness alternate. To get to the next level of social structure or social power, an individual must pass through a status of powerlessness. He or she has to lay aside previous social roles and responsibilities in order to take up new and more important ones. In this way, society controls who gets power and when they do get it.

By observing the ritual power of the inferior social subjects (not the neophytes), those who have less power within the social structure during the liminal stage of the rites of passage, Turner notices how the balance of power is achieved in a traditional society. By investing ritual power in socially and politically less powerful individuals, the reigns of power are brought under communal or social control, for the benefit of society as a whole.[13] Through this control of ritual power, less powerful members of society gain authority to criticize those in social and political power, and thus influence social and political decisions for the common good. Turner draws illustrations from not only the Ndembu people he studied but also from other regions around the globe. In this way, Turner shows clearly the universality of the phenomenon.[14]

Turner also notices that "transitional qualities" that find expression in the rites of passage in traditional society are not lacking in the industrial world. Rather, they are institutionalized. He further finds that the qualities of the "liminal" status that give rise to *communitas* are present in wider societies or social groups like the hippies of the 1960s.[15]

His comparison of the liminal status to the unstable social situations that give rise to such social groups is particularly interesting. In the African situation, for example, the democratic dispensation that swept across the continent since 1989 created a situation of "communitas" as the old social-political values that held society crumbled. Lack of a common structured basis in terms of social-political values has led to the rise of a new wave of extremist social-political groups who

---

[11] Ibid.

[12] Ibid., p. 97.

[13] Another way in which this principle is inculcated into the neophytes, especially leaders-in-the-making, is by subjecting then to physical discomfort so that they become aware that ultimate power belongs to society at large. See Ibid. pp. 103-04.

[14] Ibid. pp. 100-03

[15] Ibid. pp. 110-13.

value their own political ideologies as supreme. The conflict in Africa and other areas of the developing world is mainly a result of conflicting ideologies that can best be understood in terms of Turner's *communitas* cultural theory.

A Critical Assessment

While Turner's positive conceptual contribution to ritual theory and its implication to wider society deserves recognition, his methodology appears to be weak in certain respects. First, Turner reflects too much dependency on his extensive research on a single people group. If he replicated his study in other traditional societies, would the findings be the same? How would differences affect his theoretical analysis, one wonders. Second, the strategy of soliciting what he calls the "Ndembu inside view" and the impact of that view on his theoretical analysis do not seem to be fully developed in his study. He seems to be more interested in shaping his theoretical analysis to conform to the general theoretical framework constructed by more generalized studies of his predecessors and contemporaries. A third weakness is that his emphasis on the Ndembu practice of seeking meaning from etymological analysis of terms does not seem very helpful since word meanings do change over time and in new contexts, making original meanings unstable and sometimes irrelevant to a new situation. The problem of meaning in ritual and symbolism which we have noted here in relation to Turner's methodological procedure leads us to a consideration of the works of Clifford Geertz and Talaal Asad.

Geertz, Asad and Meaning in Ritual and Symbolism

To understand Asad's severe criticism of the cultural theories that suggest that ritual symbols represent meaning that lies outside the symbolic behaviour itself, and his attack on Geertz, one needs to be aware of the dichotomous treatment of meaning and its symbolic representation that pervades much scholarly work and is clearly represented in the work of Clifford Geertz.[16] By attacking Geertz, Asad seeks to highlight what he sees as a methodologically fundamental weakness in ritual and symbolism studies.

In his approach to the study of culture, Geertz sees ritual as a means for understanding the cultural world of a particular people. He understands culture as "historically transmitted patterns of meanings embodied in symbols, a system of inherited conceptions expressed in symbolic forms by means of which men communicate, perpetuate and develop their knowledge about and attitudes towards

---

[16] In the critical discussion of Geertz's theory that follows, I am mainly dependent on Catherine Bell's assessment in her *Ritual Theory Ritual Practice*, New York and Oxford: Oxford University Press, 1996.

life"[17] A symbol is "any object, act event, quality or relation which serves as a vehicle for a conception—the conception is the symbol's meaning."[18] Basically, therefore, in Geertz' view the symbolic representation is different and separate from the conceptual meaning it points to. What is significant for us is that this dichotomy between symbolic dispositions and the conceptual meaning they represent underlies the whole theoretical structure that governs almost all studies that seek to understand ritual as a springboard for a broader understanding of a particular culture.

In her seminal work, Bell has attempted an analysis of this fundamental dichotomy in ritual studies, not only as undertaken by Geertz but also as conducted by other scholars of culture. Bell has clearly shown that there is a fundamental dichotomy at each of the three layers of the theoretical approach that Geertz adopts and develops, and that this fundamental dichotomy affects the nature of meaning that is constructed at the end of the process through which cultural meaning is constructed.

At the first level of the theoretical structure is the state of dichotomy itself. This is the basic theoretical separation between thought and action in the ritual process.[19] In Geertz' definition of culture and symbol quoted above, it is clear that Geertz posits a dichotomy between conceptions or the symbols' meaning and the symbols themselves. The symbols act as "vehicle for a conception—the conception (being) the symbols' meaning."[20] Geertz further explains these contradictory aspects by using such terms as "ethos" and "world view."[21] Ethos represents the "dispositional" dimension. These are the activities that constitute the ritual process. They include "the moral (and aesthetic) aspects of a given culture, the evaluative elements,"[22] and every activity in the ritual process that constitutes a "vehicle" for conceptual meaning.[23] Bell correctly observes that ethos as an activity is understood as secondary, in its relative significance, to "world view" in Geertz' theoretical framework.[24] If "ethos" is to "action" on the action-thought fundamental dichotomy, "worldview" is to "thought," signifying the higher plane of conceptual perception. Indeed, Geertz defines "worldview" as "cognitive, existential aspects" of the ritual process. This is the conception of complex symbolic meanings to which ethos as

---

[17] Clifford Geertz, *The Interpretation of Cultures, Selected Essays by Clifford Geertz*, New York: Perseus Books Group, 1973, p. 89.
[18] Idid., p. 91.
[19] For a more detailed discussion, see Bell, *Ritual Theory Ritual Practice*, pp. 30-31.
[20] Geertz, *The Interpretation of Cultures*, p. 91.
[21] For a detailed discussion of these terms, see Ibid., pp. 126-41, especially pp. 126-27.
[22] Ibid., p. 126.
[23] Ibid. pp. 89-92.
[24] Bell, *Ritual Theory Ritual Practice*, p. 31.

activity points, "a fund of general meanings in terms of which each individual interprets his experience and organizes his conduct."[25] Thus, the first weakness in Geertz' theoretical approach is the irreconcilable dichotomy between the dispositional symbols and their conceptual representations.

The second layer of Geertz' theoretical framework suggests that the ritual process has a synthetic function. Ritual is seen as a functional mechanism for reintegrating the thought-action dichotomy of the first layer of the theoretical framework. Geertz writes: "sacred symbols function to synthesize a people's ethos-the tone, character, and quality of their life, its moral and aesthetic style and mood-and their worldview - the picture they have of the way things in sheer actuality are, their most comprehensive ideas of order."[26] Thus Geertz sees in the ritual process a convergence of "ethos" and "worldview" or dispositions and concepts. This convergence leads to a kind of resolution of the basic action-thought dichotomy[27] that underlies the whole theoretical framework. In Geertz' theoretical framework both the dichotomous character of the dispositions and concepts, and their resolution in ritual, although temporarily, are fundamental.

Bell obverses that this theoretical framework in which the ritual process is both an activity and a mechanism for integrating thought and action or activity necessitates the introduction of a third structure into the theoretical framework, "one in which the dichotomy underlying a thinking theorist and an acting actor is simultaneously affirmed and resolved."[28]

The introduction of the theorist-scholar into the basic structure of the theoretical framework further perpetuates the basic thought-action dichotomy and complicates the process of meaning construction. The construction of meaning becomes dialectic and ambiguous. Indeed this ambiguity is also reflected in the other layers of theoretical structure due to the dialectic nature of the ritual process itself as both activity and "fusion" and hence convergence or resolution of the thought-action dichotomy.

The consequence of this ambiguity is the construction of meaning in two fundamentally different ways.[29] Since the ritual process offers convergence of the dichotomous dispositions (ethos) and concepts (worldview), and also functions as an "activity," it offers the theorist-scholar the necessary materials for meaning construction. The theorist brings the concepts with him or her and views the ritual process as a dispositional activity. Equipped with a conceptual framework of his or

---

[25] Geertz, *The Interpretation of Cultures*, p. 127
[26] Ibid., p. 89.
[27] Bell, *Ritual Theory Ritual Practice*, p. 27.
[28] Ibid., p. 31.
[29] Ibid., p. 28.

her own, and the ritual process as an activity, he or she observes, the dichotomy of the dispositions and concepts collapses and she or he is able to perceive and construct meaning out of the symbolic systems being enacted in the ritual in light of his or her own conceptual framework as a theorist.[30] This then becomes the scholarly authoritative meaning that becomes available to the academia.

Another form of meaning is constructed by the ritual actors themselves as their own worldview and ethos converge in the same ritual process. Here, the ritual process is not merely an activity as is the case in the previous model of meaning construction. The process is here seen as an integrating mechanism for the ritual participants' own ethos and worldview, and thus equally offering them the necessary dispositions and conceptual tools for meaning construction, just as it is the case with the previous model of meaning construction.

In Geertz' theoretical approach, therefore, the construction of meaning becomes ambiguous and problematic, although the meaning constructed by the theorist model is usually not only accepted in academia but also rendered authoritative. Although Geertz seems to acknowledge the limitations of the theorist model of meaning construction in that the scholar may not sufficiently penetrate into the ritual performers' own worldview.[31]

The subtle assumption behind the choice between the two forms of meaning probably remains what Durkheim suggested long ago that the "primitive," as we might call the ritual performers, "think like a child."[32] Therefore the meaning they construct can safely be rejected or neglected by scholarly minds.

It is in the context of such persistently dichotomous character in Geertz' theoretical approach to culture studies, an approach which is embraced by many other scholars, that Talaal Asad's criticism needs to be understood. It is clear that the introduction of the theorist-scholar into the basic structure of Geertz' theoretical approach, and the acknowledgement of the limitations that inevitably face the theorist in the process of meaning construction exposes a major weakness in the whole theoretical approach.

Asad, therefore, seeks to show that the choice of meaning construction model that favours the theorist's meaning needs also to fully account for the "actors" meaning, drawn from the ritual process in which their own "ethos" and "worldview"

---

[30] Ibid., pp. 31-2
[31] Geertz, *The Interpretation of Cultures*, pp. 113-14. Bell, *Ritual Theory Ritual Practice*, p. 28, also observes that the theorist-scholar can construct meaning "in so far as he or she can perceive in ritual the true basis of its meaningfulness for the ritual actors."
[32] Emile Durkheim, *The Elementary Forms of Religious Life*, transl. Carol Cosman, Oxford: Oxford University Press, 2001, p. 51.

converge.³³ To achieve such a balance in meaning construction, Asad suggests that such terms as "local people" with reference to ritual performers or research subjects do suggest and encourage the existing imbalance in the power to construct meaning. The "local" are "primitive," "simple" and consequently powerless to meaningfully share in the construction of meaning for their own culture. Asad argues that scholars need to be constantly aware of the subtle power that they hold in this relationship and how that power affects the process of meaning construction.³⁴

The main focus of Asad's criticism against Geertz' theoretical approach is the thought-action dichotomy which pervades the whole of Geertz' theoretical framework. Asad particularly objects to the separation between symbol and its meaning.³⁵

He also argues that this meaning which is, for him, inseparable from the symbol, must be constructed in light of the prevailing historical and cultural context. Asad, in this way, argues against the fundamental dichotomy which lies at the heart of Geertz' approach, namely, the dichotomy between symbol as activity and conceptions as meaning; the privileged role of the theorist in the construction of meaning, and the use of the theorist's external conceptual framework to the neglect of the cultural context, best represented by the worldview of the performers themselves.³⁶ Despite its sharp criticism, therefore, Asad's engagement with Geertz' theoretical framework does highlight areas in the theory that call for reconsideration.

Conclusion

In conclusion, it is significant to note that the three scholars discussed in this chapter, Turner, Geertz and Asad, have all made significant contributions to the study of anthropology. Turner's insistence on basing theories on specific results from intensive field work rather than making generalizations is a recommendable effort. His most noticeable contribution, however, is his concept of *communitas* which does help us understand certain cultural phenomena even outside the ritual

---

[33] For a discussion on the need to account for the social-historical context in which a particular ritual is performed, in order to determine its meaning, see =Talal Asad, *Genealogies of Religion, Discipline and Reasons of Power in Christianity and Islam*, Baltimore and London: John Hopkins University Press, 1993, pp., 29, 31, 52-54.

[34] For a discussion on how the subtle authoritative power of the theorist affects the construction of meaning, see Asad, *Genealogies of Religion*, pp. 34-39.

[35] Ibid., pp. 31-32, 43-44, 130.

[36] For a discussion on the problem of translating information from the culture of anthropological inquiry into the language of scholarship where the theorist must construct meaning based on observation, but without much background regarding the conceptual world in which a particular ritual was performed, see Asad, *Genealogies of Religion*, pp. 171-99.

context. Although Geertz' theory for culture research does have fundamental weaknesses resulting from its dichotomous character, it is still, to my knowledge, the best model that attempts to fully account for both action and meaning. Asad's merit lies in his pointing out the weaknesses that we find in Geertz' model, especially as it relates to the one-sided dependence in the process of meaning construction, namely, its over-dependence on the theorist-scholar, paying little regard to the challenges that even limit the scholar's ability to construct meaning that would fully account for the original ritual context. Asad, however, does not offer us a satisfactory theoretical alternative. His suggestion that the distance between symbol and its representation be collapsed so that the two become inseparable does not seem to offer us a clear interpretive key to cultural phenomena. His insistence on the need to account fully for the local context in which ritual takes place is, nevertheless, highly commendable.

Although Bell's work is not a subject for our discussion in this chapter, like Asad, Bell shows us the fundamental problems inherent in Geertz' approach. However, her theory of ritualization seems to place too much emphasis on the "action" element of the action-thought dichotomy, and sees the construction of meaning as inherently fluid and unstable. In her theory, the whole question of searching for meaning collapses. There is no final meaning to look forward to. Bell asserts that "one is never confronted with 'the meaning' to accept or reject; one is always led into a redundant, circular, and rhetorical universe of values and terms whose significance keeps flowing into other values and terms."[37] Thus, for Bell, ritual does not point to meaning socially and historically constructed and preserved and pointed to through the ritual performance. Rather, each ritual performance is a creation of meaning, a process to which there is no end as meaning replaces meaning, value replaces value and term replaces term. In the end there is no meaning we would call "the meaning" for a particular ritual performance.

Despite the merits of Bell's theory, it fails to address the problem of meaning construction. Geertz' theory, despite its own weaknesses still offers a better theoretical framework for the construction of meaning for any particular ritual process.

---

[37] Bell, *Ritual Theory Ritual Practice*, p. 106. For a fuller discussion of her theory, see Ibid., pp. 94-117.

Chapter Fourteen
The Use of 'Hallelujah' (הללויה) and the Malawian Context

Introduction

The term "Hallelujah" is probably the most commonly used Christian expression in contemporary Christian evangelistic rallies. The term Hallelujah is from the Hebrew word "Hallelû Yāh" (הללויה)[1] and literally means "Praise Yah".[2] The "Yah" (יה) in the term is a short form for the name "Yahweh."[3] Other contracted forms for the name "Yahweh" found in the Old Testament are "Yahw," (יהו), "Yo" and "Yau".[4]

This chapter is an attempt to examine its Biblical significance and usage in the worshipping community of Israel and the implication of such usage in the history of the church with special focus on its use in contemporary Christianity, particularly in the Malawian context.

What is in the Name?

In Biblical times when peoples of the world worshipped both known and unknown gods[5] it was necessary for the worshipper to call upon a god by his or her name. This was done for at least two reasons: first, to establish a relationship between the worshipper and the god concerned.[6] The significance of a name in the ancient world becomes even clearer when one considers, for instance, the ancient Egyptian thought that "the name was the thing; the real object we separate from its designation was identical with it."[7] Secondly it was done as a way of revealing the nature and character of that particular deity. Therefore, to know and call upon the name of a

---

[1] See G.W. Anderson, "Psalms," *Peake's Commentary on the Bible*, London: Routledge, 1990, p. 430.
[2] See Ibid.
[3] See Bernard W. Anderson, *The Living World of the Old Testament*,. Essex: Longman, 1975, p. 61.
[4] See D.M.G. Stalker (1990), "Exodus," *Peake's Commentary on the Bible*, p. 212.
[5] Benhard W. Anderson points us to an excellent example of a Sumerian worshipper who offers a prayer to "any god and all gods, whether known or unknown" in his *The Living World of the Old Testament*, p. 60 by way of a footnote as he quotes from Pritchard's "Prayer to Every God" in his *Near Eastern Tests* (1), pp. 391-92.
[6] See Anderson, *The Living World of the Old Testament*, p. 60.
[7] See J.M. Roberts. *Penguin History of the World*, London: Penguin, 1990, p. 38.

god means, for the worshipper, to have access to a privileged relationship with a particular god in terms of the attributes of that deity as revealed in the name.[8]

A similar religious significance of the name of a deity is also generally found in Africa. The name of a deity usually suggests what that particular society conceives as being the character of a god. E.G. Parrinder in his *African Traditional Religion* observes that most African societies refer to the "Supreme Being" by using divine names which emphasize various aspects of his being, for instance, as a Creator. Other names would refer to his omnipotence. Yet still others would suggest his eternal being or his providential care for his people, the believing worshippers[9] Malawi is no exception in this regard. Each of the various Chichewa divine names, for example, also point to a specific divine attribute. For instance, the name "Mulungu" refers to the supreme Being as Creator. The name "Chisumphi" points to Him as one who hears and, therefore, answers the prayers of his people.[10] This supreme being was traditionally personified in "Make Wana," literary the "Mother of all," of the Nsinja cult.[11] "Leza," another divine name among the Chewa, refers to the loving care that his worshippers enjoy.

Just as in the Egyptian religious tradition previously referred to as well as the general African tradition with Malawi inclusive, the Israelites in the Old Testament times used a number of names when referring to the God of Israel with each name emphasizing a particular attribute of the deity. For instance, they used the name "Elohim" when they thought of him as the powerful God of creation and judgment.[12]

The names "El" and "Elyon" were used when they were thinking of his exalted nature as the "God Most High,"[13] a general divine title which would also be employed by Gentiles (Gen 14:18-20, Lk. 8:28). The name "Adonai" (אדני) was used when they thought of Him as the one who rules all people. However, the term has a wide range of meaning from "Lord" or "Master" through "Governor" and "Prince" to "King." But it is worthy to note that emphasis is on the "respect" and "authority" of

---

[8] See F.B. Huey Jr., *Exodus*,Grand Rapids: Zondervan, 1977, p. 29.

[9] For a discussion on some divine names and the divine attributes they stand for in some African religions see E.G. Parrinder, *African Traditional Religion, Third Edition,* London: Sheldon, 1974, pp. 33-43.

[10] See J.W.M. van Bruegel, *Chewa Traditional Religion*, Blantyre: CLAIM-Kachere, 2001, pp. 29-34.

[11] Ibid, pp. 45-50.

[12] See W.H. Griffith Thomas, *Genesis, A Devotional Commentary*.Grand Rapids: Kregel, 1988, pp. 63, 79.

[13] Ibid. p. 132.

the One addressed.[14] Thus, the God of Israel was a respected King whose authority is exercised over all peoples of the world.

Of interest to us here, however, is the name "Yahweh" (יהוה) which is found in the term "Hallelujah." (הללויה) The historical origin of this name still remains an inconclusive issue despite much scholarly efforts. There have been several explanations as to the origins of the name.[15]

Significance and Sovereign Character of the Name "Yahweh" (יהוה)

Etymologically, it is generally taken that the name "Yahweh" is derived from the Hebrew verb *hayah* which means "to be." In Exodus 3:14, we see *'ehyeh* being used. This is a simple first person form of the verb to be.

Therefore, the literal meaning of *'ehyeh* is "IAM" or "I Will Be." However, since beneath this present simple verb to be lies the older form with its causative connotation, the simple form can also be literally translated "He who Causes to Be" or "He Who will Cause to Be." The sacred *Tetra Grammato* YHWH (יהוה), is, therefore, derived from a third person singular of the verb "to be," meaning : "He Is" or "He Will Be"[16] or "He Causes to Be" or "He will Cause to Be." The third person singular form of the verb to be is used in Exodus 3:15 because Moses, when speaking to the Israelites, would say "He Is" has sent me, not "I AM" has sent me.

Theologically, there are a number of major views on what this revered name meant to Moses and the Israelites. An understanding of the theological significance of the name "Yahweh" is necessary. It is through the unique and exalted character of this name in the worshipping community of Israel that the expression "Hallelujah," in which there is a contracted form of this name, attains a highly exalted status.

Some scholars hold that the original meaning of the Hebrew root letters meant "to fall" or "to blow." In this view the meaning of the Hebrew simple verb "to be" would be "He Who Falls" or "He Who Blows."[17] In the causative form, then, the

---

[14] For a fuller treatmet of the meanings of the word "Adon" (or "Adonai") see H.B.P. Mijoga, "Some Biblical Terms as they have Come down to Us in Chichewa" in "*Religion of Malawi*," No. 2 Vol. 1 (1988), p. 28.

[15] For a discussion of the various explanations, see Anderson, *The Living World of the Old Testament*, =Essex: Longman, 1975, p. 65.

[16] Ibid. p. 62.

[17] See Stalker's "Exodus," *Peake's Commentary on the Bible*, p. 32. This view seems to be supported by Scriptures more readily. The God of Israel is usually associated by some ordinary natural aspects like clouds, lightning, wind. Thus, for instance, He is represented as coming in a thick cloud (Exodus 19:9) as causing lightning to fall to indicate his presence

root would mean "He Who Causes to Fall" or "He Who causes to Blow." If this view is correct then God of Israel is to be understood as one who powerfully intervenes in the natural phenomena and influences the course of events in the created order.

Another view centers on the causative nature of the verb "to be" as it particularly appears in its older form ("haway" (הוה) which in the first person takes the form *ahyeh* instead of the simple present first person verb to be *'ehyeh*. In this view, God of Israel is understood mainly in terms of his creative activity as distinctive from his participatory role in the creative order emphasized in the preceding view. Thus God is not only seen as One who intervenes and participates in the affairs of the created order but is also understood as the origin of all things. All natural phenomena and historical activity have their beginning and end in his will.[18] This view indicates that the God of Israel is not only the Lord of Nature but also the Creator of all things.

A third view regarding the meaning of the name is based on the simple present form of the verb to be, *'ehyeh*. The verb is understood in its active and dynamic sense with reference to the continued divine activity. Here, God is understood as performing all things "zealously" and "sovereignly" toward the achievement of his own purposes according to his own will. All that "happens" has its origin in him.[19]

The most significant Jewish understanding of the name revealed to Moses is, probably, the view which interprets the name not just in terms of God's creative power and his continued activity in sustaining the created order in nature and history. Rather, through the name God reveals himself as one who *will* always be with his people. His continued presence with his people is promised. It is, therefore, through this name that a covenant relationship is sealed and underlined. Israel is to understand God not as the great, impersonal God of the seemingly endless expanse of the universe. Israel is to understand him as *their* God. Through this covenant name Israel becomes a special people for God. Through the name Yahweh reveals himself as Israel's Personal and Living God who is both Creator and Saviour,

---

(Exodus 19:16; 2 Sam 22:15) and sending wind or causing wind to blow across the sea (Exodus 15:10). It must, however, be noted that in this view the God of Israel is not seen as a "nature god" who is himself part of and controlled by aspects of the created order like the fertility cults of the ancient world who had to die and resurrect annually in harmony with nature. Rather He is viewed as the "Lord of Nature."

[18] See Anderson, *The Living World of the Old Testament*, p. 63. Other scholars have rejected this view, asserting that the view is too advanced for the Mosaic period, drawing parallels from Egyptian, Babylonian and Canaanite religions. However, the fact that such understanding of a particular deity is not found in other religions does not necessarily prove that such a view could not exist in the Mosaic tradition, which, in many respects differed from other ancient religions.

[19] Ibid. p. 63.

making himself continuously known to his people in their experience throughout the ages.

It is significant, at this point, to discuss the sovereign character of the name "Yahweh." We have to note that once God revealed himself as the Personal God of the Israelite community(Exodus 3:13-15), he announced his divine freedom to act as he wills. Though he is their personal God he is not subject to human control or manipulation. This attribute of sovereignty is clearly stated in the context in which Moses demands the presence of God to accompany Israel (Exodus 33:12-23). While God promises his Presence to accompany Israel, he announces:

> "I will be gracious to whom I will be gracious and I will have compassion on whom I will have compassion" (Exodus 33:19).

But his divine freedom does not mean that he can act contrary to his will. "Since he is himself changeless and faithful to his nature they will find him ... in every situation and adequate to it."[20] He is not the god who is "capricious and whimsical... that he can or will suddenly change his mind (about the covenant he makes with his people)."[21] Thus, though he is beyond human control or manipulation by whatever means, he is faithful to his own promises and must be trusted.

In line with this divine sovereign character, God also warns Israel against any disrespectful use of his name and makes this point part of the "Ten Words" (Ten Commandments) given to Israel as a regulating factor for the newly established covenant relationship between him and Israel (Exodus 20;1-17).

The Third Commandment, which relates to the use of the covenant name of God:

> Is associated with profanity or any careless or irreverent use of God's name, but its implications go far beyond this limited interpretation. 'In vain' means 'groundless,' 'empty,' 'without basis' and includes any frivolous, insincere, or unjustified use of God's name. The command may be violated by profanity, by using God's name when there is no genuine faith or commitment... or to manipulate people.[22]

It is, therefore, clear that God expects his name, as revealed to Moses at the establishment of his covenant relationship with his people Israel, to be treated with great reverence and awe. It is not surprising that at the centre of his Being according to Israel's understanding was his sovereign character in holiness, in righteousness, in faithfulness, in power, in wisdom and in the rest of his attributes (1 Chro 29:11).

It is through his self-revelation in the name that God of Israel becomes unique and distinctive. He is not the "Supreme Being" of the pre-literary traditional peoples, the "sky divinity" who is an uninterested observer of human affairs and who is only

---

[20] See Stalker, "Exodus," *Peake's Commentary on the Bible*, p. 212.
[21] For a similar view see Alister McGrath, *Affirming Your Faith: Exploring the Apostle's Creed* (Leicester: InterVarsity, 1991) pp. 29-30.
[22] See F.B. Huey Jr., *Exodus*, Grand Rapids: Zondervan, 1977, p. 88.

worshiped when everything fails.[23] He is not "the one abstract, all-pervading reality" of the Hindu faith from whom the whole universe "emanates."[24] Neither is he the god who created and then left the universe to function on its own like an old watchmaker who made and wound a clock, then left it to run by itself, [25]=nor is the God of Israel the "Absolute Self" (Mind)" postulated by the philosophers.[26]

Thus, it will be observed that the way Israel uses the covenant and personal name of God will largely depend on her current understanding of the theological significance of the name itself.

The Use of the Term: "Hallelujah" (הללויה)

The interest here is to see how the term is used in the Bible, in the older Christian traditions, and in contemporary Christianity.

Biblical Usage of "Hallelujah" (הללויה)

The expression "Hallelujah" is frequently found in the Psalms. In pre-Christian writings the word appears in the Deutero-canonical book of Tobit 13:18. In the New Testament it appears only in Rev 19:1-6 where it occurs four times.

In the Book of Psalms there are three main groups of Psalms which use the expression "Hallelujah." In fact the names of their categorical groupings are derived from the term. The first group is called the "Egyptian Hallel" and consists of Psalms 113-118. These celebrate God's power and redeeming grace shown in the redemption of Israel from Egypt.

The second group is simply referred to as the "Hallel." They praise God for his various divine activities like his readily available help to the needy who trust in him, his providence, his creation, his salvation for his people and his judgment over his enemies. This group also includes summons to praise him for all things. The group includes Psalms 146-150.

---

[23] For this understanding of God see Edward G. Nowing, "Religions of Pre-literary Societies" in Norman Anderson (ed), *The World's Religions* (Leicester: InterVarsity, 1975) p. 38.

[24] For a thorough treatment of this concept of God (Brahman), advanced by the Vedanta philosophical school of Hinduism, see Bruce J. Nicholls, "Hinduism," in Anderson (ed), *The World's Religions*, pp. 141-142.

[25] For this view of God which was very popular in the 18th century, see McGrath, *Affirming your Faith*, p. 34.

[26] For a thorough discussion on the philosophical view of God as the "Absolute Self (or Mind)," see Georgie R. Knight, *Philosophy & Education: An Introduction in Christian Perspective* (=Michigan: Andrew University, 1989) pp. 47-48.

The third group which employs the term "Hallelujah" is known as the "Great Hallel." There are differences among scholars with regard to the composition of this group. Some scholars include Psalms 135-136, others include Psalms 120-136, while others only recognize Psalms 136 as the Great Hallel.

If the suggestion that Psalms 120-136 were used by the Jews going to attend one of the annual festivals (the Passover, the Feast of Harvest and the Pentecost) in addition to the New Year Festival and the Day of Atonement, at a central sanctuary which later became Jerusalem, is correct, then the term could as well date back to the Israelite Tribal Confederacy period. In this case the "Hallelujah" Psalms together with the "Yahwistic-Davidic" Psalms of Book One (Psalms 1 - 41) and the "Yahwistic" Psalms (Psalms 84-89) would be among the earliest Psalms.

This then would indicate that the expression "Hallelujah" in the context of worship was often employed during the early period of Israel's Temple worship. Possibly, this trend continued to the days of Isaiah of Jerusalem before the sacred name was withdrawn from common language, for Prophet Isaiah used a contracted form of the sacred name, "Yah" (יה) (Isaiah 26:4) ,though he preferred the title "Holy One of Israel."

In the Psalms then the term is used in the following ways:

1. When the community of worship adores the majesty and glory and splendor of the Person of God Himself. They sing the Hallels and shout "Hallelujah" as they meditate upon the greatness of God in wonder and awe.

2. When the worshipping community recalls the mighty works of God. These would include the wonders of creation, the salvation of his people from Egypt, the destruction of the Egyptian army at the Red Sea, God's provisions of food during the Exodus, the provision of the Mosaic Law, his leading role in the wars of establishment in Canaan, the establishment of kingship and the everlasting promises to David.

3. When the community of faith, on behalf of the whole nation, cries out to God for help in times of national disasters like invasions by foreign armies, famine, plagues, death of a prominent king and many more. At such times the term could be employed in the context of communal prayers of lament.

Thus, in Psalms, the term is being used by the faithful in the context of solemn worship as they pour out their shouts of joy for who God is and what he had done, and as they express their deep sorrow for the suffering situation they would be in.

Just as the name "Yahweh" was withdrawn from common language out of reverence for its holy character during the period of the Second Temple, following the Babylonian Exile (500 BC), there is also a relative absence of the term "Hallelujah" in latter Biblical books. The personal name of God, "Yahweh" was never employed again in the Biblical tradition following its withdrawal. Similarly, the expression "Hallelujah" is not employed again in latter Biblical works of the Old Testament, though it appears in the LXX translation of the Psalms in its Greek form.

In the pre-Christian writings, the term appears in Tobit 13:18, where the term appears in a context of a prayer which is written in response to a semi-visionary experience (a series of incidents in which Raphael, "One of the seven holy angels," taking the form of an ordinary man, proves to be very helpful to Tobias and his family) at the end of which, Raphael, the angel, urges Tobias and his father, Tobit, to give praises to God for what God has done to them through Raphael, his angel, before disappearing. The prayer, therefore, in which the term "Hallelujah" appears, is written to express joy and praise to God. Within the context of the prayer itself Tobit, in a prophetic vision, foresees the glory of the rebuilt Jerusalem.

In the pre-Christian writings, then, the term "Hallelujah" is employed not in the context of communal worship as was the case with earlier Old Testament period but in an apocalyptic sense in an individual visionary setting.

In the New Testament, the expression is only found in Rev 19:1-6 where it appears four times in a visionary eschatological setting in which the saints in heaven praise God for the destruction and defeat of Satan and all evil with him. They praise him also for the salvation of the Church, Christ's bride, as he brings her into the heavenly Jerusalem for a wedding celebration in the very presence of God the Father.

Just like in the pre-Christian writings, the term "Hallelujah" is used in the New Testament not in the context of communal worship of Israel but in a visionary eschatological setting in which only the prophet can "see" the multitude of saints and "hear" their shouts of Hallelujah at the end of time when the Kingdom of God reaches its ultimate consummation.

The absence of any usage of the term "Hallelujah" in a context of communal worship both in pre-Christian writings and in the New Testament suggests that the term was not restored into common usage, once withdrawn along with the personal name of God, "Yahweh" throughout the rest of the Biblical era. If this suggestion is correct, then the only "natural" setting in which this revered expression would appear is in the context of a prophetic visionary experience as it rightly does.

Thus, by the end of the Biblical era the usage of the expression "Hallelujah" radically changes in terms of both context and frequency. This suggests a remarkable change in Israel's conception and attitude towards the majesty and holiness of God. The term is used sparingly and that only in eschatological visionary contexts.

Traditional Christian Usage of "Hallelujah" (הללויה)

Coming to the traditional Christian usage of the term, we look at a few Christian hymnbooks. Although these hymns are in the vernacular, almost all of them are translations of older hymns dating back to the 18th and 19th Century AD or even earlier. They are therefore a good reflection of the theology of the older church, whose roots go back to the Reformation and beyond. A study of the Roman Catholic Chichewa hymnbook, *Buku la Nyimbo,* shows that of the 243 hymns, only 4 can be described as "Hallelujah" songs (songs in which the term occurs at least once) making the hallels 1.6% of the total. These are hymn No. 8 which celebrates the birth of Christ; hymn No 37 which praises God for Christ's resurrection; hymn No 49 addressed to Mary as the Mediator between the Church and Christ. Hymn No. 40 celebrates the resurrection of Christ, his decisive victory over all Satanic forces, freedom from sin and the spiritual peace he brings into the hearts of people who acknowledge his lordship. The last "Hallelujah" hymn in the book is hymn No. 42 which exalts Christ as Saviour-King both in heaven and on earth, and calls upon all people to worship him.

In terms of context, the Roman Catholic usage of the term compares well to the original Biblical context, namely: in a worshipping community of Israel. But the frequency seems to be higher in the early Biblical tradition than the Roman Catholic Church allows. However, the Roman Catholic Church differs greatly in its use of the term from the apocalyptic usage of the term in the later Biblical tradition.

It is also necessary to note a further liturgical use of the term "Hallelujah" in the *Buku la Nyimbo*. The term is also used in a context of prayer offered during the Paschal period, in which the leader sings a prayer line and then the congregation responds by singing the next prayer line in chorus. This has a touch of an ancient Christian practice since the early Church hymns were conducted by a leader to whom the congregation responded in song. The term is again used in the context of the Sacrament of Confirmation where the leading priest calls upon the Holy Spirit to come and fill the congregation anew with his love.

If this minimal usage of the term represents usage in the ancient Christian Church (the Roman Catholic Church being the oldest "denomination") then it would be said that the term was rarely employed in the worshipping Christian community. But this position, though highly probable, is difficult to establish at this point because it would require further research to establish the date of the composition of these hymns wherever possible, so that those with an ancient origin can be identified and studied.

The *Song of Praise,* a hymnbook for contemporary young Catholic students includes 14 hallels out of the 78 hymns and choruses it incorporates, bringing the hallels to 18% of the total. Of the 14 hallels, 8 are in praise of Christ for his redemptive work and the rest are praises to God in general for his goodness, faithfulness, power and glory, for the creation, and for giving to the world His Son and the Holy Spirit. In this small hymnbook the term "Hallelujah" appears in songs of praise in the context of communal worship similar to the context in which the hallels of *Buku la Nyimbo* are placed. The only difference is that of numbers. The percentage of hallels in *Buku la Nyimbo* is 1.6% while it is 18% in *Song of Praise*.

If this concentrated usage of the term in the hymnbook for the Roman Catholic student youths represents the current direction in contemporary Roman Catholic usage of the term, then it can be said that there is a departure in terms of frequency from the Roman Catholic tradition in which the term rarely occurs.

The Anglican hymnbook *Mapemphero ndi Nyimbo za Eklezia* which shares much liturgical forms with the Roman Catholic *Buku la Nyimbo,* shows a higher percentage in its usage of the term. Although it does not include any Biblical hallel in its section of 62 "Psalms," out of its 250 other hymns it has 34 hallels, making the hallels 14% of the total excluding the "Psalms." Of these 27 hallels are specifically Christological with 13 celebrating the resurrection.

In other liturgical sections the term occurs in three places. The first of these occurrences (p. 19) is in the context of the Eucharist where and the term appears as part of a benediction. The second occurrence is in the context of the Paschal period at which God receives praise for the joy his people have because of Christ's resurrection (p. 132). The third special occurrence of the term in the hymnbook takes place in the context of a messianic banquet. It is in fact quoted from Rev 19 where a wedding feast for the Lamb and his bride, the Church, is celebrated.

Thus, the Anglican tradition uses the term in the same way as the earlier Biblical tradition as well as the early Christian Church tradition reflected in the Roman Catholic traditional usage: namely in the context of a worshipping community of his people. Only a single usage departs from the traditional context of community worship. It has an eschatological and prophetic context (p. 355). This rare contextual background to the term is easily understood when one realizes that the background text is in fact a quote from Rev 19, which is itself eschatological. It only differs from the Roman Catholic traditional usage in that it has more hallels, and therefore, uses the term more than the former.

The Presbyterian hymnbook, *Nyimbo za Mulungu,* includes 20 hallels in its 384 hymns, making the hallels 5% of the total. Of these hallels 15 celebrate the redemptive work of Christ, 4 are praises to God in general, while one gives praises to the Father, Son and the Holy Spirit, specifically mentioning their Persons in the Godhead. In this hymnal, the term is employed in the same context as the Roman Catholic and Anglican traditions. However, the major difference is that the term is entirely absent in the liturgical section of this hymnal.

Sumu za Ukhristu, a Presbyterian hymnbook for the Livingstonia Synod also includes 22 hallels out of 401 hymns, making the hallels 5% of the total. 11 of these hallels are Christological with 6 celebrating the resurrection of Christ. Thus the Presbyterian usage of the term "Hallelujah" is similar to the Roman Catholic and Anglican traditions discussed above, in which the term is primarily employed in songs of praise in the context of communal worship. However, its absence in the liturgical section suggests that in Presbyterian tradition the term is not usually employed in the context of prayer. In this respect the Presbyterian usage would differ from the early Biblical usage of the term in which it is employed both in the context of songs of praise during worship and in the context of communal prayer.

It is probably noteworthy, at this point, to study the usage of the term by the Christian traditions, which arose in the aftermath of the Reformation movement. For this study we turn to the Seventh-day Adventist Church and the Baptist Church Traditions.

Khristu mu Nyimbo, the SDA's hymnbook, includes 7 hallels among its 350 hymns and choruses, making the hallels 2% of the total. 5 out of these 7 are Christological, focusing on Christ's suffering mission, kingship, his gift of the Holy Spirit, the salvation he brings and his promised return at the end of time. Thus the usage of the term by the SDA tradition is not different from the Roman Catholic Church and the Reformation churches in terms of both context and frequency

Nyimbo za Chigonjetso, a hymnal for the Baptist Convention also includes 13 hallels among its 200 hymns making the hallels 6.5% of the total. 10 of these hallels are Christological, focusing on his passion, his resurrection and his promised return. The usage of the term in the Baptist tradition also compares favourably with the early Biblical tradition as well as the other Christian traditions discussed above.

From this analysis of the liturgical material of the Roman Catholic Church, the Church of Central Africa Presbyterian, the Anglican Church, the Seventh Day Adventist and the Baptist Church, it would be concluded that the term "Hallelujah" was not widely used in the early Christian Church tradition. Both the Reformation churches and those which arose in the aftermath of the Reformation Christian movement maintained the traditional usage of the term, limiting its context to the songs of praise and prayer during worship.

This common usage of the term by the churches discussed above can probably be accounted for by the fact that these churches or the missionaries who brought them to Africa, and Malawi in particular, shared some common liturgical material or drew it from common liturgical sources. This practice is explicitly mentioned in the preface to the 1916 edition of *Nyimbo za Mulungu.*

The suggestion of a common liturgical heritage is further strengthened when we look at the percentages of hymns in some of the hymnbooks discussed above that are also found in *Nyimbo za Mulungu.* 10% of the hymns in the Anglican *Mapemphero ndi Nyimbo za Eklesia* are found in the Presbyterian *Nyimbo za Mulungu* while 15% of the Seventh-day Adventist *Khristu mu Nyimbo* are also found there. 58% of the hymns in the Baptist *Nyimbo za Chigonjetso,* as well as 62% of its hallels are also found in the Presbyterian hymnbook.

It can be concluded, then, that there was a common Christian liturgical tradition which provided a common context for the usage of the term "Hallelujah." This traditional usage of the term is still largely maintained in the churches discussed above. It has been noted that the use of the term "Hallelujah" was somehow brought back into Christian usage just as the name "Yahweh" was re-introduced in a sense in the form of "Jehovah." The phenomenon of the re-introduction of the terms "Yahweh" (in the form of "Jehovah") and "Hallelujah" into the Christian tradition, despite the silence of the latter Biblical tradition on these terms, may probably be accounted for by the need and desire to acknowledge and emphasize the divinity of Christ. By singing "Hallelujah" to Christ, the Church places Him at par with Yahweh of the Biblical tradition. The fact that most hallels are Christological is suggestive of this conclusion.

What is significant concerning its usage in both Biblical and Christian traditions discussed above is the atmosphere of reverence and awe, which always surrounds the contexts wherever the term occurs. Both traditions recognize the solemnity and awesomeness of the glory and majesty of the One evoked by calling upon these terms. It is probably in view of this awesome character of the term that in both the pre-Christian writings and the New Testament the name "Yahweh" is never mentioned while "Hallelujah" is limited to the context of a prophetic visionary experience.

"Hallelujah" (הללויה) in Contemporary Malawian Context

In order to understand the current trend in the usage of "Hallelujah" in evangelistic meetings or rallies we turn to the findings of a field research which was designed for the purpose involving 25 evangelists with three ministers (a Catholic priest and two pastors of different denominations) among their number.

Before we look at a detailed analysis of the study, two general observations can be made:

1. The use of the term, in a manner to be observed soon, runs across denominational boundaries. Evangelists with a variety of denominational background use the term more or less in the same way. They use the term freely.

2. Pastors and ministers are more sensitive when handling the term. They may employ the term or not depending largely on the tradition of their denomination. They are "denominationally" conscious whenever they deal with the term.

With regard to the meaning of the term "Hallelujah," it was found that 80% of them understood it as meaning "Praise God" or "May God be Praised." However, 5% did not understand the meaning. Suggestions which were put forward were that it means "peace" or that it implies "concurrence with God's Word being preached."

This then would suggest that many evangelists understand the meaning of "Hallelujah." However, there are some who do not know it. Probably this could be accounted for by the lack of theological training, which many local evangelists have to cope with.

It was also learned that evangelists employ the term to serve a number of purposes. Whether the evangelist knows or does not know the meaning of the term seems not to matter at this point. Apart from using the term as an expression of praise to God for whatever reason there is, the word is also used to draw attention of the audience to the preacher. This is sometimes done in an effort to quieten the audience so that everyone is able to listen to the sermon. 43% of the evangelists interviewed consented to this usage. Sometimes it could be used as an introductory exclamation as well as a conclusive remark, especially when a number of preachers take the stage in turns. 86% supported this usage.

It was also suggested that the term could be used frequently, in the course of the sermon, in order to allow for short moments of rest for the preacher. Such frequent usage could also help in sustaining the interest of the audience as the sermon progresses. 71% accepted this application of the term. Another 43% felt the term could also help the audience to move, along with the message, to a climactic point, a point of decision for Christ. 92% of them also consented to the usage of the term in order to emphasize significant points in a sermon or testimony.

A non-documented source which was found after field research suggests three further uses of the term in evangelistic rallies. First, it claims that a preacher would use the term in order to gain people's approval of what he is saying irrespective of whether the facts are correct or not. Secondly, it asserts that the leader may use the term to show excitement with the sermon or song. Thirdly, it suggests that it is sometimes used to show one's spiritual stature, that one is more "spiritual" than others.

Whether there is substance in these last three claims cannot be resolved in the present study. But that the suggestions are more egocentric, and therefore not very good Christian reflection, though highly practical, cannot be doubted. Whatever the case these indicate that there may be other ways in which the term is employed which still lie beyond the reach of this study.

The study also establishes, apart from the "purposes" discussed above, a number of "appropriate" contexts in which the term could be used. 68% suggested that the term could be used in a greeting to the congregation or the audience. 32% felt the term could be employed when giving a story of one's conversion experience, commonly known as one's "testimony." Another 76% consented to its use in the context of prayer, while 40% said it could also be employed in songs. Another 36%

suggested it could be used after casting out demons from a possessed person. In the course of preaching, 76% thought the term could be used, while consent to its use during "praise and worship"[27] was 100%.

It can therefore be concluded that in contemporary Christianity, particularly in evangelistic meetings and rallies, the term can be used in various settings and for various purposes. Such a multiplicity of settings and purposes seems to erode its significance and meaningfulness as an expression of solemn praise to God. Because of this multiplicity of contexts and purposes for its usage, it begins to acquire other meanings and connotations, which may even be strange to the Christian faith in general.

Conclusion

It can now be concluded that the term "Hallelujah" is used sparingly in both Biblical and Christian traditions as has been discussed above. It is an exclamation of praise addressed to the very person of God. Since to call upon the name "Yahweh" in whatever form (in this case the contracted form "Yah") is to acknowledge His personal being in all its totality, to mention his Name is to honour and glorify his majesty. The appropriate attitude, therefore, is to call upon his holy Name with great respect and honour because he is "Majestic in holiness, awesome in glory" (Exodus 15:11).

This attitude is the one reflected in both Biblical and Christian traditions. The contexts in which the term "Hallelujah" occurs always reflect a conscious realization in the worshipper of the awesomeness and reverence of the One evoked in the term. It is, therefore, clear that any use of the term other than for the purpose of giving praise to God, any use of the exclamation that does not take into account the glory and majesty of Him who is addressed, blurs its theological significance and is not only unbiblical but also contrary to earlier Christian usage. It can, therefore, be concluded that it is the lack of an informed conscious realization, in the worshipper at contemporary evangelistic rallies, of what is in the Name that makes contemporary usage very remote from Biblical and traditional stance. Only when one understands the nature of him who is in the Name does one begin to appreciate the use of the term in both biblical and traditional Christian practices.

---

[27] Special songs of praise are sung during "*Praise and Worship*," a stage in the service when God, in the person of the Holy Spirit, is solemnly evoked.

Chapter Fifteen
Gender Differentiation in the Bible: Created and Recognized

Hilary B.P. Mijoga

Introduction

The thesis of the chapter is that according to the Bible, gender differentiation is created and recognized (accepted).[1] In light of this assertion, it will be demonstrated that apparent marginalization of the women folk in society[2] based on their feminine gender is not inherent in creation.[3]

---

[1] The original version of this chapter was delivered at the Association of the Theological Institutions of Southern and Central Africa (ATISCA) conference held in Harare, Zimbabwe (December 1998). The theme of the conference was "Theology and Gender Issues."

[2] The feminist movement has often attributed the apparent marginalization of women to our so-called patriarchal societies. However, this chapter will not discuss this issue. For discussions on the issue of patriarchy, see for example, Kavesta Adagala, "Mother Nature, Patriarchal Cosmology and Gender," in Gilbert E.M. Ogutu (ed.), *God, Humanity and Mother Nature* (Nairobi: Masaki Publishers, 1992), pp.47-65; Sang Chang, "The Place of Women in Genesis 1-3 and 1 Timothy 2," in Ursel Rosenhager & Sarah Stephens (eds.), *"Walk, My Sister": The Ordination of Women: Reformed Perspective* (Studies from the World Alliance of Reformed Churches 18; WARC, 1993), pp. 34-51; Elisabeth Schüssler Fiorenza (ed), *Searching the Scriptures: A Feminist Introduction* (2 vols.; London: SCM, 1994), vol. 1, pp. 101-86; Isabel Apawo Phiri, *Women, Presbyterianism and Patriarchy: Religious Experience of Chewa Women in Central Malawi* (Kachere Monograph; Blantyre: CLAIM-Kachere, 1997); Elsa Tamez, ""No Longer Silent: A Bible Study on 1 Corinthians 14:34-35 and Galatians 3:28," in Rosenhager & Stephens, *"Walk, My Sister,"* pp. 52-62.

[3] The feminist movement has developed in part as a response to this apparent marginalization (making inferior or oppressing or suppressing) of women by the male folk. This apparent marginalization is understood as the domination of the female gender, hence the gender question. For discussion on feminist theology and/or feminist approach to the Bible, see for example, A. Yarbro Collins (ed.) *Feminist Perspectives in Biblical Scholarship* (Biblical Scholarship in North America 10; Chico, CA: Scholars, 1985); A. Yarbro Collins (ed.), *Women's Bible Commentary* (Louisville, KY: Westminster/John Knox Press, 1992); E. Schussler Fiorenza, *In Memory of Her* (New York: Crossroad, 1983); Elisabeth Schüssler Fiorenza, *Jesus: Miriam's Child, Sophia's Prophet: Critical Issues in Feminist Christology*

A philological study of the creation accounts in Genesis 1-2 reveals that gender differentiation is created, whereas a study of the rest of the Biblical narratives shows that gender differentiation is recognized. Both studies demonstrate that gender differentiation has nothing to do with the creation of the marginalization of the female gender. This chapter, however, does not discuss the issue of the treatment of women in society in general and the Bible and the church in particular. This issue, though interesting, is outside the limit of the present discussion.[4]

Gender Differentiation Created: a Philological Study

This section aims at showing that gender differentiation is created. To prove this assertion, a word study[5] of the creation accounts in Genesis 1-2 will be undertaken. Topics of the study are: (i) Hebrew word study of *'adam, ish,* and *issha;* (ii) the

---

(London: SCM, 1994); Elizabeth Schüssler Fiorenza (ed.), *Searching the Scriptures: A Feminist Commentary* (London: SCM, 1995); Alvera Mickelsen (ed.), *Women, Authority and the Bible* (Downers Grove, Illinois: InterVarsity Press, 1986); Isabel Apawo Phiri, "The 'Proper' Place of Women (Genesis 1, 1 Timothy 2): A Biblical Exegetical Study from a Malawian Chewa Presbyterian Perspective," Rosenhager & Stephens, "*Walk, My Sister,*" pp. 24-33. Rosemary Radford Ruether, *Sexism and God-Talk: Towards A Feminist Theology* (London: SCM, 1983); Rosemary Radford Ruether, *Reading Towards A Feminist Theology* (Woman Guildes; Boston: Beacon Press, 1985); E. Cady Stanton, *The Woman's Bible* (2 vols.; New York: European Publishing Co., 1885, 1898); Elaine Storkey, *What's Right with Feminism* (London: SPCK, 1985).

[4] A lot has been written on the treatment of women. The reader is advised to consult the literature in question, for example, literature in footnotes 1 and 2.

[5] Some of the tools used in this word study include, for example, William F. Arndt & E. Wilbur Gingrich, *A Greek-English Lexicon of the New Testament and Other Early Christian Literature* (Cambridge: University Press; Chicago: University of Chicago Press, 1957); F Blass & A. Debrunner, *A Grammar of the New Testament and Other Early Christian Literature* (trans. & ed. Robert W. Funk; Chicago/London: University of Chicago Press, 1961); Francis Brown with S.R. Driver & Charles A. Briggs, *The New Brown Driver-Briggs-Genesius Hebrew and English Lexicon with an Appendix containing the Biblical Aramaic* (Peabody, Massachusetts: Hendrickson Publisher, 1979); Benjamin Davidson, *The Analytical Hebrew and Chaldee Lexicon* (Peabody, Massachusetts: Hendrickson, 1850; 5th printing 1990); K. Elliger & W. Rudolph (eds.), *Biblia Hebraica Stuttgartensia* (Stuttgart: Deutsche Bibelgesellschaft, 1977); Paul Jouon, *Grammaire de L'Hebreu* Biblique (Rome: Institute Biblique Pontifical, 1923). I acknowledge that language can be used to oppress women. However, in this study language contributes positively to the debate.

common origin of humanity (1:26-27); (iii) the inter-dependency of genders for existence (2:7, 21-22).[6]

Hebrew Word Study
'adam'[7]

This word is a masculine noun which appears eighteen times in Genesis 1-2 (1:26,27;2:5,7 [2x], 8, 15, 16, 18, 19, [2x], 20 [2x], 21, 22 [2x], 23, 25). In 1:26, 27, the term refers to collective humanity, whereas in 2:5, 7, 8, 15, 16, 18, the reference is to a generic human being. In 2:22, 23, 25, the word is used in the sense of "man" (male gender) as opposed to "woman" (female gender). It should be pointed out here that one feminist reader of Genesis 1-3 has claimed that in chapter 2 *'adam* "is prefixed by the definite article *ha* and therefore should not be regarded as a masculine term."[8] She argues that the masculine point of view emerges in Gen 2:18. Grammatically, claiming that *ha'adam* is not a masculine term, does not do justice to the Hebrew term. We have to remember that there is no neuter gender in Hebrew.

The first time we come across this word is in 1:26, where the noun does not have a definite article. The absence of the definite article can either mean that the referent is a single object or, as in this case, it is indefinite.[9] The indefinite sense could explain why the term refers here to collective humanity. Other instances where this noun does not have a definite article are 2:5, 20. In all, this noun is used three times without the define article in this pericope. What this means simply is that if the noun *'adam* is understood as a collective term, then it encompasses both male and female genders.

In 2:20,[10] the indefinite noun *'adam* appears in a list containing animals which the definite *'adam* names. So from the indefinite usage and collectivity of the term

---

[6] For detailed discussion of the creation accounts in Genesis, consult commentaries on Genesis. For example, see Dietrich, *Creation and Fall: A Theological Interpretation of Genesis 1-3* (New York: The MacMillan Company, 1959), pp. 13-63; Walther Eichrodt, *Theology of the Old Testament* (trans. J.A. Baker; London: SCM, 1967); vol. 2; pp. 93-150; John Hargreaves, *A Guide to Genesis* (TEF Study Guide 3; London SPCK, 1969; 7th impression 1991), pp. 6-23; David F. Hinson, *Theology of the Old Testament* (TEF Study Guide 15; London: SPCK, 1976), pp. 18-64.

[7] This Hebrew word is translated as "man, mankind/humankind."

[8] Chang, "The Place of Women in Genesis 1-3 and 1 Timothy 2," p.46.

[9] For discussion on Gen 1:26, see for example, Bonhoefer, *Creation and Fall*, pp. 35-40; Kidner, Genesis, pp. 50-52; Leupold, *Exposition of Genesis*, pp. 85-93; Skinner, *Commentary on Genesis*, pp. 30-33.

[10] For discussion on Gen 2:20, see for example, Kidner, *Genesis*, pp. 65-66; Leupold, *Exposition Genesis*, pp. 30-33.

'adam, we observe that the question of gender differentiation partially comes into play. This is because collectivity can imply gender differentiation only that it is overlooked in preference for commonality.

The situation is clear in 2:22, 23 25 where gender differentiation is created as the use of the noun 'adam would show. Here 'adam is opposed to the noun 'issha. Grammatically, the two nouns have different genders: 'adam is masculine, whereas 'issha is feminine. In addition to the grammatical gender differentiation, there are other factors which contribute to the process of differentiation. First, 2:22 reveals that God stands at the origin of sexual differentiation when he creates 'issha from 'adam. What is obvious here is that God did not create another 'adam, but he created 'issha who was different from the 'adam, hence the differences in the nouns used. Second, 2:23[11] reveals that the 'adam contributed to the creation of the gender differentiation for in his exclamation of joy in finding someone like himself, 'adam names this being as 'issha, who is obviously different from 'adam or 'is.[12] Finally, 2:25[13] indicates that the narrator of the story also creates the gender differentiation, for he introduced two genders: husband (male) and wife (female). 1:27[14] also shows that gender differentiation is created. However, here we have the use of the different terms: zakar ("male") and neqeva ("female"). So with regard to the use of the term 'adam in Genesis 1-2, we note that gender differentiation is created by the Lord God (2:22), the 'adam (2:23), and the narrator (2:25). For this reason I argue that gender differentiation is part of creation.

From the word study then, is the marginalization of the female gender inherent in the gender differentiation? From the verses cited (1:26-27; 2:22, 23, 25), the issue of marginalization of the female gender is not inherent in the gender differentiation.[15] Commenting on Gen 1:26-27, Bonhoeffer states: "Man is not alone, he is in duality and it is in this dependence on the other that his creatureliness consists. Man's creatureliness is not a quality, something that exists, something that is, any more than freedom. It can only be defined in man's being over against the other, with the

---

[11] For discussion on Gen 2:23, see for example, Skinner, *Commentary on Genesis*, P. 69, Leupold, Exposition of Genesis, pp. 135-37.

[12] In this passage, 'is is used as a synonym of 'adam.

[13] For discussions on Gen 2:25, see for example, Kidner, *Genesis*, pp. 65-66; Leupold, *Exposition of Genesis*, pp. 93-95.

[14] For discussions on Gen 1:27, see for example, Hargreaves, *A Guide to Genesis*, pp 9-11; Kidner, *Genesis* pp.52; Leupold, *Exposition of Genesis*, pp. 93-95.

[15] Grammatically, it is easy to detect inferiority or degradation in Greek. This can be deducted from the use of the neuter gender (the diminutive). But it is difficult to do the same in Hebrew because there are only two genders: a thing is either masculine or feminine.

other and dependent upon the other."[16] Feminist scholars would accept that in Genesis 1 there is sexual differentiation between male and female, but they would argue that "there is not even a hint of any pattern of domination and subordination."[17] In other words, in God's original plan, "neither sex was superior or inferior to the other."[18]

In 2:22, the process of "building" of the "rib" (matter) of the 'adam into 'issha is similar to what happened to 'adam in 2:7 where the 'adam was "formed" from "dust" (matter) of 'adama.[19] So both genders are created from matter taken from a source of the opposite gender. In 2:23, the 'adam expresses his supreme joy at finding someone like himself ("bone of my bones and flesh of my flesh.")[20] So "[b]y a flash of intuition the man divines that the fair creature now brought to him is part of himself, and names her accordingly."[21] In other words, "[t]he most complete physical congruity of this new person with himself is at once recognized by the first person."[22] In 2:25, the narrator indicates that both the 'adam and his 'issha were naked and none was ashamed.

In short, the study of the use of the term 'adam in Genesis 1-2 reveals that gender differentiation is created, and that the marginalization of the female gender is not inherent in the usage of the term.

'ish'[23]

This term does not appear in connection with creation, except for 2:23 which is itself problematic. By creation, I am referring to God's "building" of 'adam, i.e. zakar and neqeba in 1:27, God's "forming" of 'adam in 2:7, and God's "building" of 'issha in 2:22. In all these instances, the term 'ish does not occur. However, the term is first found on the lips of 'adam in 2:23. Here, the 'adam indicates that 'issha was taken from 'ish, hence the creation of gender differentiation.[24] So the Hebrew text reveals that the "woman" was taken from the "man." What is obvious here is the fact that the

---

[16] Bonhoeffer, *Creation and Fall*, p. 38.
[17] Chang, "The Place of Women in Genesis 1-3 and 1 Timothy 2," p. 46.
[18] Phiri, "The 'Proper' Place of Women (Genesis 1, 1 Timothy 2)," p. 25.
[19] Note the paronomasia in 2:7: 'adam and 'adama.
[20] Note that there is nothing said about "flesh" in 2:21. There, the object is "rib." But how did the 'adam know that God took his "rib" (bone)? This is a clue that the account should not be taken literally.
[21] Skinner, *Commentary on Genesis*, p. 69.
[22] Leupold, *Exposition of Genesis*, p. 136.
[23] This Hebrew term is translated as "man."
[24] There is no etymological relationship between the two Hebrew words, but there is in English.

'adam makes gender differentiation between the two beings. In the Septuagint (LXX) and Targum renderings of the same verse, the "woman" is said to have been taken from "her man," hence the "husband-wife" understanding. This understanding is supported by 2:24,25, but not by the Hebrew of 2:23. It appears, therefore, that LXX and Targum renderings were influenced by 2:24,25. In this case, gender differentiation ("husband-wife") is created by the *'adam* and the translators of the LXX and Targum. Grammatically speaking, the two terms belong to different genders: *'ish* is a masculine noun, where as *'issha* is a feminine noun.

Is the marginalization of the female gender inherent in the above created gender differentiation? 2:23 only says that the *'issha* that the Lord created was named thus by the *'adam* simply because the *'issha* was taken from the *'ish*.[25] If the process of being "taken from" means that the female gender is inferior to the *'ish*, surely the *'adam* should be inferior to the *'adam*a from which he was "taken"! But the text does not suggest this. We also note that in 2:24 the *'ish* leaves his parents and joins his wife. Does this process of movement suggest that *'ish* becomes inferior in relation to the *'issha*? The text does not say this.

So the study of the usage of the term *'ish* reveal that gender differentiation is created. However, its usage does not show that the marginalization of the *'issha* is inherent in its usage.

'*issha*'[26]

The first time we come across this term is in connection with creation in 2:22. As already noted, in 2:22 God creates gender differentiation, but there is no hint that the male gender is superior or dominant over the female gender. In 2:23, the term appears on the lips of the *'adam* when he exclaims for joy as he finds someone like himself. Here, too, there is no suggestion of dominance of the male gender (*'ish*) over the female gender (*'issha*). In fact, in 2:24 it is the male gender (*'ish*) that abandons everything to cling to the *'issha*. In 2:25, both genders are naked, hence are equal in terms of nakedness.

So the use of the term *'issha* does not reveal any marginalization of the female gender. What is clear is that *'issha* is different from *'ish*. This is along the lines of gender.

---

[25] Gen 2:22-23 is interesting for another different reason. Here, what God created is called *'issha* by God, whereas the same being is called *'issha* again, but this time because she was taken from *'is*. What is apparent is that when *'adam* refers to himself, he uses the term *'ish*. This implies that *'adam* and *'ish* are synonymous.

[26] This Hebrew term is translated as "woman, wife, female."

Common Origin of Humanity

According to 1:27, God created 'adam in his image.[27] Here, the singular in v. 27a-b is contrasted with the plural in v. 27c. The addition of the phrase "male and female" in v. 27c should be understood in two ways:(a) that gender differentiation was already created (v. 27c). In other words, "God makes man but He does not make each person the same. It is His plan that there should be differences between people."[28] (b) that this is an attempt to avoid assuming that originally God created an androgynous human, as some scholars have suggested that "humanity was a dual being, male and female,"[29] for example. But "(t)he persistent idea that man as first created was bi-sexual and the sexes separated afterwards ... is far from the thought of the passage."[30] In other words, "the term 'adam is meant generically,"[31] i.e. "humanity defined as male and female."[32] Hence "all queer speculations about the first man are cut off as well as the quaint heresy that he was created androgynous, half man and half woman."[33] The bottom line is that the created 'adam is the created "male and female." In other words, "human beings are a unit and diverse in sex."[34] So "the sexes are complementary."[35] The complementarity suggests that both have a common origin and purpose. But gender dominance is not inherent in this common origin for both are created at the same time.

Inter-dependence of Genders

In 2:5,7 we observe two things: paronomasia: 'adam and 'adama and dependence of the male gender on the female gender for its creation (existence). The paronomasia here is used to suggest that the two terms are related in some ways. This relationship

---

[27] As note earlier, 'adam is a masculine noun. Philologically, does this suggest that gender differentiation (see v. 27c) was created from the male gender? What we do know is that in Hebrew, "mothers" of things are in the feminine gender. But does this "motherhood" apply to 'adam? These are difficult questions to answer in a chapter like this one. Perhaps, 'adam has neutral connotations (cf. its indefinite and collective nature), but since things are either male or female inn Hebrew, it so happens that the creation of "male" and "female" gender stems from masculine gender.

[28] Hargreaves, *A Guide to Genesis*, p. 10.
[29] Chang, "The Place of Women in Genesis 1-3 and 1 Timothy 2," p. 44.
[30] Skinner, *Commentary on Genesis*, p. 33.
[31] Leupold, *Exposition of Genesis*, p. 33.
[32] Phiri, "The 'Proper' Place of Women (Genesis 1, 1 Timothy 2)," p. 25.
[33] Leupold, *Exposition of Genesis*, p. 94.
[34] Phiri, "The 'Proper' Place of Women (Genesis 1, 1 Timothy)," p. 24.
[35] Kidner, *Genesis*, p. 65.

is evident in the fact that *'adam* is formed from the *'adama*, i.e., the *'adam* is the product of the *'adama*. In fact, it is suggested that the root of the word is "to be sought in the cognate word *adamah*."[36] In this case, the masculine *'adam* is dependent for its creation on the feminine *'adama*. And grammatically, the substance (matter) used to create the masculine *'adam* (male gender) comes from the feminine *'adama* (female gender), i.e., the *'apar*, "dust," (masculine) through which the *'adam* is formed. What is evident here is that the male gender is dependent on the female gender for its creation (existence). But is the apparent marginalization of the female gender inherent in the dependency of the male gender on the female gender?

The dependency of the genders on each other for creation (existence) is also manifest in 2:21-22. Here, the feminine matter/substance "rib" which is taken from the masculine being *'adam* is used to "build" the feminine being *'issha*. In this case, the creation of the feminine being, *'issha*, is dependent on the matter/substance from the masculine gender; hence, the feminine gender is dependent on the masculine gender for its creation.

Some interpreters have understood the creation of a woman as a "helper" to the man to mean that the woman is the assistant of the man, i.e., she occupies an auxiliary and secondary position. In response to this traditional view, it has been argued from the word study of *ezer* ("helper") and *kenegeddo* ("as his helper") that this is not correct.

Ezer is understood to mean a helping companion and *neged* denotes equality of relationship. What this means is that their "relationship is one of equality and mutuality."[37] So the marginalization of the female gender is not inherent in the use of the terms *ezer* and *kenegeddo*.

The preceding presentation reveals that there is interdependence of the genders, male and female, especially when it comes to their creation or existence. One needs the other; hence none can be dispensed with. So there is a symbiotic relationship. In such a situation, none is dominant; hence the question of marginalization or domination of the female gender does not come into play. In short then, although the Bible shows that gender differentiation was created, gender interdependence for existence argues for the equality of the genders. So, the marginalization or domination of the female gender is not inherent in the interdependence of the genders.

---

[36] Leupold, *Exposition of Genesis*, p. 88.
[37] Chang, "The Place of Women (Genesis 1,1 Timothy 2)," p. 28.

Gender Differentiation Recognized: a Narrative Study

Thus far, it has been demonstrated that gender differentiation was created. The aim of this section, however, is to show that gender differentiation is recognized by God and narrators of Biblical accounts. This recognition is evident in the use of gender terms as, for example, used in the marriage institution (man [husband], woman [wife]) and in instances where people are listed in their gender categories. This section also investigates whether recognition of gender differentiation contributes to the marginalization of the female gender. This narrative study of the Biblical accounts does not consider the creation accounts in Genesis 1-2.

Recognition of Gender Differentiation in the Old Testament

This study considers a select number of narratives from the Torah, especially from Genesis, Exodus, and Leviticus. First, we look at Genesis accounts. Genesis 3 narrates the account of the fall of humanity. In this account, two major characters are "woman" (3:1,2,4,6,12,13,16,17) and "man" (3:8,9,12,17,20,21,22,24), i.e., "husband" (3:6,8,16), "wife" (3:17), and "man" (3:22). This means that God recognizes these gender terms as labels for the two characters in the story. But God's usage of these terms does not suggest that the apparent marginalization of the female gender is inherent in their usage. In other words, God's recognition of the gender differentiation does not suggest female gender marginalization. For example, the account does not say that the serpent deceived the woman because the woman was female. This is because the woman could have rejected the deception if she chose to observe God's injunction, for she knew that God said, "You shall not eat of the fruit of the tree which is in the midst of the garden ...lest you die" (3:3). What we observe from the text is that the woman: (a) is inexperienced and credulous before the shrewd and deceitful serpent; (b) does not flee the temptation but begins a conversation with the serpent; (c) corrects the distortion of the serpent's question, but then she herself exaggerates the prohibition by including a command not to touch the fruit of the tree. 2:17 says nothing at all about touching the fruit. In her zeal to correct the serpent, she goes too far. It is as though she wanted to set a law for herself by means of this exaggeration.

What is evident in the test is that the woman fell for the deception not because she was female, but because she "saw that the tree was good for food, and that it was a delight to the eyes, and that the tree was to be desired to make one wise" (3:6). This means that other factors explain the choice to disobey God's injunction.

It has been said that the man was an innocent victim, while others have said he was a willing participant when he chose to disobey God's injunction. Feminist readers have argued that both the man and the woman fell for the deception. So the responsibility for the fall is shared. They support this position by a textual study of the account but also by silence in the text. First, it is said that in the Hebrew text the serpent always speaks in the second person plural. This implies that the serpent does not only speak to the woman, but the woman and the man were being addressed together. Second, the Hebrew text has *le'ishah 'immah*, "to her man" (husband) with her." This shows that the man was around when the serpent was talking to the woman.[38] Because it is understood that the man was present, some Greek and Samaritan manuscripts have "and they ate" in 3:6. So the conclusion drawn from this is that both were present and both ate the forbidden fruit, hence both fell for the deception. Third, following from the preceding that the man was present, it appears that the woman did not seek any advice or permission from the man. It is, therefore, argued that the man did not speak out about the temptation or the behaviour of the woman nor did he raise any question or objection. In this case, the man was irresponsible by neglecting and denying his right and responsibility as a partner to the woman.

What is obvious from the text is that the man chose to disobey the injunction not because he was male, hence gender is not an issue in the decision to eat the prohibited fruit. So both genders are at fault. In fact both the man and woman were punished for failure to keep God's injunction. In short then, the text does not suggest in any way that gender was the issue in whatever transpired in the narrative.

Gen 3:1-6 is also interesting in another way. The narrator states that after eating the fruit "the eyes of both were opened, and they knew that they were naked" (v. 7). This means that the transgression of the injunction enjoined on them led to the discovery of their nakedness. This discovery entails that they realized ("knew") that they were of different sexes. So sin leads to this recognition. It is also interesting to note from this passage that the man did not accuse the woman for this state of affairs. What happened was that "they sewed fig leaves together and made themselves aprons" (v. 7). So even here we don't see any marginalization of any sex. The narrator doesn't present that aspect.

Where does the marginalization of the women come from in this fall account? It has been said that sin and punishment resulted in the domination of man over the woman. It is pointed out that it is "in the punishment that we find division of roles according to gender between *Adam* and Eve. Eve's life revolves around pain in childbirth, sexual passion for her husband and her humiliating subservience to her husband."[39] In this case, "her partner becomes her master."[40] So the understanding

---

[38] However, it is also possible to understand the phrase differently because the beginning of the chapter does not tell whether or not the man was present when the serpent appeared on the scene.
[39] Phiri, "The 'Proper' Place of Women (Genesis 1, 1 Timothy 2," p. 28.
[40] Chang "The Place of Women in Genesis 1-3 and 1 Timothy 2," p. 50.

here is that sexuality is now distorted to become the domination of one partner over the other member of the partnership. Now, if domination of the female gender is due to sin and punishment, are we blaming God for this situation because it is God who pronounced this judgment? Is this what the feminist readers of this text are implying?

In Genesis 6-8, we have the flood narrative.[41] In this account, gender differentiation is recognized. God and the narrator give lists of people in gender categories. In 6:18, God says, "But I will establish my covenant with you; and you shall come into the ark, you [Noah], your sons, your wife, and your sons' wives with you." And in 8:16, God tells Noah, "Go forth from the ark, you and your wife, and your sons' wives with you." Here God recognizes the gender differentiation: men (Noah and the sons) and women (the wives). In other words, God recognizes the husband-wife relationship, a recognition which involves gender separation. In this account, God also recognizes gender differentiation by using gender terms in the expression: "male and female" (6:19: "they shall be male and female;" 7:3 "male and female;" see. 7:2 where the expression "the male and his mate" is used). So the foregoing reveals that in the flood account, God recognizes gender differentiation through his listing of people in gender categories but also in his use of gender terms. It is not only God who is involved in the recognition of gender differentiation in this account. The narrator also does the same. In 7:7,13, 8:18, the narrator presents people in gender categories: "Noah and his sons and his wife and his sons' wives" (see 7:7). In addition to listing according to gender, the narrator also uses an expression with gender terms: "male and female" (see 7:9). So these examples show that in the flood account, the narrator recognizes gender differentiation through his use of gender terms and the listing of people according to their gender.

Is the marginalization of the female gender inherent in this recognition then? There are two issues one can consider in trying to answer this question. First, there is the issue of order of people in the lists. One way of interpreting the order in the lists is to say the people appear in their order of importance. This interpretation obviously puts the women folk at the bottom of the ladder. But does this point to the marginalization of the female gender? What is clear in the narrative is that the narrator is consistent in the way people are lined up, but God is not consistent (see 6:18 with 8:16). This means that the order cannot be used as an argument for the apparent marginalization of the female gender. In other words, the fact that God's and the narrator's orders do not follow the same pattern, is an argument for not stressing the order of importance of gender in the lists. In addition to this, insisting

---

[41] For discussion on the flood narrative, see for example, Hargreaves, *A Guide to Genesis*, pp. 43-57; Kidner, *Genesis*, pp. 83-100; Skinner, *Commentary on Genesis*, pp. 139-69; Speiser, *Genesis*, pp. 47-56.

on the importance of the orders for the apparent gender marginalization might lead to pitying God against the narrator. Second, there is the issue of insistence on both sexes in the lists as well as the use of the expression "male and female." This alone implies that there is interest in equal gender representation. If this is true, then the recognition of gender differentiation here does not contribute to the marginalization of gender, i.e., the female gender marginalization is not inherent in the recognition of the gender differentiation.

The Decalogue also serves as an instance of recognition of gender differentiation in the Bible. As recorded in Exodus 20:1-17,[42] God singles out the wife as one of the beings not to be coveted (see v. 17). This is also the same in Deut 5:6-21 (see v. 21).[43] So in both versions of the Decalogue, there is insistence on the wife not to be coveted.[44] One way of understanding this insistence is to suggest that God recognizes the female gender ("wife") as distinct from the household or the man, for example. Obviously here, the recognition of the female gender is made for reasons of safeguarding the gender at stake.

Finally, we look at the laws of purity in Lev 12:1-8.[45] In this account God makes gender distinction: the people of Israel in contrast to the woman (vv. 1-2); "male child" (v. 2) in contrast to "female child" (v. 5).

Here, the law of purity applies to the female gender for two reasons: child bearing and menstruation. What is clear is that both situations involve secretions. So

---

[42] For discussion on the Decalogue in Exodus 20:1-17, see for example, Brevard S. Childs, *Exodus: A Commentary*, London: SCM, 1974, pp. 385-439; Alan Cole, *Exodus: An Introduction and Commentary*, Leicester/Downers Grove, Illinois: InterVarsity Press, 1973), pp. 149-61; Terence E. Frethem, *Exodus* (Interpretation: A Bible Commentary for Teaching and Preaching; Lousville: John Knox Press, 1991, pp. 220-39.

[43] For discussion on the decaloque in Deut 5:6-21, see for example, S.R. Driver, *A Critical and Exegetical Commentary on Deuteronomy (International Critical Commentary*; Edinburgh: T & T Clark, 1895; latest impression 1965), pp. 81-6; Gerhard von Rad, *Deuteronomy: A Commentary* (Old Testament Library) London: SCM, 1966, pp. 56-9; J.A. Thompson, *Deuteronomy: An Introduction and Commentary*; Leicester/Downers Grove, Illinois: InterVarsity Press, 1974, pp. 114-18.

[44] This injunction boarders along the question of the treatment of women. It is, however, discussed here because of the listing of the people according to their gender.

[45] For discussions on Lev 12:1-8, see for example, Andrew Bonar, *A Commentary on the Book of Leviticus,* Grand Rapids, Michigan: Baker Book House, 1978, pp. 228-31; Felix L. Chingota, "Sacraments and Sexuality," *Religion in Malawi* No. 8 (1998), pp. 34-40, especially pp. 39-40; R.K. Harrison, *Leviticus: An Introduction and Commentary* (The Tyndale Old Testament Commentary) Leicester / Downers Grove, Illinois: InterVarsity Press, 1980, pp. 133-36.

"[t]he legislation deals with the secretions that occur at parturition, and it is these that make the mother unclean. Thus the chapter should be read within the context of chapter 15, which also deals with bodily secretions."[46] Hence, the uncleanliness at issue does not come in because of her female gender, although biologically child bearing and menstruation are associated with the female sex. However, what is to be pointed out is that child bearing and menstruation come much later in the woman's life. For this reason, we cannot say that the woman as female is inherently unclean, the uncleanliness which could contribute to her marginalization. Perhaps, one may query the differences in time when it comes to uncleanliness due to child birth: seven days for a male child and two weeks for a female child. The account makes clear that duration of uncleanliness is dependent on the sex of the child. So gender plays a role in this situation. But one thing is clear and that is, the period is in the multiples of the number seven (cf. the first creation story): seven denotes completeness. Probably, the emphasis should be placed on the number rather than on the gender for the woman's purity. This explanation is contrary to the view which says, "[t]he female child keeps the mother unclean double the time. Perhaps one reason of this was that the male child had the advantage of the covenant circumcision, and brought thereby blessing to his mother. Another reason, however, was, 'because the woman was in transgression' (1 Tim 2:4), and led *Adam* into it. It kept up the remembrance of the Fall, and of the first sin."[47]

The foregoing narrative study of the OT texts shows that gender differentiation was recognized by God and the narrators. The study does not, however, show that gender marginalization is inherent in the recognition.

Recognition of Gender Differentiation in the New Testament

This section considers a select number of narratives from the New Testament, i.e., from the gospels and epistles.

---

[46] Harrison, *Leviticus*, p. 134.
[47] Bonar, *Leviticus,* pp. 229-30. the emphasis is his. For the doctrine of *Peccatum originale,* "Original sin," explained in terms of not imitation but of propagation or generation, see Augustine, *De peccatum meritius et remissione*, 1.9.10; CSEL 60.12: Augustine, *Contra duas epistolas Pelagianorum*, 4.4.7; CSEL 60.527-28. In fact, original sin is a term derived from the Western Latin Theology. See Joseph A. Fitzmyer, *Scripture the Soul of Theology*, New York/Mahwah, New Jersey: Paulist Press, 1994, p. 69.

Gospel Narratives

In the gospel narratives, we begin with the episode of the feeding of the multitudes. Matt 14:15-21[48] records that Jesus fed *pentakischilioi choris gynaikon kai paidion*. Literally this translates as: "five thousand [male] [i.e., masculine beings] besides women and children." In the Greek phrase, the three nouns are masculine, feminine, and neuter respectively.[49] This means that the narrator recognizes gender differentiation in this list. In other Greek manuscripts, the order of the last two nouns is reversed: "children and women." "The listing of the recipients here is meant to show the magnitude of the event. For our purposes, however, our interest is in the recognition of the gender differentiation.[50] This episode also appears in Mark 6:35-44.[51] In this version, no listing is given (see. v. 44). So, one can conclude that no recognition of gender differentiation is made by the narrator of the Markan account. The same situation is true of the Lucan account (Luke 9:10-17).[52] No gender

---

[48] For discussions on Matt 14:15-21, see for example, W.F. Albright & C.S. Mann, *Matthew: Introduction, Translation, and Notes* (The Anchor Bible) Garden City, New York: Doubleday, 1971), pp. 177-79; Douglas R.A. Hare, *Matthew* (Interpretation: A Bible Commentary for Teaching and Preaching), Louisville: John Knox Press, 1993, pp. 165-67.

[49] In Greek, there are three genders: masculine, feminine, and neuter. This is different from Hebrew which has only two genders: masculine and feminine.

[50] The order in the listing could be interpreted as the narrator putting emphasis on a particular gender over against the others. This could be true, but as we have noted the order is reversed in other Greek manuscripts. So we shouldn't emphasize on the order, but on the recognition of the gender differentiation.

[51] For discussions on Mark 6:35-44, see for example, C.E.B. Cranfield, *The Gospel according to Saint Mark*, London: Cambridge University Press, 1959, pp. 216-23; Ezra P. Gould, *A Critical and Exegetical Commentary on the Gospel according to St. Mark* (International Critical Commentary) Edinburgh: T & T Clark, 1896; latest impression 1975), pp. 115-20; John Hargreaves, *A Guide to St Mark's Gospel* (TEF Study Guide 2), London: SPCK, 1979, pp. 105-108; C.S. Mann, *Mark: A New Translation with Introduction and Commentary*, New York: Doubleday, 1986, pp. 298-303.

[52] For discussions on Luke 9:10-17, see for example, G.B. Caird, *The Gospel of St Luke* (Pelican New Testament Commentary), Harmondsworth: Penguin , 1963), pp. 1226-28; Fred B. Craddock, Luke (Interpretation: A Bible Commentary for Teaching and Preaching), Louisville: John Knox Press, 1990, pp. 124-26; Alfred Plummer, *A Critical and Exegetical Commentary on the Gospel according to St. Luke* (International Critical Commentary), Edinburgh: T & T Clark, 1922, pp. 242-46.

differentiation is made. In the case of Luke, this absence is strange for it has always been claimed that Luke is interested in women.[53]

Another version of the feeding episode has four thousand recipients. Matt 15:32-39 has this account.[54] As with the other account, the narrator recognizes gender differentiation among the recipients: "Those who ate were four thousand [male], besides women and children" (v. 38). Mark 8:1-10 also records the same episode, but the narrator here does not record any gender differentiation among the recipients. So from the feeding episode, it is evident that Matthew alone records recognition of gender differentiation among the partakers of the food. The differences in the presentation among the evangelists is partly due to their interests, i.e., why they presented a particular account. That interest would dictate what is to be included or left out. It is also partly due to their sources which may or may not have the details in question. So for our purposes, the fact is that one evangelist recorded recognition of gender differentiation in the feeding accounts.

In the parables of the lost sheep (Luke 15:3-7) and the lost coin (Luke 15:8-10),[55] we see Jesus recognizing the male (Luke 15:3) and female (Luke 15:8) genders. Both are used as good illustrations and not marginalizing any gender.

In the account of the way to the cross, the narrator singles out women (Luke 23:27) from the great multitude who were following Jesus.[56] So the presence of women is highlighted. This emphasis on the female gender argues for the importance of this gender in this particular episode. In fact, in the process Jesus makes a statement in vv. 28-31 which has far reaching consequences.

In the crucifixion account in Mark 15:40-41, women are singled out as witnessing the event. The narrator is depicting how concerned the women were. Their concern is obviously to be contrasted to that of the male folk in the same situation. After the crucifixion in Luke, 23:44-49,[57] the narrator lists people who were around: centurion, multitudes, acquaintances; they deserve a category of their own, hence gender differentiation in the process.

---

[53] This is notwithstanding that Luke recognizes the role of women in the service of the ministry of Jesus. (cf. Luke 8:1-3).

[54] For discussion on Matt 15:32-39, see, for example, Hare, *Matthew*, pp. 179-82; Mann, *Matthew*, pp. 189-90.

[55] For discussion on Luke 15:3-7, 8-10, see, for example, Caird, *Luke*, pp. 179-81; Plummer, *Luke*, pp. 527-30.

[56] For discussions on Luke 23:27, see, for example, Caird, *Luke*, pp. 249-50; Plummer, *Luke*, pp. 527-30.

[57] For discussions on Luke 23:44-49, see, for example, Caird, *Luke*, pp. 252-54; Plummer, *Luke*, pp. 536-40.

So the different episodes presented here demonstrate that the evangelists (including Jesus) recognized gender differentiation. What has emerged clearly here is the prominence of women, hence the female gender. This prominence is not for ill, but it stresses the women's concern over the situations depicted. So the fact of the recognition of gender differentiation does not in anyway contribute to the marginalization of the female gender.

Epistles

In this section, we first look at the Pauline corpus. From the uncontested/genuine letters, we cite examples from 1 Corinthians, Galatians, Philippians, and Romans. In 1 Cor 7:1-40[58] Paul addresses the issue of marriage as raised by the Corinthian Christians. Here Paul recognizes gender differentiation through the institutions of marriage. He talks about "man" and "woman" (v. 1), "man" and "wife" (v. 2), and "woman" and husband" (v. 3). According to Paul, each of these people rules over the other's body (v. 4). So while recognizing gender differentiation, Paul is keen to stress that both are equal in relation to each other's body. This means that according to Paul, the institution of marriage ensures the equality of genders, hence the question of the apparent marginalization of the female gender does not issue from this institution.

In 1 Cor 14:34-35[59] Paul enjoins silence in public on the part of the wife. But Paul's injunction is harsh. Some scholars have suggested that this text is probably an interpolation included later or a marginal note made by a reader at the end of the first century. If it was an interpolation or a marginal note, then why was it retained when the letter was accepted into the canon? Several suggestions have been made to explain the attitude expressed here, e.g., (a) there was fear of enthusiastic women's participation comparable to what was happening in some Hellenistic religions where such was the case; (b) women wishing to learn disturbed with their questions; (c) Paul refers only to Christian women.

Strictly speaking, this account hinges upon the treatment of women and this is not within the limit of this chapter. Whatever the case, a word needs to be said here. First, the woman at issue is a wife, "for in vs. 35 these female persons are enjoined

---

[58] For discussions on 1 Cor 7:1-40, see for example, Hans Conzelmann, *1 Corinthians* (trans. James W. Leich; Philadelphia: Fortress Press, 1975), pp. 114-38; William F. Orr & James Arthur Walther, *1 Corinthians: A New Translation Introduction with a Study of the Life of Paul, Notes and Commentary* (The Anchor Bible), New York: Doubleday, 1976, pp. 205-26.

[59] For discussion on 1 Cor 14:34-35, see for example, Conzelmann, *1 Corinthians*, pp. 246-47; Orr & Walther, *1 Corinthians*, pp. 311-13.

to gain church information from their husbands at home."⁶⁰ So, is this injunction made because they are female? Obviously the injunction is not made on the wives because they are female, for there are other females who are not wives. In fact, the text in v. 34 seems to have a generic referent "women." Why is this injunction made then to the wives? The intent of the command is to interdict situations in which wives publicly contradict what their husbands say or think or embarrass them by an interchange of conversation. They may thus be rejecting the authority of their husbands (which was firmly fixed in the sociology of their religion) and thereby be no longer subordinate. In 11:5 Paul indicated that women could pray or prophecy in the church, so unless Paul is contradicting himself he here enjoins silence in matters other than praying and prophesying. Since good order is a major emphasis of the context (cf. vs. 26, 33, 40) he may be referring especially to speaking in tongues or even to any sort of clamorous discussion of controversial issues which have arisen in the assembly.⁶¹ So the injunction is not a male thing.⁶²

In Gal 3:28 Paul also recognizes gender differences.⁶³ He says here that there is no distinction between "male and female." From the discussion in 1 Cor 11:2-16, it is apparent that "Paul did not intend to abolish the gender roles between men and women"⁶⁴ but what Paul wanted to do was to abolish the difference between…men and women"⁶⁵ In fact, it has been asserted that "Galatians 3:28 is the first occurrence of a doctrine openly propagating the abolition of sex distinctions."⁶⁶ Abolishing sex distinction is not the same as abolishing gender roles between men and women. What lies behind Paul's views here is the fact that there was discrimination in the community: by race (Jews and Gentiles), societal status (slave and master), and sex. So this discrimination is what Paul is trying to abolish in the Church. In other words,

---

⁶⁰ Orr & Walther, *1 Corinthians*, p. 312. Emphasis theirs.
⁶¹ Ibid., p.313. Emphasis theirs.
⁶² For other discussions on 1 Corinthians, see for example, Walter L. Liefen, "Women, Submission and Ministry in 1 Corinthians," in Mickelsen (ed.), *Women, Authority and the Bible*, pp. 134-60; Antoinette Wire, "1 Corinthians," in Schüssler-Fiorenza (ed.), *Searching the Scriptures*, vol. 1, pp. 153-95.
⁶³ For discussion on Gal 3:28, see for example, Hans Dieter Betz, *Galatians* (Hermeneia), Philadelphia: Fortress Press, 1979, pp. 181-201; Dieter Luhmann, *Galatians* (A Continental Commentary), trans. O.C. Dean, Jr, Minneapolis: Fortress Press, 1992, pp. 74-8: Frank J. Matera, *Galatians* (Sacra Pagina), Collegeville, Minnesota: The Liturgical Press, 1992, pp. 141-47.
⁶⁴ Matera, *Galatians*, p. 143.
⁶⁵ Luhrmann, *Galatians*, p. 71.
⁶⁶ Bets, *Galatians*, p. 197.

Paul is speaking of equal privileges between men and women.[67] In this account, we are not told, however, whether the sex discrimination was based on gender issues or on other factors.

In Phil 4:2-3[68] Paul mentions those people who had "laboured side by side" with him, among whom were women. Women are "very visibly and significantly present in his references to associates in ministry. Women preached and prayed in Paul's churches (1 Cor 11:5) and their names are many in Paul's remembrances of a lifetime of shared service (Rom 16:1-16). In fact, Luke says the church at Philippi was begun when Paul went to a place of prayer and 'spoke to the women who had come together' (Acts 16:13).[69] So Paul recognizes gender differentiation among his fellow workers here. The text as it stands suggests that the two women mentioned (Euodia and Syntyche) disagreed, for Paul urges them to "agree in the Lord" (v. 2). What the text does not say is that the two women disagreed because they were female. However, the text shows that these women were fellow workers with Paul, along with the men folk. So the recognition of the gender differentiation here is meant to show that the female gender was also involved in the proclamation of the gospel and so the call to agree is not made because the two were women.

Rom 13:9-10[70] alludes to the Decalogue (Exod 20:13-17; Deut 5:7-21). As we have already noted, the wife is singled out among those not to be coveted. Although Paul refers to the Decalogue, he does not mention the wife. Paul simply quotes: "You shall not covet" (v. 9). Does this omission of the mention of the wife mean anything? One thing that is clear from the quotation is that the injunctions stop at the action (verb). In the Decalogue, this is true up to the third injunction, but for the others, they are extended. So the omission of the mention of the wife could be explained as Paul wanting to stop at the action as he does also in Rom 7:7. In addition to this, it can be observed that in the Decalogue, the things/beings that are

---

[67] Tamez, "No Longer Silent," p. 53.
[68] For discussions on Phil 4:2-3, see for example, Fred B. Craddock, *Philippians* (Interpretation: A Bible Commentary for Teaching and Preaching) Louisville: John Knox Press, 1985, pp. 69-71; Ralph P. Martin, *Philippians* (The Tyndale New Testament Commentary; rev. ed.), Leicester: Inter-Varsity Press, 1987, pp. 167-69.
[69] Craddock, *Philippians*, p. 71.
[70] For discussions on Rom 13:9-10, see for example, Paul J. Achtemeier, *Romans* (Interpretation: A Bible Commentary for Teaching and Preaching), Louisville: John Knox Press, 1985, pp. 208-210; F.F. Bruce, *The Letter of Paul to the Romans* (The Tyndale New Testament Commentaries) Leicester: InterVarsity Press, 1985, pp. 226-27; Joseph A. Fitzmyer, *Romans: A New Translation with Introduction and Commentary* (The Anchor Bible); New York: Doubleday, 1993, pp. 676-81; Ernst Käsemann, *Commentary on Romans*, London: SCM, 1980, pp. 359-64.

not to be coveted are many, the wife being simply one of them. So the silence on the recognition could apply to others as well. Hence, from this silence we cannot seriously claim that Paul doesn't recognize gender differentiation here.[71]

We now turn to the disputed/contested Pauline letters (i.e. the Deutero-Pauline letters). Col 3:18-4:1[72] presents the *Haustafel* (household code). This is repeated in Eph 5:22-6:9.[73] In this code, the writer recognizes the institution of marriage (cf. reference to "wives" and "husbands" [vv. 18-19]), hence the recognition of gender differentiation through marriage: husband (male) and wife (female). The issue that raises problems in this code is the subjection of the wife to the husband, whereas the man is only told to love the wife. But the text does not indicate that the subjection is based on the wife's being female. In the Colossians' text, the wife is to be subject to her husband because it "is fitting in the Lord" (Col 3:18). The Ephesians text explains the basis of this subjection by saying they should do that "as to the Lord. For the husband is the head of the wife as Christ is the head of the church, his body, and is himself its Saviour. As the Church is subject to Christ, so let wives also be subject in everything to their husbands" (Eph 5:22-24). So according to the Ephesians text, the basis of the subjection is Christological and not gender. In addition to this, the text says, "even so husbands should love their wives as their own bodies. He who loves his wife loves himself. For no man ever hates his own flesh but nourishes and cherishes it ... let each one of you love his wife as himself" (Eph 5:28-33). So the wife and the husband are one flesh, hence the subjection is not dependent on gender.

Finally, we come to the pastoral letters which are also attributed to Paul. In 1 Tim 2:8-15,[74] the writer recognizes gender differentiation (cf. reference to "men"

---

[71] For other discussions on Romans 13:9-10, see for example, Elizabeth A. Castella, "Romans," in Fiorenza, *Searching the Scriptures*, vol. 2, pp. 272-300.

[72] For discussions on Colossians 3:18-4:1, see for example, Mary Rose D'Angelo, "Colossians," in Fiorenza-Schüssler, *Searching the Scriptures*, vol. 3, pp. 313-24; Eduard Lohse, *Colossians and Philemon* (Hermeneia), Philadelphia: Fortress Press, 1971, pp. 154-63; Ralph P. Martin, *Ephesians, Colossians and Philemon* (Interpretation: A Bible Commentary for Teaching and Preaching), Louisville: John Knox Press, 1991. pp. 126-29; N.T. Wright, *Colossians and Philemon*' (The Tyndale New Testament Commentary); Leicester: InterVarsity Press, 1986, pp. 145-51.

[73] For discussions on Eph 5:22-6:9, see for example, Martin, *Ephesians*, pp. 67-74.

[74] For discussions on 1 Timothy 2:8-15, see, for example, Donald Guthrie, *The Pastoral Epistles* (The Tyndale Bible Commentary), Leicester: InterVarsity Press, 1990, pp. 84-90; Bruce W. Knight, *Commentary on the Pastoral Epistles* (New International Greek Testament Commentary; Grand Rapids, : Eerdmans , 1992, pp. 130-49; Linda M. Maloney, "The Pastoral Epistles," in Fiorenza-Schüssler, *Searching the Scriptures*, vol. 2., pp. 361-80.

and "women"). This pericope has raised problems, especially on what the writer says in vv. 11-13. "Let the women learn in silence with all submissiveness; I permit no woman to teach or have authority over men; she is to keep silent" (cf. Col 3:18-4:1; Eph 5:22-6:9). Most feminist readers have pointed at this text as the basis for the domination of women in the church.[75] But why did the writer have such a view of women? Several possibilities have been suggested, for example, (a) the view is based on a misinterpretation of Genesis[76] and failure to discern the distinctive purpose for each narrative;[77] (b) the creation account was interpreted not in the light of the principle and experience of the equality of the gospel but by the patriarchal experience and principles of the church and society.[78]

But having said this, we should note first that this text seems to contradict what Paul said in 1 Cor 7:1-40, especially what he says in v. 4: "For the wife does not rule over her own body, but husband does; likewise the husband does not rule over his own body but the wife does." However, a careful reading of the text would show that the text of Timothy talks about a generic woman ("a woman"), whereas the Corinthians as well as the Colossians and Ephesians texts refers to "wives." Second, we should note that the text doesn't urge submissiveness or silence on the part of the women because they are female, i.e. because of gender. The reason given by the writer, according to the text, is that " *Adam* was formed first, then Eve; and *Adam* was not deceived, but the woman was deceived and became a transgressor" (vv. 14-15). So submissiveness or silence is urged in the text because of order in creation and transgression and not gender.[79]

Is the writer correct in his understanding of the Biblical situation of the woman? One of the versions of the creation accounts says that "male and female he [God] created them" (Gen 1:27), which means that both genders were created at the same time. But the other version says "and the rib which the Lord had taken from the man he made into a woman" (Gen 2:24). So the writer is referring to this version when he

---

[75] See, for example, Chang, "The Place of Women in Genesis 1-3 and 1 Timothy 2," pp. 34-41; Phiri, "The 'Proper' Place of Women (Genesis 1, 1 Timothy 2)," pp. 25-29.

[76] The one who advocates this view contradicts herself when she says the writer of this text follows Jewish interpretation (see Phiri, "The 'Proper' Place of Women (Genesis 1, Timothy 2)," p. 29.

[77] Phiri, "The 'Proper' Place of Women (Genesis 1, 1 Timothy 2)," p. 26.

[78] Chang, "The Place of Women in Genesis 1-3 and 1 Timothy 2," pp. 40-41.

[79] For other views on this text, see for example, David M. Scholar, " 1 Timothy 2:9-15 and the Place of Women in the Church's Ministry," in Mickelsen (ed.), *Women, Authority and the Bible*, pp. 193-253.

says *Adam* was created at the same time.[80] According to the fall account, it is true that Eve was deceived by the serpent. But one could argue that *Adam* was also deceived, as we have already pointed out, when he accepted to eat the fruit, for he knew quite well the injunction not to eat it. In short then, it can be said that according to the text, the submission or silence enjoined upon "woman" is not based on gender but on other factors.[81]

From the Catholic Epistles, we examine 1 Pet 3:1-7[82] (cf. 1 Cor 7:1-40; 14:34-35; Col 3:18-25; Eph 5:22-33; 1 Tim 2:8-15) where the writer also recognizes gender differentiation. This recognition comes through the institution of marriage (husband and wife). Here, too, women are urged to be submissive to their husbands (3:1). The reason for this submission, according to the text, is "so that some, though they do not obey the word, may be won without words by the behaviour of their wives, when they see your reverent and chaste behaviour" (v. 20). The example of Sarah obeying Abraham is also presented as reason to be submissive to husbands (vv. 5-6). So the injunction to be submissive to the husbands is made on other grounds apart from gender. The husbands are also enjoined to "live considerately" with their wives (v. 7). Part of the reason given in the text for this call is because women are "the weaker sex" (v. 7). Out of all the texts that we have looked at this is the only one that links gender (sex) to the relationship between man and woman. The adjective "weaker" suggests the superiority of the male sex over the female sex. But the way it has been used here is not to continue marginalizing the female sex but to uplift it because the writer says the two sexes "are joint heirs of the grace of life" (v. 7). So when it comes to the "grace of life" both sexes are on the same level. Being "joint heirs" implies both have equal opportunities in that inheritance.[83]

So the study of the narratives from the New Testament reveals that there is gender recognition. However, this recognition does not explain the apparent marginalization of the female gender.

Concluding on the narrative study, I am saying that the study of the select number of narratives from the Old and New Testaments has revealed that gender differentiation that was created in the creation accounts (Genesis 1-2) is recognized

---

[80] The writer is also overlooking the fact that God created '*adam* and not a being with a personal name of Adam.

[81] Perhaps, this passage can properly be discussed under the treatment of women in the Bible, hence it is not wholly within the scope of this chapter.

[82] For discussions on this text, see for example, Kathleen E. Corley, "1 Peter," in Fiorenza-Schüssler, *Searching the Scriptures*, vol. 2, pp. 349-60; Wayne Grudem, "1 Peter" (The Tyndale Bible Commentary; Leicester: InterVarsity Press, 1988), pp. 134-46.

[83] This passage can properly be discussed under the treatment of women in the Bible, hence it is not wholly within the limit of this chapter.

as such by God and the narrators in the subsequent accounts in the Bible. Notwithstanding 1 Peter 2:7, the study of the Biblical narratives has demonstrated that this recognition of gender differentiation in no way contributes to the apparent marginalization of the female gender.

Conclusion

Right from the start, it was stressed that treatment of women in the Bible is outside the limit of this chapter, but the issue at stake in this study is gender differentiation. The discussion of this has revealed that gender differentiation is created and recognized as such in the Bible. Being created implies that it is inherently good (see Paul's assessment of the law in Rom 7:12) and this goodness is evident in its recognition. But what is inherently good has become not good, for it has been said to be used to marginalize the female gender. We may pause and ask here as Paul did: "Did that which is good, then bring [marginalization] to [the female gender]?" Paul's answer is: "By no means!" (see Rom 7:13). But it is how gender differentiation has been manipulated today that has led to this apparent female gender marginalization. According to this study, evidence is clear: gender differentiation was created and recognized as such.

But women in the church in general have been enjoined to be silent, submissive, and not to preach, i.e. not to be ministers of the word and sacraments.[84] On the popular level, this injunction is made simply because women are emotionally unstable, uncertain at certain times, and child bearing; the Bible does not permit women to have authority over men; our culture does not allow women to have authority over men; if women were brought to leadership of the church, cases of immorality would increase among the leaders; and women cannot handle leadership roles.[85] Even if this were all true, would this not mean that the male folk in the church were denying women the ministry of the word and sacraments because of their being female? There is, therefore, urgent need to revisit the Bible in order to address the apparent gender imbalance in society in general and the church in particular.[86] Indeed, "the Bible is the engine that is keeping the church running."[87] In other words, "Scripture is the Soul of Theology."[88]

---

[84] On sacraments and sexuality, see for example, Chingota, "Sacraments and Sexuality," pp. 34-40.

[85] See Phiri, "The 'Proper' Place of Women (Genesis 1, 1 Timothy 2)," p. 32.

[86] See for example, Joan D. Flikkema, "Strategies for Change," in Mickelsen (ed.), *Women, Authority and the Bible*, pp. 255-84.

[87] Hilary B.P. Mijoga, "Bible and Church Growth in Malawi," *Religion in Malawi* No. 8 (1998), pp. 27-33, especially p. 27.

[88] Fitzmyer, *Scripture, the Soul of Theology*.

In this chapter, we have noted that feminists have attributed the apparent marginalization of the female gender to two factors: the Bible and culture. On the Bible, it is said: (a) through sin and punishment, the woman was made subservient to the man; (b) as the woman was helper, she was in fact made an auxiliary and secondary to the man; (c) as the woman was created from the man, the woman was made inferior; (d) that the text of 1 Timothy is a major contributor to the issue.[89] On the cultural factors, it is said that the patriarchal system is the root cause of the marginalization of women in society.[90] In addition to all this, it has been claimed that the Western Latin theology also contributes to this marginalization. On this, it is said that views of patristic writers like Aquinas, Augustine, Tertullian have permeated the church, hence the marginalization of women.

In short then, this chapter has attempted to demonstrate that gender differentiation is created and recognized in the Bible. This has been proved by the philological study of some Hebrew terms in Genesis 1-2 and the narrative study of a select number of episodes in both the *Old* and the *New Testaments*. These two studies have shown that the apparent marginalization of the women has to be explained otherwise, because the marginalization of women is not inherent in the creation and recognition of gender differentiation.

---

[89] The Biblical factor would only explain the Jewish and Christian situations for both religions use the Bible. Peoples of other faiths would not be covered by this factor since they don't use the Bible.

[90] The cultural factor would encompass people across the board, i.e, this would explain the situation of women in general.

www.ingramcontent.com/pod-product-compliance
Lightning Source LLC
Chambersburg PA
CBHW050906300426
44111CB00010B/1410